The Politics of Crisis in Europe

The Politics of Crisis in Europe explores the resilience of the European Union in the face of repeated crises perceived to threaten its very existence. Although it is often observed after the fact that these crises serve as opportunities for integration, this book is the first critical analysis to suggest that we cannot *fully* understand the nature and severity of these crises without recognizing the role of societal reaction to events and the nature of social narratives about crisis, especially those advanced by the media. Through a close examination of the 2003 Iraq crisis, the 2005 constitutional crisis, and the 2010–12 Eurozone crisis, this book identifies a pattern across these episodes, demonstrating how narratives about crises provide the means to openly air underlying societal tensions that would otherwise remain below the surface, impeding further integration.

Dr. Mai'a K. Davis Cross is the Edward W. Brooke Professor of Political Science and Associate Professor at Northeastern University, as well as Senior Researcher at the ARENA Centre for European Studies, University of Oslo. She is the author of three books, including *Security Integration in Europe: How Knowledge-Based Networks Are Transforming the European Union* (2011), which was the 2012 winner of the Best Book Prize from the University Association of Contemporary European Studies. Dr. Cross holds a Ph.D. in politics from Princeton University and a bachelor's degree in government from Harvard University. She is a Term Member of the Council on Foreign Relations.

The Politics of Crisis in Europe

MAI'A K. DAVIS CROSS

Northeastern University, Boston, Massachusetts

CAMBRIDGE
UNIVERSITY PRESS

CAMBRIDGE
UNIVERSITY PRESS

University Printing House, Cambridge CB2 8BS, United Kingdom

One Liberty Plaza, 20th Floor, New York, NY 10006, USA

477 Williamstown Road, Port Melbourne, VIC 3207, Australia

314-321, 3rd Floor, Plot 3, Splendor Forum, Jasola District Centre, New Delhi-110025, India

79 Anson Road, #06-04/06, Singapore 079906

Cambridge University Press is part of the University of Cambridge.

It furthers the University's mission by disseminating knowledge in the pursuit of education, learning and research at the highest international levels of excellence.

www.cambridge.org
Information on this title: www.cambridge.org/9781316602355
10.1017/9781316556498

First published 2017
First paperback edition 2017

A catalogue record for this publication is available from the British Library

ISBN 978-1-107-14783-6 Hardback
ISBN 978-1-316-60235-5 Paperback

For Robert

Contents

Tables and Figures

Acknowledgments

I would like to thank Marvin Krakow, Jane Junn, Ezra Suleiman, Jolyon Howorth, Fred Chernoff, Rob English Laura Pulido, Ann Tickner, and Laurie Brand for their enormous encouragement. My colleagues at the ARENA Centre for European Studies in Oslo, and the research funding I received from the Eurodiv project have been crucial in supporting this project. In particular, Helene Sjursen, Marianne Riddervold, Guri Rosen, Tine Brogger, Kate McNamara, Denise Garcia, Amilcar Barreto, Tom Vicino, and Kirsten Rodine-Hardy have been wonderful and helpful colleagues throughout the writing of this book.

I truly benefited from the incredibly valuable research assistance of Xinru Ma and her expertise in media content analysis. I also very much appreciate the research assistance of Molly Krasnodebska and Nicolas de Zamaroczy in the early stages of the project. In the late stages of the project, I benefited from the assistance of Klara Durkin, Emma Pendi-Robinson, Hiba Senhaj, Tommy Markevich, and Joanne Choi at Northeastern University in putting the finishing touches on the manuscript. I would also like to thank my anonymous reviewers for their very helpful advice.

I am always grateful to my wonderful parents, Michael Davis and Pamela Davis-Lee, who have made so much possible, and my brilliant little sister, Hana Davis. Most importantly, I am grateful to my husband, Robert, who brainstorms all of my ideas with me, cooks me dinner every night, shows me the great outdoors (with our golden retriever, Bailey), travels with me to the far reaches of the planet, creates beautiful photography as a record of our adventures, and unfailingly supports and cheers everything I do. His stamp is definitely on this book, and so it is dedicated to him.

I

A Europe of Crises

"People only accept change when they are faced with necessity, and only recognize necessity when a crisis is upon them."

Jean Monnet, architect of the European Union

INTRODUCTION

The European Union (EU) is plagued by episodes of what I call *integrational panic* – periods of often overblown, existential crisis in which it seems that the "end of Europe" is at hand. Since its inception in 1957, the European Union (or European Economic Community/European Community, in its previous incarnations) is often said to be in severe crisis. Doomsday scenarios abound: either certain key member states are on the verge of leaving the EU, or the European economy is on the brink of collapse, or a cornerstone policy of EU integration – the Euro, the Common Foreign and Security Policy, the common market, Schengen – is about to be thrown out. Every few years, like clockwork, it seems that the European integration project faces its demise in one way or another. The instances are many and are typically described as such, with notable examples stretching from the 1965 Empty Chair crisis to the 1999 Commission resignation crisis right up through the Greek debt and refugee crises of 2015 (Thies 2012). Whether these crises are internal in origin – such as the 2005 constitutional crisis – or external in origin – such as the 2003 EU crisis over Iraq – they are typically portrayed in the international media with a heavily negative slant. Journalists, commentators, politicians, and other public figures quickly jump on the bandwagon, often invoking predictions about the imminent demise of the EU. And yet, none of these predictions have actually come true. Doomsday scenarios continually prove to be overblown, even while these errors in perception are repeated over and over again. Each new crisis seems to be the worst, so that is what tends to stick in people's minds.

Despite this dark cloud hanging over Europe's image, the region is today arguably stronger, wealthier, and more integrated than ever. It has the largest economy in the world and is the United States' biggest trading partner and investor. Its member states continue to sign new treaties, solidifying new levels of integration in a wide spectrum of policy areas, from foreign policy to finance to internal security. The membership of the EU continues to grow with countries to the east – Ukraine, Macedonia, Serbia, Montenegro, and Turkey – formally seeking to become candidates or members. As a global actor, the EU cultivates its soft, smart, and normative power. Its new supranational diplomatic service – the European External Action Service – representing more than half a billion European citizens to the world, holds a great deal of potential. Politically, economically, diplomatically, and even militarily, the EU as a whole is a global actor of influence. Increasingly, decision makers have realized that integration through the institutional structure of the EU is indispensable, and indeed, have even taken it for granted.

So why is the EU often portrayed as an idealistic project that is stumbling from crisis to crisis? At the outset of this book, it is important to acknowledge that despite all that the European countries have achieved so far in their efforts to prevent the kind of war and conflict that plagued the continent for centuries, the EU, of course, has its share of problems and challenges. It is a work in progress, a project that is perennially in the middle of its evolution, with no clearly defined end goal. There are visible disagreements within Europe. The leaders of member states come together in Brussels and argue over what future is best. They debate policies, budgets, and treaties, and sometimes do not find common ground. They sometimes cannot speak with one voice when it comes to the important foreign policy decisions that really matter in global politics. They do not yet agree on how far integration should ultimately go. At the societal level, especially after the height of the 2010–12 Eurozone crisis, there are those with a greater sense of disillusionment with Europe. Extremist parties and groups have radicalized more citizens, those who identify as Euroskeptic are more vocal (even though Eurobarometer polls consistently show that Europeans generally trust the EU more than their particular national governments), and there are concerns about the future economic prosperity and security of the region. Some EU member states continually grapple with their own internal division, especially in countries such as Spain, the UK, and Italy, to name a few. Ultimately, the EU *could* cease to exist if crises and Euroskepticism make the degeneration of the European project a self-fulfilling prophecy. The EU *could* slide backward, away from achieving the goals that member states have set for themselves, loosening up the level of integration that they have achieved thus far.

This book does not deny all of these challenges, internal divides, and potential obstacles that the EU faces in trying to fulfill the aims of the European integration project. It does, however, argue that these issues are disproportionately and severely amplified during times of crisis, pitting Europeans against each other and driving elites to "play with fire" as they determine the future of Europe. After all, it is to be expected that within democracies – particularly within twenty-eight different democracies – there will be debate, disagreement, and political gridlock. And yet, a comparison with the United States is instructive – the polarization of just *two* political parties in the American system is often more of a problem than disagreement among twenty-eight EU member states over issues debated in Brussels. And unlike the United States, the EU's government has never shut down.

A disproportional reaction is when tensions within Europe manifest themselves as such serious crises that they could potentially derail the entire European project. When this happens, it represents a potentially serious problem for Europe. One of the central arguments of this book is that certain events which present challenges and obstacles to EU integration have built up into episodes of societal panic, or more specifically, integrational panic, in Europe. Such panic manifests as an overwhelming sense within significant sectors of society that EU integration simply cannot continue. As will be shown in subsequent chapters, many opinion shapers, various leaders, and above all, the media have contributed to the rise of integrational panic at certain key junctures in the EU's development. In effect, political and societal leaders, perhaps unwittingly, contribute to the construction of existential threats to the EU. Although some theories of crisis emergence (discussed in Chapter 2) argue that crises are the product of structural or systemic flaws, I contend that events in Europe often become construed as crises when people *perceive* them to be and define them as such. In other words, EU crises have a socially constructed dynamic to them, and once integrational panic sets in, these crises can grow to existential proportions.

At the same time, the creation and buildup of crises that seemingly threaten the very existence of the EU is only part of the story. What is perhaps equally interesting, and ultimately more important, is how Europeans then grapple with and overcome these crises. In that respect, this book makes the case that there is a clearly discernible pattern across these episodes of existential crisis in Europe. After these crises reach their height of intensity, seemingly bringing the EU to the brink of failure in the eyes of many, they dissipate and leave in their wake a renewed will to find consensus. Indeed, European leaders repeatedly take some dramatic steps toward *more* integration in the wake of existential crises. It is often casually recognized, usually with the benefit of hindsight, that European actors seem to use crises as opportunities to further shape European order beyond what can be achieved incrementally. An *Economist* article quipped that "Europe's model of change has long been based on lurch then muddle" (*The Economist* 2012). The 1986 Single European Act, 2003 European Security Strategy, 2009 Lisbon Treaty, and 2011 Fiscal Compact, among many others, all followed seemingly serious existential crises. Renewed political will to find consensus, and even major advances in European integration, seem to track these crises. Some aspects of this post-crisis *catharsis*, as I call it (see Chapter 2), are more informal and occur at the societal level, whereas others are more formal and involve signing new agreements on the basis of newfound consensus or the desire for more integration. Both are important, as even the more informal forms of integration are crucial for the EU's sustainability over the long run in terms of crafting a common identity and shared public sphere.

Theories of international relations have yet to offer an explanation for why EU crises might ultimately serve as opportunities, as I argue in this book. While incremental processes of day-to-day integration, punctuated with major treaties and other agreements, are well documented in the literature,[1] almost no research has actually examined EU crises in a comparative framework.[2] Nearly all research on EU crises considers them in isolation from one another, even while acknowledging that a pattern of some kind seems to exist across them. There are a number of articles on various EU crises (Crowe 2003; see also Gleissner and de Vreese 2005; Gamble 2006; Lewis 2009), but they tend to focus exclusively on single case studies. In short, the meaning and impact of crises in the history of the EU is poorly understood. *The Politics of Crisis in Europe* seeks to fill this gap in our knowledge of these key events in the evolution

---

[1] Indeed, much of my research to date focuses on incremental integration through the work of epistemic communities. See, for example, Cross (2011).

[2] One exception is Jo (2007).

of the EU. Gaining a better understanding of the role of crises in the European region has significant implications for the EU's image, power, and status as a global actor – both negative and positive.

APPROACH OF THE BOOK

Three European crises of the twenty-first century stand out in terms of their severity and are the focus of this book: the 2003 crisis over the Iraq war (Chapter 3), the 2005 constitutional crisis (Chapter 4), and the 2010–12 Eurozone crisis (Chapter 5). Of course, the nature of each of these crises is distinct from the others, ranging from external war to treaty reform to financial turmoil. Nonetheless, and perhaps surprisingly, the causes and consequences of these crises have important elements in common.

To briefly sketch out this pattern: first, there is an event of some kind that can be interpreted as a trigger for crisis, depending on societal perceptions and reaction. Second, the event leads to a sense of crisis, building in severity, alongside clear signs of integrational panic – including overreaction to events and amplification of preexisting tensions. Then, in the third phase, the crisis reaches its height with open talk of the "end of Europe," which often triggers a self-fulfilling prophecy dynamic. In other words, as each crisis builds and reaches its height, tangible manifestations of crisis emerge – such as social breakdown, economic turmoil, political gridlock – because of the integrational panic that preceded. Fourth, the crisis subsides and there is a period of catharsis that results in the fifth phase: a renewed will for consensus, typically resulting in more integration. Figure 1.1 lays out the broad-level pattern across these crisis cases, which is explained more fully in Chapter 2.

To examine this pattern in detail, I break down the case studies examined in Chapters 3, 4, and 5 into three main parts. First, I critically analyze the various arguments in the literature that have been advanced to explain each crisis. My intention is to use the existing literature surrounding each crisis as a point of departure to then investigate the socially driven causes of crisis, an aspect that has been neglected in these analyses. Second, I describe how events came to be defined as a major crisis for Europe, particularly in light of negative media coverage and frenzied attention. In particular, the socially constructed aspect of crises often contains exaggeration, extrapolation from the specific to the general, a misconstruing of significance, and negative forecasting in the media. Third, I use a narratives approach – looking at how Europeans talk about each crisis – to shed light on the process of crisis

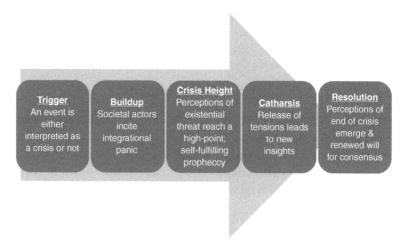

FIGURE 1.1 EU Existential Crisis Pattern

buildup and resolution, with specific attention to societal reactions and perceptions, and how they are framed. In each case of crisis, I argue that none of the three crises *necessarily* had to develop into a full-blown existential crisis for Europe. Rather, the role of the media, elites, and the public in defining an event as a crisis is crucial. In contrast to other approaches, I argue that a narratives perspective is essential to fully account for the origins of EU existential crises.

While I am at first concerned with explaining why these crises emerge, I also seek to explain how Europeans resolve these crises, turning them into windows of opportunity. Thus, I analyze how the crisis becomes an opening for finding new areas of consensus, often moving integration forward in some significant way. In particular, I explore the evidence for what I call post-crisis *catharsis*: that is, a crisis-induced process of openly airing tensions within European society – East vs. West, North vs. South, public vs. elite, and so on – that would otherwise largely remain below the surface. To this end, I identify the main pre-crisis societal tensions of the time and compare them to the content of the crisis narratives – both at the elite and public levels. The expectation is that if European society airs these tensions, then some degree of catharsis is achieved. I consider media coverage during the crisis as an indicator of the main crisis narrative, as well as Eurobarometer polls to establish the changes in attitudes before and after the crisis. Finally, I assess to what extent leaders decide to find new areas of consensus as they seek to resolve each crisis. I show that if the main narrative about a crisis is predominantly constructed around preexisting societal tensions, leaders are more likely to push forward with EU integration. In other words, crisis resolution that includes catharsis is what enables crises to become opportunities rather than setbacks for EU integration.

Thus, going beyond standard approaches that explain major crises, my emphasis is on societal actors – the public, opinion shapers, media, politicians, and Brussels elites – involved in constructing and resolving EU crises. As will be seen, in each case the international media clearly plays a strong role in defining relatively average events or routine obstacles to integration as major crises for the EU. The media is not the only actor framing events this way, but in the twenty-first century, the media has served as a kind of threat multiplier, amplifying negative ideas about events that eventually impact perceptions about the future of Europe, and thus fueling a self-fulfilling prophecy dynamic.

SIGNIFICANCE OF THE STUDY

Conventional wisdom tends to claim that the EU has always suffered from systemic and structural problems because it is deeply and inherently flawed in fundamental ways. The assumption is that every once in a while, these flaws rise to the surface and take Europe to the brink of breakdown. In contrast, my aim is to show that these crises need not have escalated to the point that they ultimately threatened the very existence of the EU. And crises do not need to do so in the future. However, in order to see how this works, it is necessary to look at the societal dimension and social narratives about each crisis, rather than simply stopping at structural conditions and assuming after the fact that these conditions made crises inevitable at certain junctures. Explanations of major EU crises over the decades have relied too heavily on assumptions about the flaws in the design of the EU, and it is important to examine whether other factors better explain repeated instances of crisis in Europe.

This book acknowledges the wealth of research that has gone into understanding each of these crises individually, but seeks to go beyond mainstream accounts of crises through the use of a comparative approach. Since there is a wide-ranging debate surrounding each of these crises in its own right, I have written each case study so that it can stand alone, and I consider the competing arguments for each case study separately. Although some of these competing arguments have some weaknesses, others are compelling. Nevertheless, it is through the overarching comparison of these crises to each other that the importance of crisis narratives becomes apparent. Societal narratives about crises coming from the media, elites, and the public show how these crises end up becoming far more severe than one would anticipate. Moreover, it is eventually in the substance of these crisis narratives that a degree of catharsis is achieved, tensions are released, and solutions are found. Time and time again, the EU as a whole turns these crises into opportunities for more integration.

Ultimately, the book shows why the EU has staying power, and why it will likely continue to play a major role in the region and in international relations in the years to come. In this sense, the book seeks to correct ongoing misperceptions about the EU's image, identity, and influence. It also provides new insights into the role, impact, and reaction to crises in international relations, taking into account the powerful role of the media in the twenty-first century. Indeed, the approach for understanding crises set forth here could also potentially shed light on the causes and consequences of crises in international relations more generally, especially considering the increasing incidences of media-driven (and social-media-driven) frenzies and even uprisings. Such an analysis may be useful in explaining why society tends to perceive certain events as crises and not others, as well as the opportunities that result from these critical junctures. With the information revolution and the international media's power to stir up episodes of societal panic, crises with a socially constructed dynamic are likely becoming more prevalent in many cases worldwide.

THE PUZZLE OF EU EXISTENTIAL CRISES

Most casual observers of European politics are aware that the EU is frequently described as in trouble for a variety of reasons. News headlines would make this impossible to ignore. Before delving into the core cases of this book – three major EU crises near the beginning of the twenty-first century – it is worth revisiting the historical basis for the question: why has the European region seemingly stumbled from crisis to crisis on its path toward more integration? Numerous and significant crises have peppered the history of the EU, from the 1950s to today. These have included the collapse of the European defense and political communities in the 1950s, Charles de Gaulle's vetoes of UK membership in the 1960s, the 1965 Empty Chair crisis, the failures of the precursors to the European Monetary System, and the September 1992 "Black Wednesday" crisis, among others. The crises that have plagued European integration throughout its development have not all necessarily been of the same severity, but many were perceived to be critical junctures at the time, during which the viability of the European integration project came into serious question.

When looking at the historical record, how can we recognize when an event constituted an existential crisis? Crises must be distinguished from failures or setbacks. As discussed in detail in Chapter 2, crises are relatively unusual events, and they must be serious enough to pose a threat to the existing social, political, or institutional order. Thus, a crisis is not simply an event that shows the limits of what can be achieved – in this case, European cooperation and integration; it is an event that appears to bring societies to the brink of a fundamental break with the existing way of life. Crucially, in line with the argument of this book, a crisis must be defined and perceived as such.

It would be too ambitious of an undertaking to analyze all of Europe's crises at the level of detail that I reserve for Chapters 3 through 5, but a brief overview of these more historical cases adds weight to the puzzle addressed here, and demonstrates the concrete need to understand the impact of these events on the development of the EU, beyond day-to-day processes of incremental integration. Looking back chronologically, it is evident that numerous events have been seen as significant crises for Europe. While some may rightly argue that the events mentioned here do not comprise an exhaustive list, my goal as stated at the outset of this book is simply to show that there is indeed a historical record of crises in the development of the EU that deserves an explanation.

The 1950s

The crises of the 1950s must be seen in the context of newfound hope for the achievement of a bold and far-ranging political structure in Europe that would be designed specifically to bind European countries together and make another war among them impossible. On the one hand, the idea of including the newly established Federal Republic of Germany as an equal member in a new proposal to subsume coal and steel production under a common High Authority was a major step, however uncomfortably it sat with some so soon after the devastation of the Second World War. On the other hand, the goal of launching a radically new form of European political organization that would cast aside national sovereignty and embrace pan-Europeanism under a federal structure had gained considerable traction, and a narrow focus on coal and steel seemed to fall short of this aim. The idea of a federal Europe had been discussed for some time, even before the war, with its roots in Altiero Spinelli's manifesto calling for a "Federal Union among the European peoples" (Dinan 2010: 9–11). This continued after the war, when, to name just a couple of examples, Jean Monnet (the head of France's economic planning office) wrote that a federation among European countries was necessary, and Winston Churchill called for a United States of Europe, albeit one without Britain.

Thus, at this early stage after World War II, when expectations were high that there would be a dramatic transformation of some kind, any failure to achieve far-reaching agreement presented a crisis in the attainment of these goals. The six founding member states – France, Germany, Italy, and the three Benelux countries – signed the Treaty of Paris on April 18, 1951, establishing the European Coal and Steel Community (ECSC), the precursor to the European Economic Community (EEC). Little more than a year later, on May 27, 1952, the same six countries signed a treaty to establish a European Defence Community (EDC), which would be an alternative to German membership in NATO and would constitute a pan-European army. Alongside this, a plan to launch a European Political Community (EPC) to support the EDC and ensure democratic accountability drew initial support. The Council of Europe had early on proven itself too weak to be invested with any real political authority, so a great deal of hope was placed in the fledgling ECSC. Ultimately, even though it was the French prime minister, René Pleven, who proposed the EDC, the French parliament rejected it (319 to 264) on August 30, 1954, deeming it a threat to national sovereignty and fearing the re-militarization of Germany so soon after World War II. The treaty had the support of the other five countries, but with the loss of French backing, the EDC, and along with it the EPC, was left to die on the vine.

Many in the European political elite saw the collapse of the European defense and political communities in the 1950s as an existential crisis for the ECSC. The sense among some was that the failure of the EDC and EPC meant that the minimal requirements for forming a political community had been seriously undermined. Those in favor of a federalist Europe referred to the negative parliamentary vote as "the crime of August 30" because one country had effectively halted a process that was headed toward more supranationalism. J. Spaey, a member of the Belgian section of the European Movement, argued at the time that this was about more than the debate between confederalists and federalists; it was about the reality that no single nation within Europe could defend itself or achieve economic prosperity (Spaey 1953). Some saw this failure as squandering the momentum behind the European Movement (Dinan 2010: 21). The tone in Western Europe and the United States was one of profound disappointment, and the perception was that France, the country that had been the pioneer in launching European integration, had failed the rest (CVCE 2012). Naturally, the disagreement within the French parliament was reflective of a broader societal debate on EDC, primarily within France but also across Europe and in the United States.

In the end, Europeans and Americans wondered whether the ECSC would be enough to serve as a fulcrum for supranationalism and the safeguarding of peace in Europe. As it turned out, the ECSC *was* enough, but the failure of EDC and EPC to get off the ground was a setback and created a sense of crisis at the very inception of the European project. Even though the French parliament rejected EDC because of the fear of rearming Germany, the latter was nonetheless rearmed shortly after through its admission into NATO in 1955. The EDC's replacement – the Western European Union – was far weaker than the EDC would have been, but numerous other areas of supranationalism, especially in the economic realm, flourished beyond expectations.

The 1960s

There were at least two major crises of note in the uncertain period of the 1960s. In 1957, with the signing of the Treaty of Rome, the ECSC had grown into the much broader European Economic Community (EEC), which included a customs union and a Common Agricultural Policy (CAP). The first crisis came out of the latter in the form of the so-called 1965 Empty Chair crisis. In these early years of the European Community, the CAP was absolutely crucial in symbolizing unity among the Six and the willingness to bind together their ever-important agricultural sectors, which had become heavily guarded through subsidies and protection. French President Charles de Gaulle was a big supporter of CAP because the sheer size of French agriculture would benefit greatly from European (as opposed to national) subsidies, even though it meant that France would sacrifice some national sovereignty and become permanently locked into European integration.

However, as the sensitive negotiations over CAP proceeded, de Gaulle became increasingly alarmed over the Commission's visible effort to seize more budgetary power for itself in financing the CAP. De Gaulle balked, but Commission President Walter Hallstein persisted. France withdrew its minister and permanent representative from Brussels, leaving an empty chair in all Council meetings, a boycott that de Gaulle indicated would continue indefinitely. This amounted to an ultimatum as Brussels governance was frozen without a French vote. Desmond Dinan describes this crisis as "the most serious constitutional conflict in the EU's history" (Dinan 2010: 37). The French foreign minister at the time, Maurice Couve de Murville, referred to it later in his memoirs as "undoubtedly the most serious crisis that the Common Market had ever experienced" (de Murville 1971: 329–339). It was the first time in the history of the European project that a member state had brought European governance to a standstill. It demonstrated major divergences among member states on the extent to which their common project would be supranational or intergovernmental, and federal or confederal. It also brought to the fore a profound sense of distrust (Jo 2007: 69–72), striking at the very heart of how the Six had governed the community thus far (Dinan 2010: 63).

Six months later, in 1966, de Gaulle finally sent the French representatives back to Brussels. The crisis was ultimately resolved with the Luxembourg Compromise, which introduced the rule that if one member state deems an issue to be of vital importance, a unanimous vote would be required. The atmosphere immediately after this crisis was decidedly less in favor of integration than previously – de Gaulle got his way – but once the stalemate was behind them, the European Community signed into being new agreements on CAP and renewed its quest to achieve a single market for Europe. This crisis episode, among other domestic and international factors, signaled the beginning of the end of de Gaulle's presidency, and his departure from office two years later led to a relaunch of integration efforts on several fronts, including monetary policy, foreign policy, and enlargement.

Another major crisis of note during this period was the question of enlargement, and specifically Britain's application to join the EEC. This crisis began with the French veto of Britain's bid in 1961, and stretched into the early 1970s. In the short two-year period from 1958 to 1960, the economies of the Six had grown by 50 percent, and the UK was regretting its isolation from the community. Although this amounted to a relatively short-lived crisis, Paul-Henri Spaak referred to the day that de Gaulle spoke out against British membership (January 14, 1963) as "Black Monday" in that it represented a crisis for both European integration and for the transatlantic alliance (Dinan 2010: 41). It had been US President John F. Kennedy who had encouraged British membership in the EEC, but this endorsement ended up backfiring when de Gaulle interpreted it as American interference in European affairs. Besides the US position on this, de Gaulle and other leaders of the member states were concerned that Britain would dilute the level of integration that had already been achieved and turn the EEC into merely a free trade area.

Even though Germany, Italy, and the Benelux countries had some reservations regarding British accession, they were shocked by France's unilateral veto. This precipitated a crisis atmosphere and a desire in Brussels to isolate France. A German daily newspaper, *Süddeutsche Zeitung*, reported hostile reactions on the part of the others toward de Gaulle (Paulus 1963). The day after de Gaulle's "Black Monday," each member state issued a firm statement in favor of British membership, sharply separating the rest of the community from France. The sense of crisis for the new EEC was palpable, given that the Treaty of Rome stipulates that any European country can apply for membership and that Britain was willing to adhere to the key provisions of the common external tariff, customs union, and CAP, as well as the necessity of leaving the European Free Trade Area (EFTA), to which it belonged, upon entry. In May 1967, Britain again applied for membership, and again was met with a French veto, creating a brief resurgence in crisis over enlargement of the EEC, and the question of how to deal with disagreement among member states over this important issue. If enlargement could not proceed, especially to include one of the most powerful countries in Europe, then this was indeed a problem for the viability of the European project. Ultimately, this crisis too reached resolution. On January 1, 1973, Britain, along with Denmark and Ireland, joined the EEC, expanding membership beyond the Six for the first time. As with the Empty Chair crisis, resolution of the crisis once again helped move Europe toward closer integration, and many of the questions surrounding the criteria for future rounds of enlargement were resolved as a result of this crisis over Britain's bid.

The 1970s and 1980s

By 1970, the plans for monetary union were in place; nonetheless the period from the mid-1970s to the 1980s is often described as one of "Euro-sclerosis" and "Euro-pessimism" (Dinan 2010: 53–72). Rather than stemming from internal obstacles, such as the crises of the 1950s and 1960s, external circumstances triggered much of the turmoil for Europe during this period. The international monetary system itself was undergoing a series of crises, and some of the main principles of the Bretton Woods System were collapsing. In particular, the decline of the dollar and its 1971 decoupling from the gold standard signaled major problems for the system that had structured global trade since 1945. Indeed, beginning in the mid-1960s, the EEC and Japan had become significant economic actors, and Europeans decided that the time was ripe for them to create their own monetary system in 1972, known as *European currency snake*. The nine member states of the EEC were soon in crisis with the failure of this system, combined with exogenous oil shocks (Arab countries quadrupled the price of oil and put an embargo on the port of Rotterdam in the wake of the 1973 Arab–Israeli war), the inability to work together to resolve the problems with the snake, and the clear monetary and economic differences among member states. As a result, the EEC quickly plunged into its first major episode of serious inflation and economic recession. It eventually climbed out of this crisis with the advent of the European Monetary System (EMS), which was an improved version of the snake, and one that included a provision to launch an eventual common currency.

The British budgetary crisis was another major event for this period that seemingly threatened the continuity of European integration through the 1970s. At last, after 1973, the UK was finally in the EEC, but the new British prime minister who returned to power in the following year, Harold Wilson, now wanted to change the terms of his country's membership agreement. Among other things, he wanted to renegotiate the UK's contribution to the common budget as it seemed that the British were putting more into it than they were getting out of it. Wilson was eventually able to gain some concessions, but they were largely superficial, and this set the stage for a resurgence of the crisis in 1979 when Prime Minister Margaret Thatcher came to power. Without a more fundamental change to the calculation of Britain's contribution to the budget, there was well-grounded fear that British public opinion would eventually turn against membership. However, because the other European member states felt the issue had been closed with Wilson's renegotiations, they developed a sense of distrust toward Thatcher. On top of that, she was not the easiest person with whom to negotiate, given her somewhat aggressive personality.

This crisis continued on into the 1980s and became far more complex than it should have been. As Dinan puts it, "[T]he 'Bloody British Question' ... nearly wrecked the EC and filled a reservoir of ill feeling toward Britain in Brussels" (2010: 62). The sense of crisis was so strong that there was discussion among European leaders of having to create a "two-speed" Europe so that the British could be on a different, slower path than the rest of the community. The antagonism and division among European countries was sharply felt. Indeed, the disillusionment over the various crises in this period was so profound that the *Economist* published an issue in March 1982 whose cover bore a cartoon of a tombstone with the EEC carved onto it with the inscription "born March 25, 1957, moribund March 25, 1982," and below that "*Capax imperii nisi imperasset*" (It seemed capable of being a power, until it tried to be one). Despite this extreme pessimism and public image of doom, this crisis was resolved in the years that followed, and the fear of a seriously altered two-speed Europe did not come to pass. Once the British budgetary question was dealt with, EEC leaders were able to move forward with their plans to complete the single market and launch the common currency. European integration was back on track, and the period of Europessimism and Eurosclerosis came to a close. As R. Daniel Keleman describes:

> *The Economist* declared the EEC to be in a near-death coma, at risk of collapsing into prolonged crisis or total stagnation ... Three years later, Jacques Delors became Commission President and launched the Single Market program that breathed new life into the EEC and paved the way for the SEA and Maastricht's Treaty on EU. In the ensuing years, the EEC (later the EC and then the EU) both widened – adding fifteen member states – and deepened – extending majority voting, enhancing the powers of the Parliament and the ECJ, gaining new powers in existing areas of economic policymaking and extending its authority to a host of new areas outside the purely economic realm. (2007: 51)

Once more, the predictions that the European project was on its last legs proved to be unfounded. With the 1986 Single European Act, the European Community entered its strongest and most vibrant period of integration since its founding.

The 1990s

The mid-1980s and the decade that followed ushered in many advancements in European integration, including the adoption of a new name – the European Union (EU). But even this period was not without punctuations of existential crisis. Early on, some ambitious plans were once more derailed. The 1992 Maastricht Treaty, solidifying the agreement on European Monetary Union (EMU), quickly encountered a major crisis (beyond the uncertainty surrounding ratification of the treaty discussed in Chapter 6). On September 16, 1992, the British government withdrew from the Exchange Rate Mechanism (ERM), an event known as "Black

Wednesday." The EU was quickly plunged into a currency crisis, as Italy withdrew, Spain devalued, and markets punished the French franc. International confidence in the EU and EMU sharply dropped; Spain, Portugal, and Ireland further devalued; and the Danish krone barely maintained its position in the ERM.

The crisis really took its toll on public perceptions and confidence in the plan to complete the single market and eventually adopt the euro. EU finance ministers were able to deal with the crisis by dramatically widening the ERM's band of fluctuation. Instead of requiring member states to stick within a 2.5 percent fluctuation, they could now comply with a 15 percent band. This enabled the EU to fend off harsh speculation from international markets against their economies and continue with their plans. The crisis ultimately showcased the strong political will of European and member-state leaders to maintain their loyalty to the EMS and to deal effectively with setbacks. The EU had once more weathered a highly visible storm and came out strong in the end.

At the same time, a major foreign policy crisis – the war in Yugoslavia and its successor states – plagued the EU and prompted serious questions about the very purpose of its existence, especially given the military role already played by NATO (Pond 1999). Since the early 1990s and the end of the Cold War, the EU had begun to see itself as *the* major actor in Europe. And in 1991, when rising ethnic nationalism in Yugoslavia threatened to break up the country, the EU felt a sense of responsibility to use its power and influence to restore stability. At this point, the EU was just on the cusp of being able to play a role, with its intense discussions on the implementation of the Common Foreign and Security Policy (CFSP). The United States was occupied with other problems in the Middle East and expected Europeans to step up to the plate this time.

In this case, the growing sense of EU crisis did not stem primarily from disagreement among member states on how to respond, but rather from the EU's ultimate inability to act and get results in the face of this serious conflict in its own backyard. Mario Zucconi argues that there were three phases of EU action in response to the war in Yugoslavia (Zucconi 1995). First, the EU's goal was to try to keep Yugoslavia united, despite growing ethnic nationalism. Some member states – Hungary, Denmark, Germany, and Austria – supported Croatian and Serbian independence, but the collective EU goal to keep Yugoslavia as a single state remained. In the second phase, beginning in the spring of 1991, the EU put forth several proposals to take control of Yugoslavia in the face of armed conflict. These included the Common Declaration for a Peaceful

Solution to the Yugoslav crisis, the Carrington-Cutileiro peace plan, and the Vance-Owen plan. But at this stage, the EU's lack of resources to put action behind its words in the foreign policy arena became evident. The various proposals were never implemented or agreed upon. Finally, in the third phase, beginning in 1992, the EU scaled down its ambitions, and in the end, the UN and NATO essentially took over control of the situation in the Yugoslav region, signaling a clear crisis in the EU's ability to be a real player beyond its own borders.

Elizabeth Pond argues that this crisis "was existential. It put to the test all the continent's gains of the previous fifty years, and especially of the post–Cold War 1990s. It challenged the assumption that at last, at the end of a terrible century, voluntary cooperation had triumphed over Nazi and Communist coercion" (Pond 1999: 77). After half a century of integration, Europeans had assumed that they now controlled the peaceful and democratic destiny of their continent, and that the Balkans were part of this destiny. The realization that this was not entirely the case constituted a European crisis. Nonetheless, this crisis paved the way for the 1998 Saint-Malo declaration between Prime Minister Tony Blair and President Jacques Chirac, which finally reconciled British and French differences on European defense, and made possible the European Security and Defence Policy (ESDP), which included for the first time an autonomous EU military capability.

The 2000s

The crises of the early twenty-first century are the focus of the main case studies in this book: the 2003 Iraq crisis for Europe (Chapter 3), the 2005 constitutional crisis (Chapter 4), and the 2010–12 Eurozone crisis (Chapter 5). In many ways, these crises appear more severe than those that came before. Part of the reason for this is that as the years go by and the EU integrates further, there is more at stake. With twenty-eight member states, a population of over half a billion, the largest economy in the world, and areas of cooperation or integration that encompass nearly every conceivable policy area, the EU has clearly demonstrated a high level of ambition when it comes to solidifying this common project. Another significant reason for the severity of these crises is the information revolution and the rise of the twenty-four-hour news cycle. The well-known cliché that "bad news sells" rings true, with news outlets continually trying to outdo each other in sensationalizing conflict. Nonetheless, the general pattern of crises that seemingly threaten the very existence of the EU continues through the decades up to today.

While crises have still been relatively unusual over the course of EU integration (i.e., many other events occurred in the rapid transformation of Europe after World War II, but did not become crises), they have nevertheless seemed to happen with surprising regularity over the years. This is especially remarkable considering that none of these crises, howsoever dire they may have seemed at the time, actually ended up taking Europe off the path toward building an ever-closer union. We know in hindsight that the EU has successfully expanded its membership and strengthened its common institutions and policies. There has even been an emerging European identity over the decades. Thus, it is noteworthy that the EU has faced many tests to its very existence, while at the same time maintaining its momentum toward ever-greater integration.

Of course, other cases could be considered as part of this list, such as the Fouchet crisis, various treaty ratification crises, the resignation of the Santer Commission, Kosovo's bid for independence, and the Russia–Georgia war, among others. Indeed, some of these other possibilities will be discussed in Chapter 6 as belonging to the category of "dogs that didn't bark" – that is, events that had similar triggers to the ones described in the rest of the book, but which were *not* perceived to be existential crises at the time.

A look at this big-picture trajectory in Europe presents two puzzles. First, why has Europe – the region that has constituted by far the most successful experiment in international cooperation since World War II – seemingly stumbled from crisis to crisis? And second, why have Europeans come out of these crises with more resolve and a strengthened will to stay together and integrate their societies and common governance even further? To answer these questions, it is necessary to take a closer look at particular crisis cases, as I do in the three main case studies of this book.

ORGANIZATION OF THE BOOK

Chapter 2 describes the framework of analysis of this book, situating my work in the existing literature on crises and discussing the methodological approach used. Specifically, I define the concept of integrational panic, explain why it emerges, and lay out the process by which crises are resolved in the European context. Chapter 2 also advances the argument that EU crises have a socially constructed dynamic to them that is often under-recognized. I argue that integrational panic – an adaptation of the widely cited sociological theory of *moral panic* – occurs in the buildup to these episodes of crisis. In particular, societal actors, especially the media, spread the perception that the current social order is under threat and cannot continue. I also explain why the concept of catharsis is useful in understanding how Europeans are ultimately able to turn these crisis events into opportunities. More generalist readers may choose to skip this conceptual chapter (which is intended to ground my approach in the scholarly literature) and move directly to the case studies after reading this introduction.

In Chapters 3, 4, and 5, I examine the three recent and most prominent crisis cases – Iraq 2003, constitution 2005, and 2010–12 Eurozone – to fully detail the pattern that spans across these different crises. Chapter 3 explains how the US invasion of Iraq in 2003 came to represent a major crisis for Europe because EU member states were divided over whether to join America's so-called coalition of the willing. As the belief became widespread among political elites that disagreement over Iraq would derail the planned enlargement of EU membership to include ten Central and Eastern European countries, it was construed as an existential crisis for the EU. The dominant crisis narrative focused on East–West tensions, which were then openly aired, especially during the height of the crisis. European leaders then resolved the crisis with several new advances in the field of security integration, including new areas of cooperation and agreement on the first European Security Strategy.

Chapter 4 argues that the ratification process of the 2005 Constitutional Treaty was seen at the time as a crisis that threatened the very existence of the EU and its ability to achieve more integration going forward. The treaty's anticipated rejection was interpreted at the time as signaling the need to scale back the ambitions of the European project and to even undo previously achieved levels of cooperation. The dominant crisis narrative was mainly about public–elite tensions. Ultimately, as social tensions were released through the course of the crisis, a renewed sense of common destiny in Europe emerged. As a result, there was open talk of a reinvigorated European public sphere and shared identity, among other things. The 2009 Lisbon Treaty followed, bringing about nearly all of the changes toward greater integration that had been proposed in the draft constitution.

Chapter 5 discusses the causes of the 2010–12 financial crisis, which brought Europe to the brink with concerns that the common currency would have to be abandoned, and with it, EU membership for several long-standing member states. This period of crisis was perhaps the most severe as it completely undermined international confidence in the future viability of the EU. In this case, as compared to the others, a self-fulfilling prophecy dynamic was most hard felt as markets reacted strongly to the crisis narrative within Europe and in the international media. The dominant narrative here was about tensions between Northern and Southern member states. The narrative about this divide became so severe that for the first time since the founding of the ECSC back in the 1950s, there was open talk of "the German problem." And yet, the end of this existential crisis heralded a new fiscal compact, a new European Stability Mechanism, a new banking union, a stronger European Central Bank, and many more significant steps toward far closer integration.

Chapter 6 concludes the book by summarizing its findings and considering non-cases of crisis, or the "dogs that didn't bark." Here I describe several instances of potential existential crisis in which societal actors, such as the media and political elites, were *less* prominent in framing crisis narratives, and show how potential crisis triggers can fail to intensify in the absence of integrational panic. At the same time, when potential crises are not used as opportunities to release tensions, a leap forward in integration is not expected. Examples in this chapter include the Maastricht Treaty ratification difficulties, Kosovo's bid for independence, Europe's reaction to the 2008 Russia–Georgia war and to Libya in 2011, the Russia–Ukraine crisis, and the British referendum on membership (Brexit), among others. When the three main cases considered in this book – Iraq, constitution, and Eurozone – are thrown into contrast with the various "non-cases" outlined in Chapter 6, the importance of societal actors in constructing existential crises becomes even more evident.

This final chapter also takes a broader look at the crisis pattern in Europe and considers the implications for this. Why do Europeans continually seem to get caught in this "crisis trap"? I argue that there is a metanarrative in the international community's understanding of the EU, which is deeply flawed and detrimental to the goals that Europeans share in common. I conclude with a note of caution: integration by crisis is a potentially dangerous means of advancing the European project, even though it paradoxically boosts the political will behind this. Ultimately, incremental integration has met with more success in terms of achieving long-term stability and augmenting Europe's role in the world.

References

Cross, Mai'a K. Davis. 2011. *Security Integration in Europe: How Knowledge-based Networks Are Transforming the European Union.* Ann Arbor: University of Michigan Press, 2011.

Crowe, Brian. 2003. "A Common European Foreign Policy after Iraq?" *International Affairs* 79(3): 533–546.

CVCE, 2012. "The Refusal to Ratify the EDC Treaty." *Centre Virtuel de la Connaissance sur l'Europe*, September 11.

de Murville, Maurice Couve. 1971. *Une politique étrangere (1958–1969).* Paris: Plon. Translation CVCE.EU by UNI.LU

Dinan, Desmond. 2010. *Ever Closer Union: An Introduction to European Integration*, fourth edition. Boulder, CO: Lynn Rienner Publishers.

The Economist. 2002. "The European Union: Restoring Europe's Smile." October 24.

Gamble, Andrew. 2006. "European Disunion." *British Journal of Politics & International Relations* 8(1): 34–49.

Gleissner, Martin and Claes H. de Vreese. 2005. "News about the EU Constitution: Journalistic Challenges and Media Portrayal of the European Union Constitution." *Journalism* 6(2): 221–242.

Jo, Sam-Sang. 2007. *European Myths: Resolving the Crises in the European Community/European Union.* Lanham, MD: University Press of America.

Keleman, R. Daniel. 2007. "Built to Last? The Durability of EU Federalism," In *Making History: European Integration and Institutional Change at Fifty*, Oxford: Oxford University Press, 51–66.

Lewis, Jeffrey. 2009. "EU Policy on Iraq: The Collapse and Reconstruction of Consensus Based Foreign Policy." *International Politics* 45(4): 432–450.

Paulus, E. G. 1963. "Starke Verärgerung über de Gaulle." *Süddeutsche Zeitung.* Münchner Neueste Nachrichten aus Politik, Kultur, Wirtschaft und Sport. Hrsg. Dürrmeier, Hans; RHerausgeber Proebst, Herman. Nr. 14; 19. Jg. München: Süddeutscher Verlag., January 16, p. 1.

Pond, Elizabeth. 1999. "Kosovo: Catalyst for Europe." *The Washington Quarterly* 22(4): 77–92.

Spaey, J. 1953. "What Has Become of the Political Community?" *La Voix Fédéraliste*, (Spring): 13–15.

Thies, Wallace. 2012. "Is the EU Collapsing?" *International Studies Review* 14(2): 225–239.

Zucconi, Mario. 1995. "The European Union in the Former Yugoslavia." In *Preventing Conflict in the Post-Communist World: Mobilizing International and Regional Organizations*, edited by Abram Chayes and Antonia Handler Chayes. Washington, DC: Brookings Institution, 237–278.

2

Explaining Existential Crises

INTRODUCTION

Crises are opportunities for change. And both crises and change are at the heart of the study of politics and international relations. Yet, as John Ikenberry writes, "our scholarly theories need to grapple more effectively with the problem of continuity and change in the international political order" (Ikenberry 2008: 7). The dominant accounts that explain change in international relations tend to rely more on statist structural frameworks of explanation (Hellmann 2008: 28–52). As a result, there is a tendency to neglect the role of human agency in scholarly attempts to explain and understand international crises.

Delving into the vast landscape of theories about crises is akin to opening up Pandora's box. Almost any event of interest in international relations can be characterized as a crisis at one point or another: war, coup d'état, ethnic conflict, humanitarian disaster, regime change, resource scarcity, climate change, power transition, and so on. On some level, the study of crises can almost be equated to the study of international relations itself.[1] Thus, this chapter must, by necessity, focus on certain aspects of this literature, and not provide an exhaustive account. Specifically, the aim here is to situate my approach – with its emphasis

---

[1] In the field of international relations, most work on international crises addresses incidences of violence and war as forms of crisis. For example, Michael Brecher (1993) extensively analyzes the nature of military-security crises that often result in war. In a later book, Brecher, together with Jonathan Wilkenfeld (1997), exhaustively examine dozens of case studies of international crises around the world that have a variety of triggers resulting in violence.

on the importance of social narratives about crises – in the literature that seeks to understand crises. I argue that to a significant extent, crisis narratives shed light on the buildup of existential crises in Europe because they reveal these crises' socially constructed underpinnings. In this chapter, I introduce a framework of analysis based on what I call "integrational panic" to explain the origins of EU crises, and similarly use the concept of catharsis to shed light on the process of crisis resolution.

Defining "Crisis"

While the term "crisis" is used frequently in everyday situations to refer to a wide range of events, a baseline understanding is that a crisis must be seen as a relatively *unusual* event in the history of an organization, institution, or society (Seeger, Sellnow, and Ulmer 2003: 4). I adopt a widely accepted definition of "crisis" here:

> a serious threat to the basic structures or the fundamental values and norms of a social system, which – under time pressure and highly uncertain circumstances – necessitates making critical decisions. (Rosenthal, Charles, and 't Hart 1989: 10)

Because a crisis is unexpected, it triggers some urgency for leaders to respond in new ways to manage and then resolve it. Ikenberry defines *"international* crisis" in a similar way:

> a historical juncture when conflict within the political order has risen to the point that the interests, institutions, and shared identities that define and undergird the political system are put in jeopardy. The settled rules, expectations, and institutions that constitute the political order are rendered unsettled. Conflict has pushed the very existence of the political order to the brink. (Ikenberry 2008: 3)

Going further, Ikenberry argues that in recognizing a crisis, one or more of the following must occur:

> (1) a fundamental disagreement breaks out over what at least one side believes is a core interest; (2) a sharp break occurs in market and social interdependence; (3) an institutional breakdown occurs regarding the rules and norms of process; (4) and/or a breakdown occurs in a sense of community. (Ikenberry 2008: 12)

Many international crises are explained by variables associated with power and security (i.e., power shifts, divergent strategic cultures), economic interests (i.e., growing economic interdependence can spark conflict), institutions, law and sovereignty (i.e., legal rules that provide "normative grist for disagreement"), or values and political identity (i.e., a breakdown of shared community or conceptions of democracy)

(Ikenberry 2008: 14–26). But there is a difference of degrees between conflict and crisis, and additionally between crisis and *existential crisis*. If a crisis is constructed through negative and heightened characterizations of events involving conflict, then an existential crisis can be understood as when these heightened characterizations also anticipate a fundamental change or end of a certain way of life. In the context of understanding EU crises, an existential crisis is marked by widespread belief that the EU's very existence and/or core characteristics are seriously under threat.

Explaining EU Crises: Causes and Consequences

The first task of this chapter is to explain why EU crises emerge and build in intensity. In advancing the perspective that crisis narratives – how people talk about crises – shed light on this dynamic, I show in the three main case studies examined in this book (Chapters 3 through 5) that EU existential crises are perceived as such because they are to some extent *socially constructed*; that is, society (at the public and/or elite levels) recognizes and defines an event as a crisis. This argument rests on the power of ideas in influencing how people respond to events and shape their meanings. As Craig Parsons puts it, "[I]deational logic suggests that certain historically situated people develop their own ways of interpreting the world around them, and that this shapes how they act" (Parsons 2007: 102).[2] In other words, beliefs shape actions and steer people in certain directions.[3] For example, when EU member states disagree on foreign policy decisions, these events are often treated as routine: it is generally expected that on occasion EU countries will have different opinions on these issues, and they will not be able to speak with one voice. However, in the case of the 2003 Iraq crisis, key societal actors defined disagreement over whether or not to side with the United States as a crisis for EU integration and enlargement (see Chapter 3). In other cases, such as when EU member states disagreed over intervention in Mali in 2012, commentators, political leaders, and other opinion shapers chose to define this as a "shortcoming" of EU

---

[2] Of course, as Parsons explains, there are limits to how far such interpretation can go, as people have certain filters and subjective lenses through which they form their beliefs in a given context. Moreover, there is an objective environment that they are interpreting in the first place, and this creates some boundaries for beliefs (Parsons 2007: 97).

[3] An example of this kind of argument is William Reddy's study of the French textile trade in nineteenth-century Europe. People believed labor markets appeared in this context, and even though they had not, people behaved as if they did (Parsons 2007: 103).

capabilities, rather than as a crisis (German Marshall Fund 2013). To put it counterfactually, if the Iraq crisis had not been perceived as a crisis that threatened the very existence of the EU, then it might have passed by as just another foreign policy shortcoming for Europe.

Building upon these observations, I argue that there is a discernible pattern in the evolution of crises in the European region. The initial development of crises depends upon societal perceptions. As such, there is always an *interpretive stage* of some kind during which it is determined whether or not an event will be seen as a crisis. As I will elaborate, with the powerful role of the media in today's world, the interpretation of events is filtered, amplified, and often defined through media coverage of events. Then, depending on how social actors, such as the media, interpret potential crisis triggers, these events can become self-fulfilling prophecies. That is, after the initial interpretation of the event, during which society forms perceptions of it, new developments can contribute to the buildup of crisis, and can gain traction mainly because a crisis atmosphere already exists. For example, during the 2011 Eurozone crisis, when speculators began to bet against the viability of the euro, borrowing costs went up in many EU member states that had previously had healthy economies, leading to tangible problems for businesses and employers (see Chapter 5). Moreover, when policy makers then reacted with a strict turn to austerity, this clearly exacerbated the crisis, making it worse than even initial negative perceptions had predicted. Once a crisis builds momentum in this way, it then becomes difficult to distinguish which events may not have developed into a crisis if only people had perceived and behaved differently at the time.

The second task of this chapter is to explain the circumstances surrounding how Europeans tend to deal with crises once they happen. A multitude of actors, from expert groups to politicians to bureaucrats, may weigh in on what to do about a crisis. But it is, by definition, an *urgent* discussion in which exigency prevails. After all, the very continued existence of the EU comes under question during these times. Discussions surrounding how to resolve existential crises are thus emotional, direct, and oftentimes, raw. As I show in Chapters 3 through 5, it is in the very urgency of this crisis atmosphere that the impetus toward crisis resolution takes place. Specifically, I argue that a kind of catharsis occurs, releasing tensions that would otherwise remain more under the surface, impeding the achievement of European integration goals. By using crises as opportunities to release these tensions, EU actors are then able to move forward with a renewed will to work together to find lasting solutions.

Layout of the Chapter

The remainder of the chapter elaborates upon this book's framework of analysis, situating it in the existing literature on the subject. I divide this analysis into the two overarching explanations introduced earlier in this chapter: (1) the origins of crises and (2) the resolution of crises.[4] The first section that follows discusses when and why an event becomes defined as a crisis in the first place. One key debate in the literature is whether crises can be objectively measured or whether it is necessary to take subjective interpretations about crises into consideration. I argue that the latter fits better with understanding the nature of EU existential crises. Societal perception and reaction is indispensable to any explanation about the initial causes of crises, especially because societies are essential to not only defining crises as such, but also in constructing them. In this respect, I introduce a new concept, integrational panic, which builds upon the sociological literature on moral panic, as a framework for understanding the social construction of crises in the European context.

In the second section, I examine the dynamics behind how societies manage and resolve crises, as well as the end result. I argue that the concept of catharsis is a valuable tool for understanding why EU crises result in more integration. This will set the stage for the rest of the book, which explains why the EU has seemingly suffered from numerous existential crises, and yet has repeatedly turned these episodes into opportunities for growth and innovation. Of course, there are literally hundreds of books and articles across numerous fields of study wholly devoted to conceptualizing different kinds of crises. It would be impossible to survey this vast literature in detail here, but I endeavor to outline some of the broad brushstrokes in order to situate my approach in the scholarly debate about the causes and consequences of crises.

PERSPECTIVES ON THE ORIGINS OF CRISES

In the social sciences, there are at least three perspectives – systemic, behavioral, and sociological – that grapple with crises and seek to explain how and why they happen (Geva, Mayhar, and Skorick 2000; see also Schmitt 1922/2004; Gamble 2006; Neal 2009). When it comes to

---

[4] Some scholars in the crisis literature describe three phases: pre-crisis, crisis, and post-crisis. For example, see Seeger et al. (2003). However, if the focus is on explanation, then it seems appropriate to divide the analysis into origins and resolution.

explaining the origins of EU existential crises, I suggest that the socio-logical approach, which prioritizes the importance of perception and societal interpretation, offers the most explanatory power. A closer look at each of these perspectives will show why.

Systemic/Structural Perspectives

One major approach to understanding the origins of crises is the systemic/structural perspective, which argues that crises result from "unfolding events" that enable "destabilizing forces" in the international system to disturb routine patterns, undermine institutions, and ultimately threaten the nature of the existing structure (Crozier 1964; Young 1968: 6–15; Almond, Flanagan, and Mundt 1973; Linz and Stepan 1978). The argument is that crisis events simply occur, and then decision makers must find a way to reinstate stability, which may require fundamentally changing the system in place. This approach takes as a given that crises are objective, structural phenomena, and that human perceptions do not matter (Young 1968; Verba 1971; Gourevitch 1984; Jo 2007). It assumes that crises originate from structural factors that are built in and "that come to represent an undeniable threat to the system" (Boin et al. 2005: 5). New institutionalist accounts can also be situated within this structural approach. Paul Pierson, for example, argues that critical junctures are not only produced by exogenous factors, but could also stem from endogen-ous factors such as path dependence, threshold effects, cumulative causes, extended causal chains, and so on (Pierson 2003).

The structural approach, however, encounters potentially serious diffi-culty in that there are numerous instances in which potential triggering events, and even systemic change, are neither seen as crises nor treated that way. For example, this approach would not work well in explaining the 2005 EU constitutional crisis as this crisis was actually fully under way *before* the results of the negative referenda in France and the Netherlands (see Chapter 5). A systemic analysis would assume that the negative referenda were the objective points at which the EU could be said to be in crisis. But this would miss the earlier socially constructed dimension – clearly visible in international media coverage at the time – that Europe was in existential crisis well before the negative referenda. In other words, the structural/systemic approach tends to discount the role of human perception and reaction to events in understanding the causes of crises, and thus may miss numerous cases in which the structure of the system would anticipate a crisis, but the crisis failed to materialize. Or it may miss cases where there was nothing in the structure to indicate a potential crisis, yet human interpretation defined an event as a crisis anyway.

Behavioral Perspectives

A second approach to explaining the origins of crises is the behavioral perspective. Rather than assuming that the ingredients for crises are somehow embedded in the structure of the system, this approach prioritizes the behavior of individuals as they relate to the system around them, particularly in how they are constrained by a set of utility-maximizing preferences. From this perspective, Charles Hermann argues that crises emerge when an event:

(1) threatens one or more important goals of a state, that is, the group of authoritative policy makers who constitute the state, (2) allows only a short time for decision before the situation is significantly transformed, and (3) occurs as a surprise to the policy makers.   (Hermann 1972:187)

Behavioralists see the study of crises as objective in that these are measurable events with certain *thresholds* that can be determined through analysis of the observable "facts" involved. Billings et al. argue, that the threshold depends on "the perceived value of possible loss, probability of loss, and time pressure" (Billings, Milburn, and Schaalman 1980: 303–304). They define "loss" as the difference in one's state of being before and after the triggering event. So, from this perspective, there is a measurable point at which an event becomes a crisis based on the calculation of the costs involved.

Beyond more systemic or structural crises, behavioralism tends to emphasize individual cost calculation and scientific measures of crisis triggers and thresholds. It tends to underplay the social processes that are often so fundamental to the construction of nonstructural crises. This emphasis on rational cost calculation does not fit well with the pattern of EU crises. For example, investors and speculators took advantage of market fluctuations during the Eurozone crisis, which in turn aggravated the crisis, but this should not be confused with rational behavior. These investors and speculators acted based on perceptions about the viability of the euro and the media-driven belief that the union might fall apart. Moreover, Europeans often willingly take on *more* cost during and after crises to keep integration moving forward, as they did with the repeated bailouts during the Eurozone crisis. To understand cost or loss calculation, it is necessary to investigate what people value, which in the case of the EU may also be the *idea* of a supranational entity (Cross 2012: 229–246).

Sociological Perspectives

A third major perspective on crises draws upon sociology and fully delves into the socially constructed and "subjectively perceived" nature of crises (Hay 1999: 317–344). Colin Hay, for example, argues that shared narratives about crises are what bring them into existence, not calculations of loss or cost. Similarly, Carroll Estes argues that social construction "does not deny or ignore the existence of objective phenomena . . . . Social action, however, is inseparable from the socially constructed ideas that define and interpret these phenomena" (Estes 1983: 446). This sociological approach, which takes human interpretation into account, has valuable explanatory power because it can tell us why various events have built up into crises while others have not, as well as those that grew into major crises in part because of societal perception. Thus, Ikenberry's "extraordinary moment" of crisis occurs when society *perceives* that an event represents a threat to the current political or social order.

Within this sociological perspective, a central question becomes: which constituent of society is most central to the social construction of crises? Classic Marxist theories tend to emphasize the power of elites to engineer crises out of minor issues to serve their own selfish purposes, such as to divert public attention away from real issues of concern. This argument assumes that the general public has little agency of its own and that their issues of concern do not ultimately matter unless elites exploit them in some way (Chambliss and Mankoff 1976; Hall et al. 1978; Reinarman and Levine 1997; Goode and Ben-Yehuda 2009: 62–66). From this elite perspective, the media echoes elite-constructed narratives because they have a kind of embedded respect for elite views and have access to them in reporting a story (Hall et al. 1978: 57; Goode and Ben-Yehuda 2009: 55–57).

On the opposite end of the spectrum, scholars who subscribe to a more grassroots model emphasize the importance of the general public in constructing crises (Morin 1971; Victor 1993, Brunvand 2001: 55–57; Goode and Ben-Yehuda 2009: 64). The argument is that instead of elites engineering the terms of crisis narratives, they are actually feeding off of the sentiments that already exist in the regular public. If the media or elites were to attempt to construct concern around issues that did not already strike a chord with society, the public would not take the bait. Thus, from this grassroots perspective, the most elites and the media can do is echo and amplify public perception to a limited extent.

In between these two extremes is the argument that interest groups in the middle of the social hierarchy matter most in constructing crises.

Interest groups, in this sense, are defined as groups of opinion makers, such as the media, epistemic communities, NGOs, businesses, lobbying groups, professional organizations, and so on. They may construct crises either for material or normative reasons. For example, the media may choose (consciously or not) to frame events as crises because "bad news sells," whereas a professional organization of human rights experts may spread a crisis narrative about the need to stop trafficking in humans because it is quite simply the right thing to do.

These three arguments within the sociological approach – emphasizing the role of elites, the regular public, or interest groups such as the media – differ merely as a matter of emphasis. In every case study and context, one or another societal actor may be most important in defining events as crises, but all three should be considered in understanding the nature of these events. As will be argued later in this chapter, contemporary crises in particular seem to have a heavy media-driven component, and it may be true that in most cases an event comes to be defined as a crisis for the first time in news coverage. Only then does it take on a broader crisis narrative within the general public that can turn into a self-fulfilling prophecy.

This sociological approach to crises, which takes human interpretation and agency into account, has valuable explanatory power because it can tell us why various events on the road to EU integration have built up into crises while others have not (as discussed in Chapter 6). Of course, most crises have elements of all three of the societal levels just discussed. Indeed, many events might have become crises if leaders had not ignored them. And, conversely, it would often be quite difficult for the general public to rally around a crisis issue without opinion makers to help guide them toward specific narratives. The sociological approach is also important because it takes into account a potential gap between how events are perceived and the actual conditions of events on the ground. In addition, this approach is not so broad as to encompass systemic changes while not so narrow as to only consider the effects on specific organizational structures. From this perspective, examining the narrative(s) about the origins and nature of the crisis is the most reliable way to gain insight into these critical junctures.[5]

---

[5] Naturally, an approach that seeks to capture subjective interpretation is not as easily executed from a research perspective as those that rely on "objective" measures. However, as Bovens and 't Hart (1996) argue it is necessary to understand why some events become perceived as crises even while potentially more destabilizing events pass by without much attention.

To explain the origins of EU crises, my framework of analysis is situated within this sociological approach. In particular, I identify the analytical tools from the field of sociology that can tell us about the most severe form of crisis: existential crises. That is, when a crisis is perceived to be so severe that it threatens an actor's very existence.

Integrational Panic

How specifically are EU crises socially constructed and subjectively perceived? What explains their repeated occurrence? To grapple with these core questions, the sociological concept of *moral panic* is a useful point of departure for understanding this dimension of EU existential crises.[6]

From Moral Panic to Integrational Panic

The theory of moral panic, first developed in the 1960s, seeks to explain specific instances of societal overreaction to what is perceived to be a growing problem within that society (Rohloff and Wright 2010: 404). As Charles Krinsky writes, "A moral panic may be defined as an episode, often triggered by alarming media stories and reinforced by reactive laws and public policy, of exaggerated or misdirected public concern, anxiety, fear, or anger over a perceived threat to social order" (Krinsky 2013: 1). Thus, the purpose of the approach is to show how and why societal actors, especially the mass media, construct concern or anxiety over a social issue that constitutes an out-of-proportion reaction. This reaction can build up to such an extent that it poses a threat to the principles underlying a given society. In other words, moral panics are crises, according to the standard definition – they are seen as "a serious threat to the basic structures or the fundamental values and norms of a social system" (Rosenthal, Charles, and 't Hart 1989: 10).

Even though the theory of moral panic was developed to explain how some actors *within* society come to be defined as threats to dominant social values, an adaptation of this concept – integrational panic – is valuable in understanding the pattern of major EU crises. Unlike in the case of moral panic, societal concern that arises from integrational panic is not about a threat to morality or shared values; instead it is about a threat to the common European project of integration. I define "integrational panic" as a social overreaction to a perceived problem with EU

---

[6] As Cohen (2002) argues, "panic" is not to be taken literally, but as a metaphor for the overall social reaction to an episode or event.

integration[7] and argue that it is the key phenomenon that characterizes the social construction of existential crises in Europe. In other words, these major episodes of crisis have taken on an existential quality precisely because integrational panic is what is driving them.

Numerous events such as disagreement over foreign policy, questions over whether a new treaty will be approved, or a debt problem in a small member state occur frequently and relatively routinely, but only some grow into perceived existential crises for the EU. As I will demonstrate in the case studies, social processes, especially the role of the media, determine when this occurs. As with cases of moral panic, the central quality of integrational panic is the disproportionate reaction to events. The media is not the only social actor stirring up crises, but in the twenty-first century, it serves as a kind of threat multiplier, amplifying negative ideas about events that potentially threaten the onward trajectory of EU integration.

The rich sociological literature on moral panic is helpful in many respects in terms of understanding the origins and buildup of crises, as well as the identification of the actors involved. I now turn to a more specific look at how we can recognize integrational panic when it happens, which actors are involved, and what characterizes their actions in the early stages of crisis.

Who Panics?

Sociologists who have researched moral panics have tried to operationalize the various components of it (Goode and Ben-Yehuda 2009: 2). Some key questions that arise are as follows: Who panics? In other words and for our purposes here, must *all* of European society panic to qualify as integrational panic, or can the panic be confined just to elites, or just to the mass media? What type of behavior is characteristic of this type of panic? And what types of events trigger integrational panic?

Stanley Cohen's approach to moral panics is useful in breaking down the societal dynamics in integrational panic. He sees segments of society as actors in a drama. These actors may be different depending on the nature of the crisis, but consistent players in these dramas are the media, the public, and agents of social control (Cohen 2002; Goode and Ben-Yehuda 2009: 22). Integrational panic follows similar lines, but since these panics are political in nature, political leaders at the national and EU levels can be

---

[7] In the language of moral panic theory, EU integration itself is repeatedly defined as the scapegoat, or "the 'folk devil' onto whom public fears and fantasies are projected" (Hunt 1997: 631) during crises.

thought of as the "agents of social control" in Cohen's conceptualization. Thus, the societal levels involved in integrational panic are the regular public, the media (and other interest groups), and political leaders. The interaction between and among different societal actors contributes to the perception of crisis. They make claims about whether an event constitutes a crisis, and the meaning behind this (Critcher 2003). And while many societal actors interact to contribute to the perception of crisis, it is not necessary for all to be involved for events to lead to integrational panic.

The Media

It is unlikely that the public *on its own* would be able to craft a coherent narrative about problems with EU integration. Arguably no societal actor is as powerful as the media in enabling public perceptions of crisis to build around specific narratives. The media has the unique ability to pick up and amplify the perceptions of other societal actors, especially other opinion shapers and leaders. As Critcher argues, "[Media discourses] define, describe and delimit what it is possible to say and not possible to say" (Critcher 2003: 170). Figure 2.1 represents how interconnected these three types of actors are, and the disproportionate role played by the media in inciting integrational panic.

On a practical level, the media has the power to disseminate information to and reach a large audience in a way that no other actor does. However, beyond the media's power to reach many people, the manipulation, exaggeration, or misinterpretation of events is common, particularly in light of the intense pressure to provide news first, and to update that information more quickly than the competition. In the process, communications scholars have shown that the media tends to spin events in

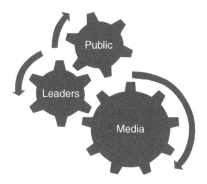

FIGURE 2.1 Interaction among the media, the public, and leaders

a negative direction (Critcher 2003). The cliché that "bad news sells" bears out in practice, especially when it comes to crises. As Seeger et al. write:

> Media coverage of crises has become more aggressive and frequent, with the proliferation of news magazines and 24-hour news programs. Typically, the media seeks information about scope of harm, cause, blame, responsibility, and remedial efforts. Generally, the broader the scope of harm and the more dramatic and visual the event, the more extensive the media coverage.
>
> (Seeger, Sellnow, and Ulmer 2003: 8)

In the early stages of a potential crisis, the media can play a particularly strong role. In these situations, it tends to overreport, exaggerate, and distort events as well as predict that the worst is still to come (Goode and Ben-Yehuda 2009: 23). It also uses the power of language to create ready symbols of a crisis (Critcher 2003: 12). Since the public needs information about a crisis in order to react, the media is at the core of whether publics understand an event to be a crisis or not (Cohen 2002). Moreover, news reports often cite official sources, which make their coverage seem more convincing to the regular public, even if there is a distinctive bias to the stories (Hall et al. 1978; Thompson 1998: 68–69; Critcher 2003: 14). Naturally, journalists do not craft such stories out of thin air. There is an interaction effect between media framing and public or elite narratives about an event. Perhaps a leader makes a statement, or an interest group – like rating agencies or lobbyists – speaks a little louder about an issue of concern. Nonetheless, the media can either make or break a potential crisis depending on its collective choices about framing and volume of coverage.

In effect, the media typically serves as the "primary definer" of a crisis (Critcher 2003: 15). In the fields of communications and media studies, this is often referred to as *framing*. As Valkenburg et al. define it, "A media frame is a particular way in which journalists compose a news story to optimize audience accessibility . . . They use certain frames to simplify and give meaning to events, and to maintain audience interest" (Valeknburg, Semetko, and de Vreese 1999: 550–551). Studies of media framing in the field of communications show that the Western media often uses a *conflict frame* in its coverage (Semetko and Valkenburg 2000). Journalists tend to cast problems as "us vs. them," often emphasizing winners and losers, and using the symbolism of war or competition (Jamieson 1992; Patterson 1993; Valkenburg, Semetko, and de Vreese 1999). This type of framing has been shown to increase the level of cynicism readers feel about an event (Cappella and Jamieson 1996 as cited in Valkenburg, Semetko, and de Vreese 1999). In general, there is a clear causal link between the way journalists frame news and how people think about issues (Price, Tewksbury, and Powers 1997). Critcher (2003: 171) and Fowler recognize that "[t]he press inevitably use a form of cultural shorthand, instantly recognizable to journalists and to their audience, so that 'stereotypes are the currency of negotiation'" (Fowler 1991: 17).

Thus, if media coverage of EU events defines a crisis as such, frames it as potentially derailing EU integration, and emphasizes a kind of "us vs. them" conflict, it is likely to be a contributing factor to integrational panic, and subsequently, to the social construction of crisis. Key indicators that the media is playing a role in constructing an existential crisis for Europe include the use of symbols (such as "war" among member states or "death" of the EU), exaggeration of the scope of the problem, predictions that the end of Europe is at hand, and disproportional coverage of a specific event compared to other noteworthy news items or compared to previous coverage of the same or a similar issue.

Beyond day-to-day decisions about how to frame the news, when reporting on Europe specifically, the international media has internalized a grand or metanarrative that Europe is nearly always stumbling from crisis to crisis. Thus, it becomes a kind of knee-jerk reaction for the media to pay attention to the region mainly when crises are seemingly brewing. Also, this metanarrative includes the perception that the EU is an elitist project in which Brussels bureaucrats do whatever they want and are out of touch with regular people. This message comes across in the way the media reports on issues, which then exacerbates this elitist impression. As Chien-Yi Lu argues, "The prevailing journalistic styles of reporting EU news, which inform citizens about legislation only after their adoption and leave out the vital details of what influences had been exerted and by whom, only reinforce the perception that public opinion matters little" to EU decision makers (Lu 2008: 443). This metanarrative also includes the belief that the EU is inherently difficult to understand, especially for journalists, economists, and the general public. Moreover, and partially as a result, they consistently underestimate the degree to which European integration is actually occurring (Lundestad 2005: 21). Whatever the facts are surrounding a particular story, this metanarrative is easy to fall back on: the failure of Europe, the unwieldy nature of its institutions, and the complicated rules and procedures that seem so inefficient. These assumptions are not grounded in reality, but they further help legitimize the confusion that nonexperts have about the history and functioning of the EU.

A crisis builds when social reactions to a potential crisis grow from being relatively average events into a sense of threat to the continuation of the system. It is difficult to generalize about what motivates the media to pick up and amplify one event as compared to another (Gleissner and de Vreese 2005: 221–242; Baum and Groeling 2009; Krzyzanowski and Galansinska 2009), but it is not enough to say that disagreements within Europe lead to crises because there are always disagreements, and they do not always lead to crises. Society cannot react unless it has the information that forms its perceptions in the first place (Cohen 2002: chapter 2). Some kind of catalyst must define a crisis as such, and the media is often the main actor that has the power to shape perceptions in this direction.

The Role of the Public and Leaders

The media, however, is not the beginning and end of the story of EU crises. If the media were to escalate an issue through overreporting and exaggeration, but this elicited little public concern, then the fuel for crisis would likely burn out (Cohen 2002: 65–70; Goode and Ben-Yehuda 2009: 25). But how does the public matter? One challenge of examining the grassroots level is that it is difficult to talk of "the public" and "society" as if they are somehow monolithic. After all, there are so many motivations and social currents at work in any given interaction or reaction. How does public response consolidate around specific themes and viewpoints? In the field of sociology, social reaction theory recognizes that important events such as crises result in multiple reactions, some related to the real problem or tension that has occurred, and others wholly unrelated (Garland 2008: 23).[8] As Cohen points out, in the very disproportionality of moral panics is the symbolic indication that there exists some deeper source of tension within or across societies (Cohen 2002). The same is true for integrational panic. In effect, the crisis event that the media talks up becomes an excuse for the European public to air preexisting tensions. In each of the three detailed case studies described in this book, integrational panic is not just about a reaction to the crisis event itself – such as disagreement over foreign policy or a treaty that may not pass referenda – but about a range of underlying societal tensions: East vs. West (in the 2003 Iraq crisis), public vs. elite (in the 2005 constitutional crisis), and North vs. South (in the 2010–12 Eurozone crisis).

---

[8] For example, the notion of *risk society* describes a public preoccupied with concern over what the future will bring in modern society, such as over-reliance on technology, environmental degradation, changing norms of lifestyle, and political repression. Some of these perceptions about these risks are objective, and others are subjective (Beck, 1992: 50).

Similarly, at the intersection of psychology and sociology, the literature on crowd psychology, which examines how groups of people take on a different dynamic than if they were to react as individuals, is also valuable in understanding the role of publics in the social construction of crises. Gustave Le Bon (1895) argues that in crowds, individuals feel more insulated from the repercussions of their actions – they feel anonymous – and therefore are more likely to react emotionally or at the extreme end of the spectrum. Sigmund Freud (1921) argues that emotional responses within crowds tend to tack toward the least common denominator, meaning that responses become more basic, simple, or even primitive. Group unity enables overall weak social restraint since no individual within the group is the focus of attention.[9] With widespread use of the Internet, the crowd effect has gone virtual as well. Members of the public may read their news online, and then anonymously post their responses, feeding into the tensions that are increasingly strengthened and solidified in the press. The anonymity associated with online posting encourages responses that are far more sharply worded and controversial than would be the case if participants were meeting face-to-face (Christopherson 2007). Even long before the existence of the Internet, Plato, in his parable about the ring of Gyges, argued that anonymity or invisibility could encourage extreme behavior (Zhuo 2010).

All of these factors can contribute to the rise of tensions in crisis narratives. Thus, it is the very fact that individuals act in groups that enables them to cohere around specific ideas. These individuals may be different in many other ways, but they come to embody certain basic arguments they wish to advance. Naturally, there are numerous instances in which publics react in routine ways to EU issues of concern – both vocal and quiet reactions can help move the system forward and provide legitimacy. But in cases of integrational panic, there is clear interaction between public perception and media-packaged information. The pattern in this interaction often plays out as illustrated in Figure 2.2.

As Figure 2.2 indicates, leaders certainly play their part in this dynamic as well, especially as they exist at both the elite, political level, and at the activist or grassroots level. They may be experts on the issue involved in a particular crisis, or official bureaucrats charged with addressing the matter. Like the media, what leaders share in common is the ability to shape public opinion.

---

[9] Although much of the literature focuses on how crowds become aggressive or violent, they also recognize that group actions can be either positive or negative.

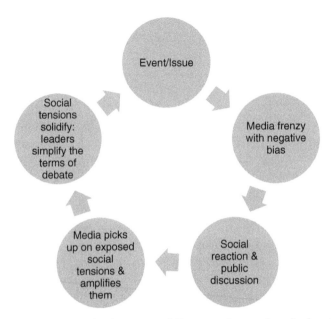

FIGURE 2.2 Interaction between public perceptions and media framing

During the buildup of crises, elite opinion makers are instrumental in persuading others of the nature of the problem and oftentimes in assigning blame. Later on, they become the key agents for resolving crises.

In particular, publics rely on leaders to articulate their concerns. In the studies of social reaction and crowd psychology alluded to earlier, publics often play off of the leaders' narratives about events. Emergent norm theory suggests that most individuals within a crowd are actually followers, and thus they require some kind of leadership to guide them and create coherence in their messages (Turner and Killian 1957). David Garland writes,

A precondition for the recurring investment of the mass media and the political class in panic-producing processes is, no doubt, the emotional energy and collective excitement that are unleashed whenever a mass public can be provoked into feeling passionate outrage, together with all the opportunities that this energy provides.   (Garland 2008:18)

Indeed, Joseph Nye finds that leadership "involves relationships of power within groups" because a leader "helps a group create and achieve shared goals" (Nye 2008: 18). His central claim that leaders tend to lead from the middle and that they become leaders when followers recognize them as such further emphasizes the importance of the interaction of the various societal constituents in constructing crises.

Leaders are just one societal group in a crisis drama, and while they may be more influential than publics at shaping opinion, they too are subject to the overwhelming power of the media, which continually selects and interprets their statements. What leaders say to the public is nearly always filtered through the media. The end result is that sometimes leaders can be ignored, and at other times certain statements they make can be disproportionately amplified. For example, when member-state leaders publicly affirmed their commitment to the ongoing existence of the euro during the Eurozone crisis, they were largely ignored in the press. But when US Defense Secretary Donald Rumsfeld referred to "old Europe" and "new Europe" during the buildup of the 2003 Iraq crisis, this had a disproportionate impact because of the media frenzy that ensued. There can sometimes be a kind of spiral effect between leaders and the media, creating intensification of panic (Critcher 2003: 15). However much leaders try to shape public opinion, they still rely on the media to get their points across. Whenever journalists react with exaggeration or disproportionality, they define the terms of the debate for leaders. In this sense, the media is often more influential than leaders in defining crises.

Crises are complex phenomena, but they are fundamentally *social* phenomena. They have multiple social causes, and these factors interact with each other, leading to the origination and buildup of crises that may often be unanticipated.

PERSPECTIVES ON THE RESOLUTION OF CRISES

Much of the literature on crises deals with their resolution and addresses a range of important questions in this respect: How do various actors respond to crises once they emerge? Which actors matter most? What types of reactions are more likely to aggravate or ameliorate their evolution? Why do existential crises end, and what are their potential outcomes? Explanations of crisis resolution range from the more sinister "shock doctrine," with its antidemocratic underpinnings, to the more optimistic projections of the "high reliability" approach, which puts its faith in well-designed institutions to absorb any disturbances to the system.

Moral panic theory predicts that crisis episodes of social upheaval will dissipate as quickly as they appear, as there is little real basis for them to continue once the media becomes occupied elsewhere (Critcher 2003).

Similarly, with integrational panic, I anticipate that the perception of existential crisis could also end as quickly as it appears, even if societies and institutions are still dealing with the aftermath for some time to come, as in the case of the Eurozone crisis.[10] Since there is a socially constructed dynamic involved, when the public loses interest or media coverage shifts its attention to other issues, the sense of existential threat can quickly dissipate. At the same time, however, because integrational panic is about more than a threat to morality, it carries with it the possibility of a self-fulfilling prophecy. For example, if a crisis trigger involves financial markets, there is a high degree of vulnerability to external perception or misperception that can lead to real actions based on fears of market failure. In the process, these actions in turn can make market failure more likely, and then lead to the distinct possibility that no resolution to the crisis might be found.

How and why do EU crises ultimately resolve instead of succumbing to the tensions and fears that surface with integrational panic? There is often casual reference to the notion that crises create a window of opportunity for EU integration, whether it is through making competing preferences explicit (Menon 2004), providing an opportunity for self-definition (Everts and Keohane 2003), seeking a return to policy coherence (Natorski 2015), or creating a European public sphere through a politicized citizenry (Risse 2010). These studies suggest that various crises seem to have enabled Europeans to clarify the issues at stake, and to make consensus a clear priority (Crowe 2003: 533–546; Gleissner and de Vreese 2005; Gamble 2006; Lewis 2009). Such newfound political will in Europe may not have otherwise emerged in the absence of crisis.

The broader literature on crisis resolution is also valuable in understanding the pattern evident across various European crises. There is actually much complementarity and coherence in this literature, and so it is useful to synthesize it rather than separate it into schools of thought. In this synthesis, I divide crisis resolution into roughly three phases: (1) the broadening of policy choices, (2) the elevated power of elites to decide,

---

[10] In referring to the resolution of crises or the end of crises, I am not trying to explain how *all* aspects of these crises go away entirely. The impact of a crisis may linger for some time, and there may be many loose ends that still have to be resolved. Rarely do the factors involved in a crisis simply disappear. Rather, I am interested specifically in how the existential threat that comes with a crisis is resolved, such that society no longer displays characteristics of integrational panic, the crisis narrative weakens, and there is no longer anticipation of the "end of Europe."

and (3) the potential outcomes.[11] I will ultimately argue that the concept of catharsis fills an important gap in these explanations of crisis resolution, and is particularly relevant to cases of EU existential crises.

In the first stage of crisis resolution, the range of possible actions in response to the crisis becomes very broad. Leaders craft their own ideas about what should be done, experts and epistemic communities put forward a variety of policy solutions, and the public also often weighs in. As Peter Haas argues, "New ideas will be solicited and selected only after crises, for crises will alert politicians to the need for action and will seek to gather information about their interests and options" (Haas 2001: 11581). While this statement is somewhat of an exaggeration – new ideas arguably matter at all times – crises do bring with them uncertainty precisely because they enable a much larger range of possible actions than during non-crisis periods. Capoccia and Kelemen write that critical junctures have two main outcomes: "the range of plausible choices open to powerful political actors expands substantially and the consequences of their decisions for the outcome of interest are potentially much more momentous" (Capoccia and Kelemen 2007: 343). In addition, at the societal level there is often a sense of unity in the wake of a crisis. Drabek and McEntire point to two immediate crisis effects that are common: "individuals and groups typically become more cohesive and unified during situations of collective stress" and "new behaviors and organizations appear after disaster" (Drabek and McEntire 2003: 99). When the citizenry is more unified in its response, public input can have a stronger than usual contribution to broadening the range of possible choices in response to crises.

In the second stage, it becomes clear that leaders – as opposed to other actors – have the primary responsibility to decide what action to take. Indeed, the role of elites is greater than in non-crisis periods as the public relies on them to make important choices. Arjen Boin et al. write:

In times of crisis, citizens look at their leaders: presidents and mayors, local politicians and elected administrators, public managers and top civil servants. We expect these policy makers to avert the threat or at least minimize the damage of the crisis at hand. They should lead us out of the crisis; they must explain what went wrong and convince us that it will not happen again.

(Boin 2005: 1)

---

[11] These three stages may happen virtually simultaneously, but it is helpful to think of them as distinct processes for analytical purposes.

Even though leaders have a wide range of options at their disposal, resolving crises is easier said than done.[12] Indeed, organizational theory finds that crises are often exacerbated because system disruptions make it difficult for organizational managers to perform well. In effect, once the impact of the crisis is felt, decision makers can make it worse when they do not deal with the crisis effectively. Seeger et al. write,

> Organizational members, crisis stake holders, and the public often experience intense emotional arousal, stress, fear, anxiety, and apprehension, which may compromise their ability to make effective decisions. These responses are often maladaptive and may significantly complicate the effects of a crisis by inhibiting crisis management and response capabilities. (Seeger, Sellnow, and Ulmer 2003: 9)

Much is at stake in the crisis context. If leaders appear to be ineffective, then the crisis could intensify, enhancing the possibility of a self-fulfilling prophecy. Leaders can very quickly lose legitimacy in the eyes of the citizenry, and when that happens, the legitimacy of the state could also be undermined (Boin 2004: 166).

At the same time, many scholars recognize the *opportunity* inherent in the process of crisis resolution. Some refer explicitly to a kind of "silver lining effect" (Seeger, Sellnow, and Ulmer 2003: 6; Meyers and Holusha 1986). Crises require change to be overcome, and what decision makers do with this opening provides the potential to make things better in some way. As University of Chicago economist Milton Friedman writes:

> Only a crisis – actual or perceived – produces real change. When that crisis occurs, the actions that are taken depend on the ideas that are lying around. That, I believe, is our basic function: to develop alternatives to existing policies, to keep them alive and available until the politically impossible become inevitable.
> (Friedman 1962: ix)

In the case of the EU and its pattern of crises over time, it is clear that crises have served as opportunities to achieve more than was possible before. In the wake of disagreement over the Iraq invasion, the 2003 European Security Strategy took a significant step forward in establishing a European security identity. After the 2005 Constitutional Treaty crisis when the French and Dutch voted "no," a new European public sphere flourished, and Europeans debated issues across borders as a common citizenry. Similarly, in reaction to the Eurozone crisis, the EU agreed to

---

[12] The crisis management approach also tends to focus on attributing blame for the crisis as well as determining the victims and how they should be compensated (Seeger, Sellnow, and Ulmer 2003, chapter 1).

unprecedented economic and fiscal integration for the long-term. But how do we know whether leaders will make more effective or ineffective choices in these post-crisis periods of augmented leadership power? The answer to this comes in the third stage of crisis resolution.

In the third stage, leaders with decision-making authority take action, and the outcome of a crisis becomes apparent. Most arguments about crisis resolution naturally prioritize the role of elites or leaders in finding ways out of crises, but they differ in terms of what elites choose to do. One possibility is that leaders will take advantage of the crisis to get what they have always wanted. They strategically use crises for political ends, such as for increasing state power or furthering EU integration (Sala 2010). Naomi Klein introduces the idea of the shock doctrine to refer to the sinister ways in which leaders get away with pushing through unpopular policies while the public is distracted by crises (Klein 2011). She argues more specifically that there is a strong connection between "superprofits" and "megadisasters," and examines numerous cases in which socially unpopular policies of privatization, deregulation, and cuts to social spending were imposed as crises struck so that the ability for popular protest against these measures was severely diminished (Klein 2011: 9). Examples range from the disappearances in Argentina in the 1970s, the Falklands War in 1982, the Shock and Awe campaign in Iraq after 9/11, and more recently, Hurricane Katrina in New Orleans. Klein argues that all of these crises contribute to a pattern of "exploiting crises" on the part of those who support this capitalist model. She concludes that "the history of the contemporary free market – better understood as the rise of corporatism – was written in shocks" (Klein 2011: 18–19). Similarly, Carl Schmitt argues that sovereign decision makers may actually *create* crises to justify certain political actions (Schmitt 1922/2004: 5). When a sovereign identifies a crisis, he or she can then disregard the natural principles and laws that normally bind the sovereign's actions, and protect the interests of the people (Schmitt 1922/2004: 8). Andrew Neal also argues that liberal states can act illiberally when statesmen take advantage of the exceptionalism of crises to change the existing order (Neal 2009: 1).

Another possibility, however, is that leaders could respond to crises through rebuilding and transforming institutions, creating a better-functioning institutional and normative environment. Indeed, some organizational theorists argue that crises are actually an inherent and natural part of organizational development. Organizations need change and improvement, and crises provide that opportunity (Seeger, Sellnow, and Ulmer 1998: 232). As Gene Rochlin argues, the human errors that crises bring to light allow the creation of better-designed and maintained organizations (Rochlin 1996). The organizational approach tends to see crises as being subject to standard operating procedures. Built into the setup of institutions is a "crisis mode" for when something goes wrong. These events are thus planned for in advance. Rosecrance, for example, suggests that systems that survive repeated crises have a strong variety of regulatory mechanisms in place (Rosecrance 1963). Thus, if institutions already have built-in safeguards and mechanisms for handling crises, leaders are more likely to make adjustments to the system in place rather than try to transform the existing order entirely.

In cases of international crises that seemingly threaten cooperation or integration among states, leaders are often less constrained because the sovereignty and well-being of their own territory and citizens is their priority. Thus, they could *roll back, freeze,* or *push forward* cooperation and integration.[13] Leaders might choose to roll back cooperation if they interpret a crisis as a signal that their cooperative arrangement no longer works. For example, some experts argued that the Eurozone crisis was evidence that the euro had been doomed from the start and should be dropped in favor of national currencies. Alternatively, leaders might choose to freeze the level of cooperation where it is if they interpret a crisis as a signal that pushing for more cooperation would be dangerous. For example, in the 2003 Iraq crisis when there was an initial failure to achieve a common stance, some elites argued that any enhancement of the Common Foreign and Security Policy (CFSP) would be impossible, and that Europeans were not capable of improving their approach to foreign policy. Another reaction to a crisis could be for leaders to push forward with more integration in response. In theory, this would seem to be the least likely reaction because in an international system based on state sovereignty, we might expect leaders to take a "safer" route that restores sovereignty in order to avoid future crises and to reduce the vulnerability that comes with interdependence. And yet, it is precisely this third sort of reaction that has proven far and away the most common in the case of the EU. This presents a puzzle. In short, why have crises served as opportunities to push integration forward time and time again in the case of the EU?

---

[13] This distinction is similar to Ikenberry's argument that "[c]risis can lead to resolutions that reestablish the old rules and institutions of a political system, it can lead to a transformation of that political system, or it can lead to a fundamental breakdown and disappearance of the old political system" (Ikenberry 2008: 3).

Catharsis

Organizations, leaders, and elites are important actors in finding solutions to crises, but there are also broader societal-level processes at work that must be considered in order to explain why some crises become opportunities for change. The concept of catharsis fills a significant gap in the existing literature on crisis resolution, and is valuable in explaining this puzzle.[14] The field of psychology defines catharsis as the process of releasing tension after undergoing a personal crisis. To be sure, there are many definitions of "catharsis," but it generally refers to a kind of Freudian-style process in which individuals seek to more fully recognize and express emotions about past events that they typically repress. The purpose of this is to release and move beyond these sources of psychological stress. Catharsis often entails new and sudden insight, a more positive attitude about oneself, and the end of destructive or counterproductive behavior that deviates from the norm. This can happen at the group level as well (Hodgskin 1941).

Thus, as EU crises build and reach their height, we should expect societal actors – both at the public and elite levels – to craft narratives about how they interpret these crises. Discussions surrounding the nature of a crisis should take on an emotional edge. If catharsis is at work, it is in the very urgency of this crisis atmosphere that the impetus toward crisis resolution takes place. Crises provide opportunities for a kind of *group catharsis* to take place, releasing tensions that would otherwise remain under the surface and impede the achievement of European integration goals. While some pundits in the United States believe that "elections are America's way of letting off steam" (Luce 2012: 9), the same can be said of EU crises.

When these tensions are aired, actors seek to replace the turmoil and uncertainty inherent in existential crises with coherence of some kind. Michal Natorski argues, "[C]risis resolution can be understood as a political struggle over the representation of a coherent vision of crisis episodes and ways of overcoming the contradictions that they reveal" (Natorski 2015: 5). He observes that crises tend to "reinforce previous policy developments" (Natorski 2015: 2). Going further, Federica Bicchi (2007) argues that crises lead to innovations on

---

[14] To be clear, my use of the concept of catharsis is more of a broad analogy for what the EU, as a whole, experiences during times of existential crisis than a literal description of European crisis resolution.

previous policy tracks, Nicolaïdis (2010: 25) refers to the EU's "addic-
tion to institutional reform" in the face of problems, and Natorski and
Pomorska (2017) show how crises may precipitate new levels of trust
in EU institutions.

In using crises as opportunities to release steam, so to speak, EU leaders
are then able to move forward with a renewed will for consensus or
further integration. How key actors frame a crisis, what they say during
a crisis, how publics in various member states respond, and how these
interpretations feed into the crisis resolution are important factors to
consider. When preexisting tensions shape the terms of each crisis's
dominant narrative, these episodes become opportunities to speak frankly
and, in so doing, overcome certain differences that would have otherwise
served as obstacles to moving forward with the European project.
I suggest that this explains why as EU leaders face a wide range of choices
in seeking to resolve crises they end up enhancing their will to work
together and even integrate further.

At the same time, the concept of catharsis does not imply that once
Europeans release tensions such tensions are gone forever. Obviously,
there are countless narratives and tensions that pervade any society, and
it is rare for any single theme to disappear entirely. Rather, I contend that
the most prominent tension of the time does recede to a significant extent
in the wake of a crisis. There is something therapeutic about being able to
talk honestly about doubts, divisions, and even prejudices. There is always
the possibility that these tensions may arise again, but in the immediate
wake of a crisis, there is a period of relative harmony that allows certain
barriers to integration to recede.

The existing literature on crisis resolution makes clear that crises are, in
effect, critical junctures that broaden the range of possible outcomes. They
also give leaders more power to decide than they have normally, and in the
case of international crises, enable leaders to either give up on collective
action, freeze it, or push forward. The fact that leaders, decision makers,
and other influential elites always have a choice shows that they have the
power to turn crises into opportunities. The idea of catharsis is a valuable
analogy in this respect. The next three chapters will illustrate how this
happens in practice.

A NOTE ON METHODOLOGY

Just as the argument of this book has two fundamental parts – integrational
panic and catharsis – so must the methodology behind this research. As far

as the first part is concerned, showing that there is a socially constructed dynamic to existential crises in Europe, it is necessary to argue that structural explanations fall short. Craig Parsons writes that to support ideational claims, evidence "must show both that actions reflect certain interpretations rather than direct objective positioning, and that the interpretations are not just derived from objective positioning" (Parsons 2007: 129–130).[15]

The following three case studies bring together both quantitative and qualitative media content analysis, public opinion polls, and analysis of elite decision making – at both the national and European levels. In terms of media content analysis, the evidence was derived through reading *all* new stories that mention the keywords "Iraq," "constitution," or "Eurozone" during the relevant crisis time period in The *International Herald Tribune, Financial Times, Economist*, and *Time* magazine. The total number of articles was 465 for the Iraq crisis, 266 for the constitutional crisis, and 2,069 for the Eurozone crisis. The neutrality of an article is counted as *negative* when the anticipated consequences of the crisis for the EU's continued viability are depicted as negative, *positive* when the EU is portrayed as being able to overcome current challenges, and *neutral* if the story expresses no judgment about outlook.

To determine media framing of the dominant tensions at the time, the focus is on (1) *scope* – whether European or domestic; (2) *players* involved – whether among member states, between Brussels and member states, or within a particular member state; (3) *nature* – the substantive quality of the tension; and (4) *sub-tensions* within the dominant tension – the various reasons contributing to the major tension. These specific categories encompass a range of most likely possibilities for where news stories might consistently draw out tensions or even assign blame for the difficulties the EU faces during times of crisis buildup, including whether this is a European or a national problem, the various actors involved who might be responsible, the main tension expressed, and the causes of that tension. The analysis is restricted to the period of crisis buildup, with an

---

[15] Parsons goes on to elaborate this in stages, which I adapt for the purposes of this study. Ideational arguments must show that (1) certain ideas or beliefs are present prior to the crisis, that is, "preexisting ideational elements"; (2) people act according to these beliefs in their response toward the crisis; (3) the development of the crisis itself is affected by these beliefs; (4) competing explanations (logics) for the crisis delineate the space for beliefs to matter; and (5) the causal role of beliefs fill this space, and thus fill in the argument for the cause of the existential crisis (2007: 130).

aim to better illustrate the role of the international media in potentially contributing to the dynamics of a crisis at the outset.

This original data works in support of the qualitative dimension of the research. I rely on secondary sources for national and local media coverage as research has already been conducted in this area. The use of the international media as a source provides evidence of how the stages of crisis were built, and is also a good source of direct quotes from elites. Thus, it provides an account of actual events, quoting actual responses of people to events – but it also betrays its own identity as an actor. The media has the power to define events and shape responses through its volume of coverage, framing, and spin.

Some might suggest that the choice of English-language international presses is limiting. However, the goal of this book is not to present a comprehensive study of the media. Rather, it is to shed light on the dynamics behind repeated EU crises. The international media is an important actor, but it is only one among many, and it would be a truly mammoth undertaking to survey all sources of media. It is also doubtful that attempting to code directly a large range of other forms of media, such as those at the local and national levels, would add that much to the study, or even be feasible given the amount of time required for such an endeavor, and the need to master dozens of languages. Thus, throughout the book, as primary evidence, I focus more on the biggest international periodical publications as these have been shown to have the greatest impact on elite public opinion, and they all have very high circulation.[16] I bring in other media sources through secondary sources, or on a more limited basis. That is not to say that other sources of media do not matter. Consequently, I have chosen major international media sources with the highest level of readership as a way to "capture" the nature of the information provided to the public, and indeed, to national, local, and regional news sources. This is a way of sampling the news without trying to replicate a full reading of *all* news sources.

As far as the second part of the argument is concerned, I consult opinion polls, public narratives, and policy changes to determine whether catharsis has occurred as a result of the crisis, either at the elite or public

---

[16] For data on circulation, see: "The Economist Annual Report: 2011" and "The State of the News Media 2012: An Annual Report on American Journalism," *Pew Research Center's Project for Excellence in Journalism; Financial Times Average Daily Global Audience (ADGA), Financial Times, November 2011*; "International Herald Tribune: Reader Profile, 2012," *The New York Times Global.*

level. These sources provide an indication of societal tensions before and after each of the crises, as well as support the qualitative research of crisis narratives. I also draw upon direct quotes from elites – including European leaders, national politicians, and expert opinions – during each of the crises, with a particular focus on tone-setting statements. Using government documents and other records, I trace the processes by which elites react to and resolve these crises.

References

Almond, Gabriel, Scott Flanagon, and Robert Mundt. 1973. *Crisis, Choice, and Change: Historical Studies of Political Development*. Boston: Little, Brown and Company.

Anderson, Jeffrey, John Ikenberry, and Thomas Risse. 2008. *The End of the West? Crisis and Change in the Atlantic Order*, Ithaca, NY, and London: Cornell University Press.

Baum, Matthew and Tim Groeling. 2009. *War Stories: The Causes and Consequences of Public Views of War*. Princeton, NJ: Princeton University Press.

Beck, Ulrich. 1992. *Risk Society, towards a New Modernity*, London: Sage Publications.

Bicchi, Federica. 2007. *European Foreign Policy Making toward the Mediterranean*. New York: Palgrave Macmillan.

Billings, Robert S., Thomas W. Milburn, and Mary Lou Schaalman. 1980. "A Model of Crisis Perception: A Theoretical and Empirical Analysis." *Administrative Science Quarterly* 25(2): 300–316.

Boin, Arjen. 2004. "On Financial Crises." *British Journal of Management* 15(2): 191–195.

Boin, Arjen, Paul 't Hart, Eric Stern, and Bengt Sundelius. 2005. *The Politics of Crisis Management: Public Leadership under Pressure*. Cambridge: Cambridge University Press.

Bovens, Mark and Paul 't Hart. 1996. *Understanding Policy Fiascos*. New Brunswick: Transaction.

Brecher, Michael. 1993. *Crises in World Politics: Theory & Reality*. Oxford: Pergamon Press.

Brecher, Michael and Jonathan Wilkenfeld. 1997. *A Study of Crisis*. Ann Arbor: University of Michigan Press.

Brunvand, Jan Harold. 2001. *Encyclopedia of Urban Legends*. New York: W.W. Norton.

Capoccia, Giovanni and Daniel R. Kelemen. 2007. "The Study of Critical Junctures: Theory, Narrative, and Counterfactuals in Historical Institutionalism," *World Politics* 59(3): 343–369.

Cappella, Joseph and Kathleen Jamieson. 1996. "News Frames, Political Cynicism, and Media Cynicism." *The Annals of the American Academy of Political and Social Science* 546: 71–84.

Chambliss, William and Milton Mankoff. 1976. *Whose Law? What Order? A Conflict Approach to Criminology.* New York: John Wiley and Sons.

Cohen, Stanley. 2002, originally published in 1972. *Folk Devils and Moral Panics: The Creation of the Mods and Rocker,* third edition. London: Routledge.

Critcher, Chas. 2003. *Moral Panics and the Media.* Buckingham: Open University Press.

Cross, Mai'a K. Davis. 2012. "Identity Politics and European Integration." *Comparative Politics* 44(2): 229–246.

Cross, Mai'a K. Davis and Xinru Ma. 2015. "EU Crises & Integrational Panic: The Role of the Media," *Journal of European Public Policy* 22(8): 1053–1070.

Crowe, Brian. 2003. "A Common European Foreign Policy after Iraq?" *International Affairs* 79(3): 533–546.

Crozier, Michael. 1964. *The Bureaucratic Phenomenon.* Chicago: University of Chicago Press.

Christopherson, Kimberly M. 2007. The Positive and Negative Implications of Anonymity in Internet Social Interactions: "On the Internet, Nobody Knows You're a Dog," *Computers in Human Behavior* 23(6): 3038–3056.

Drabek, Thomas E. and David A. McEntire 2003. "Emergent Phenomena and the Sociology of Disaster: Lessons, Trends, and Opportunities from the Research Literature," *Disaster Prevention and Management* 12(2): 97–112.

Estes, Carroll L. 1983. "Social Security: The Social Construction of a Crisis," *The Milbank Memorial Fund Quarterly. Health and Society* 61(3): 445–461.

Everts, Steven and Daniel Keohane. 2003. "The European Convention and EU Foreign Policy: Learning from Failure," *Survival: Global Politics and Strategy* 45(3): 167–186.

Fowler, Roger. 1991. *Language in the News: Discourse and Ideology in the Press.* London: Psychology Press.

Freud, Sigmund. (1921/1981) Group Psychology and the Analysis of the Ego. (Translated from the German original *Massenpsychologie und Ich-Analyse* [1921] by James Strachey.) *Standard Edition,* vol. XVIII. London: The Hogarth Press. pp. 67–143.

Friedman, Milton. 1962. *Capitalism and Freedom.* Chicago: University of Chicago Press.

Gamble, Andrew. 2006. "European Disunion," *British Journal of Politics & International Relations* 8(1): 34–49.

Garland, David. 2008. "On the Concept of Moral Panic." *Crime, Media, Culture* 4(1): 9–30.

German Marshall Fund, blog, January 17, 2013. Accessed at http://blog.gmfus .org/2013/01/17/mali-intervention-exposes-europes-security-shortcomings.

Geva, Nehemia, James Mayhar, and Mark J. Skorick. 2000. "Cognitive Calculus of Foreign Policy Decision Making: An Experimental Assessment," *Journal of Conflict Resolution* 44(4): 447–471.

Gleissner, Martin and Claes H. de Vreese. 2005. "News about the EU Constitution: Journalistic Challenges and Media Portrayal of the European Union Constitution," *Journalism* 6(2): 221–242.

Goode, Erich and Nachman Ben-Yehuda. 2009. *Moral Panics: The Social Construction of Deviance,* second edition. Oxford: Wiley-Blackwell.

Gourevitch, Peter. 1984. *Politics in Hard Times: Comparative Responses to International Economic Crises.* Ithaca, NY: Cornell University Press.

Haas, Peter. 2001. "Policy Knowledge: Epistemic Communities." In *International Encyclopedia of Social and Behavioral Sciences.* Amsterdam: Elsevier, 11578–11586.

Hall, Stuart, Chas Crichter, Tony Jefferson, John Clarke, and Brian Roberts. 1978. *Policing the Crisis: Mugging, the State and Law and Order.* New York: Palgrave.

Hay, Colin. 1999. "Crisis and the Structural Transformation of the State: Interrogating the Process of Change." *British Journal of Politics and International Relations* 1(3): 317–344.

Hellmann, Gunther. 2008. "Inevitable Decline versus Predestined Stability: Disciplinary Explanations of the Evolving Transatlantic Order." In *The End of the West? Crisis and Change in the Atlantic Order*, edited by Jeffrey Anderson, John Ikenberry, and Thomas Risse. Ithaca, NY, and London: Cornell University Press, 28–52.

Hermann, Charles F. 1972. "Threat, Time, and Surprise: A Simulation of International Crisis." In *International Crises: Insights from Behavioral Research*, edited by Charles F. Hermann. New York: Free Press, 187–211.

Hodgskin, Philip T. 1941. "Group Catharsis with Special Emphasis upon Psychopathology of Money," *Sociometry* 4(2): 184–192.

Hunt, Arnold 1997. "'Moral Panic' and Moral Language in the Media," *The British Journal of Sociology* 48(4): 629–648.

Ikenberry, John. 2008. "Explaining Crisis and Change in Transatlantic Relations: An Introduction." In *The End of the West? Crisis and Change in the Atlantic Order*, edited by Jeffrey Anderson, John Ikenberry, and Thomas Risse. Ithaca, NY, and London: Cornell University Press, 1–27.

Jamieson, Kathleen Hall. 1992. *Dirty Politics.* New York: Oxford University Press.

Jo, Sam-Sang. 2007. *European Myths: Resolving the Crises in the European Community/European Union.* Lanham, MD: University Press of America.

Klein, Naomi. 2011. *The Shock Doctrine: The Rise of Disaster Capitalism.* New York: Metropolitan Books.

Krinsky, Charles (ed.). 2013. *The Ashgate Research Companion to Moral Panics.* Burlington, VT: Ashgate.

Krzyzanowski, Michal and Aleksandra Galansinska. 2009. *Discourse and Transformation in Central and Eastern Europe.* New York: Palgrave.

Lewis, Jeffrey. 2009. "EU Policy on Iraq: The Collapse and Reconstruction of Consensus Based Foreign Policy," *International Politics* 45(4): 432–450.

Le Bon, Gustave. 1895. *The Crowd: A Study of the Popular Mind*, The Project Gutenberg Etext. Available at http://www.gutenberg.org/dirs/etext96/tcrwd10.txt. (Accessed December 3, 2013).

Linz, Juan and Alfred Stepan. 1978. *Problems of Democratic Transition and Consolidation.* Baltimore, MD: Johns Hopkins University Press.

Lu, Chien-Yi. 2008. "Constitution-making and the Search for a European Public Sphere." In *The Rise and Fall of the EU's Constitutional Treaty*, edited by Finn Laursen. Leiden: Brill, 431–452.

Luce, Edward. 2012. "Welcome to the New China-Bashing," *Financial Times*, comment section, March 12, p. 9.

Lundestad, Geir. 2005. "Toward Transatlantic Drift?" In *The Atlantic Alliance under Stress: US–European Relations After Iraq*, edited by David M. Andrews. Cambridge: Cambridge University Press.

Menon, Anand. 2004. "From Crisis to Catharsis: ESDP after Iraq," *International Affairs* 80(4): 631–648.

Meyers, Gerald C. and John Holusha. 1986. *When It Hits The Fan*. Boston: Houghton Mifflin.

Morin, Edgar. 1971. *Rumor in Orléans*, translated by Peter Green. New York: Pantheon Books.

Natorski, Michal. 2015. "Epistemic (Un)certainty in Times of Crisis: The Role of Coherence as a Social Convention in the European Neighborhood Policy after the Arab Spring," *European Journal of International Relations*, OnlineFirst September 2015.

Natorski, Michal and Karolina Pomorska. 2017. "Trust and Decision-making in Times of Crisis: The EU's Response to the Events in Ukraine," *Journal of Common Market Studies* 55(1): EarlyView (Special Issue, Europe's Hybrid Foreign Policy: The Ukraine-Russia Crisis, edited by Mai'a K. Davis Cross and Ireneusz Pawel Karolewski).

Neal, Andrew. 2009. *Exceptionalism and the Politics of Counter-Terrorism: Liberty, Security and the War on Terror*. New York: Routledge.

Nicolaïdis, Kalypso. 2010. "Sustainable Integration: Towards EU 2.0?" *Journal of Common Market Studies, Annual Review* 48(Issue Supplement s1): 21–54.

Nye, Joseph Jr. 2008. *The Powers to Lead*. New York: Oxford University Press.

Parsons, Craig. 2007. *How to Map Arguments*. Oxford: Oxford University Press.

Patterson, Thomas E. 1993. *Out of Order: How the Decline of the Political Parties and the Growing Power of the News Media Undermine the American Way of Electing Presidents*. New York: Alfred Knopf.

Pierson, Paul. 2003. "Big, Slow-Moving, and . . . Invisible: Macro-social Processes in the Study of Comparative Politics." In *Comparative Historical Analyses in the Social Sciences*, edited by James Mahoney and Dietrich Rueschmeyer. Cambridge: Cambridge University Press, 177–207.

Price, Vincent, David Tewksbury, and Elizabeth Powers. 1997. "Switching Trains of Thought the Impact of News Frames on Readers' Cognitive Responses," *Communication Research* 24(5): 481–506.

Reinarman, Craig and Harry G. Levine (eds.). 1997. *Crack in America: Demon Drugs and Social Justice*. Berkeley, CA: University of California Press.

Risse, Thomas. 2010. *A Community of Europeans: Transnational Identities and Public Spheres*. Ithaca, NY: Cornell University Press.

Rochlin, Gene I. 1996. "Reliable Organizations: Present Research and Future Directions," *Journal of Contingencies and Crisis Management* 42(2): 55–59.

Rohloff, Amanda and Sarah Wright. 2010. "Moral Panic and Social Theory: Beyond the Heuristic," *Current Sociology* 58(3): 403–419.

Rosecrance, Richard N. 1963. *Action and Reaction in World Politics: International Systems in Perspective*. Boston: Little, Brown.

Rosenthal, Uriel, Michael T. Charles and Paul 't Hart. 1989. *Coping with Crises: The Management of Disasters, Riots, and Terrorism.* Springfield, IL: Charles C Thomas Pub Ltd

Sala, Vincent Della. 2010. "Crisis, What Crisis? Narrating Crisis and Decline in the European Union." Conference paper for the European Consortium for Political Research fifth pan-European conference on EU politics, June 23–26, Porto, Portugal.

Schmitt, Carl. 1922/2004. *Political Theology: Four Chapters on the Concept of Sovereignty,* translated by George D. Schwab. Chicago: University of Chicago Press.

Seeger, Matthew, Timothy Sellnow, and Robert Ulmer. 1998. "Communication, Organization, and Crisis," *Annals of the International Communication Association* 21(1): 231–276.

Seeger, Matthew, Timothy Sellnow, and Robert Ulmer. 2003. *Communication and Organizational Crisis.* Westport, CT: Praeger.

Semetko, Holli A. and Patti M. Valkenburg. 2000. "Framing European Politics: A Content Analysis of Press and Television News," *Journal of Communication* 50(2): 93–109.

Thompson, Kenneth. 1998. *Moral Panics.* London: Routledge.

Turner, Ralph. H. and Lewis M. Killian. 1957. *Collective Behavior.* Oxford: Prentice-Hall.

Valekenburg, Patti M., Holli A. Semetko, Claes de Vreese. 1999. "The Effects of News Frames on Readers' Thoughts and Recall," *Communication Research* 26 (5): 550–569.

Verba, Sidney. 1971. "Sequences and Development," In *Crises and Sequences in Political Development,* edited by Leonard Binder and Joseph La Palombara. Princeton, NJ: Princeton University Press, 283–316.

Victor, Jeffrey S. 1993. *Satanic Panic: The Creation of a Contemporary Legend.* Chicago: Open Court Press.

Young, Oran. 1968. *The Politics of Force: Bargaining During International Crises.* Princeton, NJ: Princeton University Press.

Zhuo, Julie. "Where Anonymity Breeds Contempt," *The Opinion Pages, The New York Times* (November 29, 2010). Available at https://www.bremerand whyte.com/files/nationally-syndicated-publications/11.29.10_-_new_york_ times.pdf. (Accessed December 4, 2013).

3

The Iraq Crisis

INTRODUCTION

In the lead-up to the 2003 Iraq crisis, the EU had at long last begun to make progress in realizing its goal of a Common Foreign and Security Policy (CFSP), but it still needed some kind of push to make it truly operational. The Iraq crisis for Europe would eventually serve as this catalyst. But first, it is important to revisit the historical groundwork that led to this new phase in European foreign policy, both because it sheds light on the underlying tensions of the time and because it illustrates the socially constructed roots of this crisis. History shows that there was little reason for internal disagreement over such a faraway and unprecedented foreign policy challenge to take the EU to the brink of existential threat, if not for the integrational panic that built up around a powerful crisis narrative of East–West tensions.

The specific roots of the European Union's external security cooperation can be found during the Cold War (Jones 2007). In the 1950s, when the European Coal and Steel Community (ECSC) was still in its early years, the six founding member states hoped to accomplish more. Specifically, they wanted to achieve cooperation, or at least coordination, of their foreign policies. Two failed attempts – the European Defense Community and the European Political Committee – seemed to portend purely economic cooperation. In the very next decade another attempt fell through. The Fouchet plan, a French proposal to restructure the European Community at the same time as giving it military independence from the United States, was too ambitious in some ways and flawed in others.

Still determined, in 1970, the Six (France, Germany, Italy, and the Benelux countries) were able to put into place a new institutional framework: European Political Cooperation (EPC). Although the framework stuck, it was by all perspectives underwhelming, separated as it was from European Community structures and not backed by treaty agreement. As one scholar put it, "[N]ot only was EPC's scope of action so indeterminate that it threatened to invite more conflict than cooperation, but its mechanisms to induce such cooperation were feeble and peculiar" (Smith 2004: 1). Despite this, EPC enabled more progress in political cooperation than might have been expected given its shortcomings. It did make possible some major diplomatic initiatives such as the Euro–Arab Dialogue and the Conference on Security and Cooperation in Europe, and ended up becoming more than simply a forum for discussion. Perhaps most importantly, EPC enabled Europeans to overcome their initial hesitations about security cooperation and provided a venue for the expression of their desire to turn EPC into something more (Smith 2004: 2). But it was not really until after the Cold War that security cooperation began to make real progress.

The 1992 Maastricht Treaty on European Union transformed the incremental progress brought about by EPC into the Common Foreign and Security Policy (CFSP), for the first time enshrining political and security cooperation into a treaty. With the advent of CFSP, the stage was set for possible progress in this area. It called for the EU

to assert its identity on the international scene ... including the eventual framing of a common defence policy, which might in time lead to a common defence ... The Member States shall support the Union's external and security policy actively and unreservedly in a spirit of loyalty and mutual solidarity. They shall refrain from any action, which is contrary to the interests of the Union or likely to impair its effectiveness as a cohesive force in international relations.

(Treaty on European Union, Article J 1992)

In the same year as Maastricht, as part of the quest to instill a European security and defense identity, member states – meeting under the Western European Union format – agreed on the so-called Petersberg Tasks. They stipulated that member states may use force if a crisis called for "humanitarian and rescue tasks; peace-keeping tasks; and tasks of combat forces in crisis management, including peace-making" (Petersberg Declaration 1992). Jolyon Howorth argues that the Petersberg Tasks "implied radical transformation of the EU's existing capacity to provide deployable, professional intervention forces geared to 'out of area' crisis management" (Howorth 2007: 98).

But during the first few years after Maastricht and the Petersberg Declaration, CFSP was still relatively empty. As Wyn Rees describes it, "CFSP remained weak and represented little more than a loose amalgam of the national foreign policies of the fifteen members" (Rees 2006: 5). It needed some kind of *enabler*, a way for it to become concrete. This opportunity eventually came in December 1998 during a summit in Saint-Malo, France, when French President Jacques Chirac and British Prime Minister Tony Blair agreed that the EU needed a true defense capability.[1] In other words, the two main security actors wanted the EU to "have the capacity for autonomous action, backed up by credible military forces" (Franco-British summit joint declaration on European defense 1998). Blair and Chirac were both witnessing Europe's utter inability to act in the midst of the crisis in Kosovo and the collapse of Yugoslavia. The Saint-Malo Declaration represented a big shift in British policy, as the UK had resisted the idea for decades (Lindley-French 2007: 247). In 1999, member states approved the European Security and Defense Policy (ESDP),[2] reflecting the goals of Saint-Malo. However, the question remained whether this would still be an agreement on paper only. Indeed, in 2002, as the world began to debate whether or not an invasion of Iraq was justifiable, no action had been taken under ESDP.

Finally, in 2003, after decades of struggle, the EU finally made ESDP operational, sending troops out to conduct humanitarian operations under the EU flag. For the first time, the EU had not only articulated a desire for a common foreign policy, it had actually put concrete action behind these words. I argue in this chapter that Europe's crisis over Iraq served as an important catalyst for this, and for other far-reaching advancements such as the 2003 European Security Strategy. Prior to the Iraq crisis, CFSP had stalled, just at the cusp of actually meaning something. A catalyst of some kind was still necessary (as the terrorist attacks of September 11, 2001, had served in launching internal security integration) to spur on a European security and defense policy with real weight (Cross 2011: chapter 2). Certain political obstacles among member-state leaders still stood in the way. These were, namely, differences in strategic culture, perceptions of threat, attitudes toward the use of force, and the nature of each country's relationship to NATO. It was difficult to contemplate engaging in common military operations with these tensions

---

[1] The story behind how this agreement was reached is well told in Howorth (2004) and Mérand (2010).

[2] ESDP is now known as the Common Security and Defence Policy (CSDP).

still at the forefront of everyone's thinking. To European leaders, these obstacles seemed even more difficult to surmount in light of the upcoming enlargement to include ten new Central and Eastern European countries (CEECs) in 2004 and 2007. In their eyes, not only would countries from the other side of the Iron Curtain come under the umbrella of European institutions, but membership in the EU would almost double, making future agreement more difficult. This was the climate of the times in the lead-up to the 2003 Iraq crisis for Europe.

President George W. Bush's address to the United Nations on September 12, 2002, calling for the international community to support an invasion of Iraq, served as an external triggering event for this crisis. In the speech and in the UN Security Council, Bush strongly pressured the EU to side with the United States (Tiriteu 2012: 201). Of course, the decision that eventually led to the US invasion of Iraq on March 19, 2003, stemmed from a number of issues of supposed US concern, such as retaliation for 9/11, access to oil, alleged weapons of mass destruction, democracy promotion, and so on. The Iraq invasion was certainly a crisis in many respects – for the Iraqi people, American society, and transatlantic relations – but this chapter focuses on how and why this became seen as a crisis *for the EU*. As the *Economist* put it, "Despite a tendency for commentators on both sides of the Atlantic to spy a damaging Europe-America split over Iraq, in fact it is Europe that is most deeply divided."[3] How did the externally driven Iraq invasion become an existential crisis for the EU? The EU's response to US actions provided the grounds for transforming this external crisis into a European one. But far less scholarly attention has been devoted to this aspect.

With the passage of time, it is sometimes easy to forget how significantly the Iraq crisis impacted the EU during this period. After all, there is a human tendency to overemphasize the uniqueness and importance of recent events, and so much attention has since been paid to the Eurozone crisis as if it were the only crisis that seriously threatened to undermine the existence of the EU. At the time, however, the crisis for Europe over Iraq was indeed severe. As the *International Herald Tribune* put it:

There has rarely been a more dramatic illustration of the Union's failure to speak with a common voice, despite the fact that it officially has a common defense and security policy ... This war is undermining the course of Europe toward integration.   (James 2003)

---

[3] "Dealing with Iraq: Days of Reckoning," *The Economist*, January 30, 2003.

Similarly, the Iraq crisis was described in the *Financial Times* as "one of the darkest moments in the EU's history ... The Union's divisions have torn apart its common foreign policy and hobbled its influence in reshaping the international order."[4] At the height of the crisis, the candidate member states that were about to join the EU were shut out of a summit in February 2003, and the French government openly threatened to veto their membership. There was serious talk of actually not going through with enlargement of EU membership to include the CEECs, and it was assumed that any aim to establish a substantive common foreign policy for Europe would have to be cast aside. There was a real sense that the EU had reached a breaking point, both in terms of its membership and in terms of integration. The puzzle is how the crisis got to this level of intensity in the first place.

The chapter is organized as follows. I first lay out various other explanations that have been advanced to explain the origins of this crisis. I argue that while these causes are important in understanding how the question of Iraq created the circumstances for an EU crisis, they do not fully explain why these circumstances grew to such severity. In the second section, I argue that neither the US invasion of Iraq nor the subsequent disagreement within Europe necessarily had to develop into a full-blown existential crisis for the EU. Rather, media and elite rhetoric surrounding disagreement over Iraq ratcheted up the crisis atmosphere, creating a growing sense of integrational panic at the elite level. Third, I turn to the process by which Europeans transformed this crisis into an opportunity for integration. I analyze how pre-crisis tensions at the elite level – among the so-called Big Three and between eastern and western member states – came to the surface and comprised the main substance of the crisis narrative. I argue that the open and honest expression of these tensions led to a sense of catharsis among European leaders, and subsequently to new political will to find consensus and move toward more security and defense integration.

THE CAUSES OF THE EU'S CRISIS OVER IRAQ

Many books and articles have been published on the 2003 Iraq war. Much of this literature focuses on the various foreign policy stances of the key players – the United States, the UK, France, Germany, Russia, Japan, and Canada – as

---

[4] "Europe's Torment: The EU Must Start to Pick Up the Pieces," *Financial Times*, London, first edition, March 21, 2003.

they made decisions about what to do in response to US President George W. Bush's call to invade Iraq because of the apparent existence of weapons of mass destruction (Gordon and Shapiro 2004; Andrews 2005; Lindberg 2005; Fawn and Hinnesbusch 2006; Anderson, Ikenberry, and Risse 2008; Davidson 2011; Tiriteu 2012). The amount of research devoted to under-standing how the decision over Iraq became an existential crisis for the EU is much more limited than the broader literature on the war. As Alexander Nikolaev and Ernest Hakanen write with respect to the Iraq war, "[O]nce a war begins all history leading up to it is immediately based on the war itself, in other words, the cause is explained by the effect" (Nikolaev and Hakanen 2006: 3). Indeed, the first scholarly publications analyzing this episode in international relations nearly all describe it as a transatlantic crisis, with only passing reference to the crisis *within* Europe. For example, in her analysis of the growing transatlantic divide in 2001–2, Elizabeth Pond mentions, "Almost more distressing to the Europeans, however, was their own disarray in the crisis" (Pond 2005: 33). Similarly, Gordon and Shapiro also write, "As tensions between the United States and France and Germany deepened, so did the strains among Europeans themselves" (Gordon and Shapiro 2004: 128). This type of passing reference to the crisis within Europe is perhaps understandable given that the European dimension of this crisis occurred early on and in a relatively short period of time: the entire EU crisis took place before the war in Iraq had even begun. Once the feeling of existential crisis within Europe died down, the lasting impression of this episode in foreign policy toward the Middle East was that it was really about the United States versus Europe.[5] Much of the post–Iraq war literature refers to "Europe" and "America" as though their positions over this issue were coherent and unified. This was, of course, demonstrably *not* the case.[6] If, ultimately, this event also constituted a crisis in transatlantic relations, with the United States strongly pitted against Europe, why did the EU experience such a significant crisis of its own? After all, if there is no sense of "Europe," then it is difficult to speak of a US–EU rift in the first place.

Thus, the question is why did this crisis, clearly born of US priorities and actions in the Middle East, lead to the perception that the "end of Europe" was near, and to the belief that enlargement and integration might no longer be viable? What did the impending Iraq invasion mean

---

[5] For good overviews of the effects the Iraq crisis had on transatlantic relations, see Andrews (2005); Peterson and Pollack (2003).

[6] As Gordon and Shapiro write, "It would be wrong to caricature the positions of 'Americans' and 'Europeans' in the Iraq debate" (Gordon and Shapiro 2004: 75).

for European integration? In the immediate lead-up to the invasion, there was of course much debate among leaders across the globe about what should be done, but this was especially true among Europeans who had long been core US allies. As the positions of each European country solidified, a significant divergence of opinions among leaders emerged, and this quickly became labeled a crisis that seemingly threatened to undermine the quality and character of the EU.

Focusing on the European dimension of this crisis, the story of its origins is told in a number of different ways. In this section, I visit three main explanations in turn: (1) diverging views on member states' relationships to the United States, (2) the inability for EU leaders to agree on foreign policy, and (3) deep divisions between eastern and western member states' strategic culture. While all three explanations shed light on the initial origins of this crisis, as will be discussed, they do not fully account for why intra-European disagreement over policy toward Iraq became so overblown that there was talk of the EU's demise. To understand this buildup of crisis, I argue that it is necessary to examine social narratives, especially the role of the media and elites in ratcheting up an atmosphere of integrational panic.

First Perspective: Member States See the Transatlantic Relationship Differently

One major explanation is that EU countries (both member states and candidates) saw their relationship to the United States differently, particularly since the end of the Cold War. For nearly five decades, the United States and Europe worked together on many levels to deal with the Soviet threat. As David Andrews writes:

[T]here was a broader and largely unspoken political agreement: European governments supported, or at least refrained from actively opposing, American policy activism around the world, while the United States supported, or at least refrained from actively undermining, a series of regional and global arrangements that underwrote Europe's regional prosperity and international influence. The United States was for the most part at liberty to pursue a strategic global vision; though west European capitals frequently criticized US policy, they rarely challenged it directly (and certainly not in crisis situations).   (Andrews 2005: 1)

Many scholars argue that the end of the Cold War saw the unraveling of this tacit understanding (e.g., Anderson, Ikenberry, and Risse 2008). During the 1990s, the weakening of mutual support was not as visible as it would be later because a variety of other factors helped to keep tensions at bay. But as Geir Lundestad argues, the diplomacy leading to the Iraq war represented a "fundamental break" from the previous nature of the transatlantic relationship (Lundestad 2005: 9). This was the culmination of a significant change in US foreign policy post–9/11 into a neoconservative unilateralism that relied on flexing military might with an unusual, crusading bravado (Gordon and Shapiro 2004: chapter 2).

This perspective largely focuses on the Big Three – France, the UK, and Germany – as they had the most to offer the United States in terms of military support. As Ioana Tiriteu puts it:

France decried the American hegemonic inclinations that were defiant of the *jus ad bellum* stipulations encompassed in the UN Charter; the [Federal Republic of Germany] revived its pacifist status of a civilian middle power that operates according to public international law; whereas the UK and Spain displayed clear intentions to defend the strategic utility of the transatlantic relationship.

(Tiriteu 2012: 223)

In the lead-up to the push to go into Iraq, the United States pressured EU states to either join the United States militarily, even without a UN mandate, or to reject the US call for a coalition of the willing (Tiriteu 2012: 1; Coicaud, with Gandois and Rutgers 2006: 238). This triggered many kinds of geopolitical issues that had been at the core of each state's identity and relationship to the use of force. Various constituencies on both sides of the Atlantic, who had kept their opposition to the other relatively innocuous until that point, became much more vocal. Thus, according to this perspective, the decision to invade Iraq marked a turning point (Andrews 2005: 2), and this was clearly visible across various key member states in early 2002 (Pond 2005: 33).

Germany
German leaders had been strongly Atlanticist in their orientation since at least the signing of the 1963 Elysée Treaty. Their precept was that "US-German relations must always take precedence even over the crucial French-German relationship" (Pond 2005: 44–45). The country was a consistent and significant contributor to NATO, and one of the United States' most reliable allies. After all, the United States was crucial to guaranteeing West Germany's security during the Cold War. But once the Cold War ended, German leaders gained more independence from the United States, and did voice opposition to US policies on occasion. However, the tone of these objections was nowhere near as strong as it would be in the debates leading to the 2003 Iraq invasion.

When Germany's Chancellor Gerhard Schröder began his campaign for reelection in late summer 2002, he stated unequivocally that there would be no support for the United States in invading Iraq, even if a UN resolution allowed it. This went against his previous promise to Bush not to touch the antiwar theme during his campaign, and it was the first time that a German chancellor had run against the United States since the founding of the Federal Republic (Gordon and Shapiro 2004: 101–103; Pond 2005: 37). Schröder argued that attacking Iraq with military force would only increase uncertainty in the Middle East, and even if there were a UN resolution, a peaceful approach would be preferable. The German leadership worried that the impending Iraq invasion looked more like a war of aggression than an act of self-defense (Dettke 2009: 158). Germany's Justice Minister Herta Däubler-Gmelin actually compared Bush to Hitler saying that the invasion was an attempt to "divert attention from his domestic problems," and that "[i]t's a classic tactic. It's one that Hitler also used" (as quoted in Gordon and Shapiro 2004: 100–101). It was clear that the German chancellor saw the Iraq war, and the war on terror as unrelated (Dettke 2009: 60). Thus, he was willing to use the German military to oppose terrorism in light of 9/11, but not to invade Iraq. Overall, the German view of the transatlantic relationship had fundamentally transformed at this point. Besides the major shift in US foreign policy, the Germans themselves found themselves in a new situation: reunited with East Germany, free to act as they saw fit, and surrounded by friendly countries (Lundestad 2005: 9).

France
Prior to debate over the Iraq invasion, the French often stood with the Americans too, especially when there was much at stake. There was good reason for this: the United States had promised to guarantee French security against its foes. But in 2002, French President Jacques Chirac backed out of the "total support" to the United States that he had proclaimed in the wake of the 9/11 attacks (Lundestad 2005: 9–29). This seemed to signal a more fundamental shift in the French attitude toward the United States (Soutou 2005: 102). With respect to this, Obajtek-Kirkwood writes, "This was another episode of the widening of the gap between the United States and France in their appraisal of the situation and decisions about Iraq, which engendered francophobia in the United States on a scale never witnessed before" (Obajtek-Kirkwood 2006: 141). Indeed, many scholars of Franco–American relations in this period argue that there were strong differences in terms of foreign policy approaches (multilateralism vs.

unilateralism), geopolitical interests (EU vs. NATO), and ideology (European identity vs. Anglo-Saxon liberalism), among other things (Soutou 2005: 114–122; Davidson 2011: 152).

Reflecting this deteriorating relationship, the Chirac administration opposed participation in the US-led Iraq invasion on the grounds that it was better to focus on UN weapons inspectors, and only use force if the Security Council voted in favor of it (Gordon and Shapiro 2004: 104–105). Chirac also felt that invading Iraq would be tantamount to justifying preventive war, which would set a dangerous precedent for the future. In short, such a war went against French interests because rather than getting rid of an impending threat, it would actually lead to more instability in the region. In the Gaullist tradition, French governments like to assert their independence, even if it means damaging relationships with other actors. Chirac was opposed to the unilateral action that the United States was willing to accept, but did not firmly take participation in military action off the table until January 2003 (Davidson 2011: 147).

United Kingdom

The "special relationship" between the UK and the United States is well known and well documented (e.g., see Louis and Bull 1987; Dumbrell 2006; Rees 2011). The British, of course, had always supported US military action, but this did not mean that they uniformly conformed to US preferences on other issues, such as on the Kyoto Protocol and the International Criminal Court (Lundestad 2005: 10). British Prime Minister Tony Blair had continued this tradition, and numerous studies find that Blair chose to support Bush on the Iraq issue, despite public opposition to an invasion, so that he could gain more influence with the US president (Stevens 2004; Davidson 2011: 134). He genuinely believed that the British alliance with the United States was the cornerstone of British foreign policy (Cook 2003: 2). Even though Blair did not think that Iraq played a part in 9/11 (Davidson 2011: 137), he justified intervention on the grounds that it was important to stand up to dictators and defend human rights (Gordon and Shapiro 2004: 105–106). For the British prime minister, the use of force was necessary in the name of international norms, and moreover, there *did* appear to him to be a clear linkage between terrorism and the need to destroy weapons of mass destruction (Gordon and Shapiro 2004: 105–106). He wanted to preempt potential future attacks from groups such as Al-Qaeda, but at the same time articulated his thinking behind the scenes that invading Iraq was probably the only circumstance under which Iraq would actually use weapons of mass destruction (WMD), if indeed it had them (Davidson 2011: 147). Thus, the British relationship to the

United States remained strong – despite some questions over the outcome of intervention – but increasingly stood apart from France and Germany.

Other Member States

The story is similar with other member states as they chose either to uphold their long-standing relationship with the United States or to diverge from it. In the case of Italy, for example, the Berlusconi government strongly stood by its transatlantic alliance, and politically sided with Bush, but eventually stopped short of a formal military contribution (Davidson 2011: 158). Spain, Poland, Denmark, the Czech Republic, Hungary, and Portugal also emphasized their enduring solidarity with the United States, while others joined the Franco–German camp.

However, the argument that diverging viewpoints on the transatlantic relationship caused the crisis for Europe does not alone explain why the crisis built up to such a degree. Indeed, as this perspective recognizes, the transformation in transatlantic relations had been under way for some time, and numerous previous disagreements with the United States [e.g. Suez, Berlin/Cuba, France's withdrawal from NATO, Vietnam, NATO missile deployment, and so on (Nau 2008)] did not escalate into a major crisis for Europe. I argue that just as the global financial crisis would provide the greater context for the Eurozone crisis (see Chapter 5), the transatlantic divide provided the greater context for the Iraq crisis. This is not to downgrade the importance of the crisis in transatlantic relations that overlapped with the timing of the EU's crisis, but simply to recognize that it had its own dynamic. Something more is needed to understand why the issue of Iraq became a trigger for the perception of existential crisis in Europe. Why *this* issue? Was it truly more divisive than the transatlantic differences that had come before?

Second Perspective: The EU Is Incapable of a Common Foreign and Security Policy

Another perspective on the causes of this crisis is that it was a result of the member states' inability to speak with one voice when it came to major foreign policy issues. This is, of course, related to their varying views on the transatlantic relationship, but the emphasis here is somewhat different. From this perspective, disagreement over whether to support or oppose an invasion of Iraq stemmed from differences in EU member states' strategic culture, and even identity. During the EU's crisis, which occurred before the Iraq invasion had even taken place, European member states had not yet articulated a common strategic vision in the way that they would after the crisis. Thus, according to this perspective, in the lead-up to the Iraq invasion, member states each acted on the basis of their national strategic cultures and did not prioritize a common European response. This prevented them from upholding CFSP. As with the previous perspective, this argument also emphasizes the overwhelming leadership status of the Big Three in articulating (or failing to articulate) Europe's approach to foreign policy.

Germany

Germany's strategic culture was, of course, the product of its post–World War II identity, its reunification with East Germany, and its determination to move in a dramatically new direction after past aggression (Dettke 2009: chapter 2). Christoph Meyer writes, "The powerful lesson of World War Two was after all that never again should German troops be used in a combat role on foreign soil" (Meyer 2006: 88). The country's approach to foreign policy was to bind and constrain itself through becoming embedded in international institutions, norms, and laws. This was not about gaining power and influence through multilateralism, as in the French case, but about behaving in an appropriate way. Thus, Germany willingly gave up national sovereignty to international institutions and saw this as an expression of German national interest (Müller 2006: 266–267). At the same time, the country was not opposed to the use of military force. During the Cold War, Germany had 500,000 troops permanently deployed and capable of high-intensity combat. After the Cold War, in 1994, Germany's constitutional court made it legal for German troops to serve in peacekeeping operations overseas as long as they were acting in self-defense or under a UN mandate, and the use of force was taken only as a last resort. Consequently, Germany sent troops into combat in both Kosovo and Afghanistan, and participated in peace-keeping operations in Bosnia and Macedonia. Dieter Dettke argues, with respect to Chancellor Schroeder, "The new national consciousness that he represented was that of a grown-up nation, and he wanted to be recognized as the leader of a grown-up Germany, a country that wanted to be a good ally – but also one that could say 'no'" (Dettke 2009: 152). In light of this, Germany's behavior toward the United States and Iraq in 2002–3 can be clearly understood.

Adhering to the principle of using force only as a last resort meant that German leaders had to determine whether a preemptive war in Iraq was legitimately self-defense or really a guise for US aggression. To be sure,

German views on the legitimate use of force had changed over time –
starting with being confined only to territorial defense and moving to the
view that humanitarian operations "out of area" were permissible (Meyer
2006: 68). But Germany's strategic culture dictated that the country
should not engage in "wars of choice," especially if it would create
a precedent for other powers to behave in the same way (Dettke 2009:
158). Unlike France, Schroeder argued that even if there were a UN
Security Council resolution authorizing the use of force, Germany
would still not become involved in an invasion because circumstances in
Iraq were unrelated to stopping terrorism, and thus there was no circumstance in which force would be justified.[7] Moreover, the costs to Iraqis of
military intervention would be high, including political, economic, and
social instability. In sum, Germany displayed a clear pacifist reflex in the
absence of real justification for the use of force, and this was in line with its
strategic culture.

France

In the words of Jean-Marc Coicaud et al., "[T]he reasons at the heart of
the French opposition to the war in Iraq, although neither totally egoistic
nor completely altruistic, are part and parcel of its strategic vision of the
world and the Middle East" (Coicaud 2006: 234). French presidents over
the course of the entire post–World War II era have tended to conduct
their foreign policy according to the Gaullist tradition of projecting
national interest to achieve international influence. Given that France
has not held superpower status for some time, French leaders have often
focused on the foreign policy areas and geographic regions that can max-
imize their influence. In particular, since the 1960s, France has been ideally
positioned to lead the EU in its foreign and security policy goals, and thus
French national interest has become synonymous with EU integration.
French leaders have also emphasized the importance of the UN in con-
doning EU foreign policy endeavors. French strategic culture understands
multilateralism *as* multipolarity, and recognizes the UN as the key driver
in promoting a multipolar world (Coicaud 2006: 235–236). On the military side, French foreign policy seeks to avoid the use of force, but France
will not hesitate to deploy troops in great numbers if it is deemed

---

[7] In this respect, Dettke argues that German foreign policy toward Iraq represented a break
from its traditional approach because Schroeder was actually going against the idea that
the UN provides legitimacy, the relationship with the United States is key, and that CFSP
takes priority (Dettke 2009: 169).

absolutely necessary.[8] Like Germany, the country actually supports a booming defense industry, and in 2002, it was the third biggest arms exporter globally.[9]

In light of this strategic culture, when it came to Iraq, the initial French reaction was hesitation. In August 2002, French Foreign Minister Dominique de Villepin made it clear that Saddam Hussein's defiant behavior was unacceptable and may warrant the use of force in response, but only if there was UN Security Council approval. From this perspective, the French president acted in line with French strategic culture, emphasizing multilateralism, the primacy of the UN (to mitigate US unilateralism), and the use of force as a last resort. Together with the UK and US, France pushed for UN Resolution 1441, which led to WMD inspections in Iraq. But when no evidence of WMDs could be demonstrated between December 2002 and March 2003, Chirac diverged more sharply from Bush and Blair, firmly opposing war. The rationale was not that Saddam Hussein should be allowed to continue, but that without WMD evidence there was no *justification* for invasion (Coicaud 2006: 238–239). Thus, from this perspective, the argument is that Chirac was acting according to France's long-term strategic vision as well as abiding by the norms so central to France's identity on the world stage.

United Kingdom

Again, British strategic culture has been intimately tied to Atlanticism. British Prime Minister Tony Blair spent a great deal of time cultivating trust with President Bush, especially after 9/11 (Wallace and Oliver 2005: 170). Blair, like John Major before him, proclaimed upon taking office that his overarching platform was to put the UK "at the heart of Europe" while still nurturing the country's "special relationship" with the United States. Thus, the story is not so different from the one outlined in the previous perspective, but perhaps with a stronger emphasis on New Labour's firmer commitment to European integration. The Blair administration did introduce some changes to the UK's overall foreign policy vision. Its so-called Third Way cut a middle ground between Thatcher's free market economics and traditional Labour's social democracy, as well as between the "special relationship" and EU integration (Wallace and Oliver 2005: 162). There was a greater emphasis on the importance of

---

[8] In 2004, for example, more than 40,000 troops were deployed around the world.
[9] The United States and Russia were (and still are) first and second, respectively (Stockholm International Peace Research Institute 2014).

Europe for Britain, as evidenced by the earlier Saint-Malo agreement. This political and strategic culture governed the British approach to numerous issues, but when it came to Iraq, Blair's myopic focus on Bush eventually resulted in a public backlash as the British leader seemingly ignored widespread opposition to invading Iraq.

In sum, as with the first explanation, this perspective tends to underplay the role of the CEECs vis-à-vis Iraq, and instead sees this breakdown in EU foreign policy as a symptom of a long-existing struggle among EU member states to see eye-to-eye on foreign policy. From this viewpoint, disagreement over Iraq was part and parcel of the failure to agree on the European Defence Community in the 1950s, the inability to merge European Political Cooperation into EU structures in the 1970s, the long road to CFSP in the 1980s, and finally the inability to make CFSP operational in the 1990s.

All EU countries were naturally concerned about Saddam Hussein's leadership in Iraq and the possibility that he had weapons of mass destruction, but they had different interpretations of how urgent it was to take action (Tiriteu 2012: 216). From this perspective, these different interpretations stem from member states' distinctive worldviews, and thus also explain other European foreign policy failures. The underlying assumption is that member states will prioritize their own national interest and strategic culture over finding a common EU approach. Indeed, the argument is that they care little about speaking with one voice.

Although it is true that CFSP was at times challenging for the EU, this does not in itself explain why this crisis grew to existential proportions for Europe. Precisely because the foreign policy side of EU cooperation had evolved so slowly, expectations for a common approach to Iraq should have been quite low. Especially when one considers that the EU did not even have a common foreign policy as part of its institutional structure until the 1992 Maastricht Treaty, and had not been particularly successful at speaking with one voice in reaction to past foreign policy challenges.[10] The reaction to this crisis might still have played out in far milder terms.

---

[10] It is important to note that the EU had done relatively well at speaking with one voice when it came to routine questions of foreign policy, particularly in terms of its participation in the UN and WTO. The challenge was with more unprecedented issues that could require the use of military force.

Third Perspective: Eastern and Western Member States Are Fundamentally Different

A third perspective sees the origins of this crisis in the fundamental differences that seemed to divide eastern and western countries in Europe. Unlike the previous two, this argument brings the CEECs front and center into the story. As is typical when countries are candidates for EU membership, the CEECs were already heavily entrenched in Brussels politics in the decade prior to joining, and thus their opinions and attitudes toward the CFSP were influential in the lead-up to the Iraq crisis. This perspective simultaneously emphasizes the ongoing stigma of the Cold War, as well as the significant transformation underway with the impending EU "big bang" enlargement. Proponents of this argument claim that the East–West relationship represented an underlying current of tension that eventually prompted Donald Rumsfeld to quip that the French–German axis was "old Europe."

Eastern candidate countries felt at times that western member states held all of the cards, and were thus taking advantage of their power over the East, as if the former were doing the latter a favor rather than welcoming the return of their fellow Europeans into the fold with the opening of the Iron Curtain. It took thirteen years after the end of the Cold War for the CEECs finally to be approved for admission, and they had had to accept many concessions and compromises in the terms of their membership. To them, it seemed the West was worried that the EU would become a transfer union, in that the West would have to financially support the East for some time to come, and that the new members would be expensive.

The countries to the east also displayed a strong attraction to NATO, which sent the message that they were more US-friendly than the German–French axis appeared to be. They also did not have the same fear of US unilateralism or military domination. Anne Applebaum argues, "Whereas many west Europeans remember the Cold War era as a time of economic growth and political strength, east Europeans remember it as a time of national catastrophe. There is little nostalgia for the days when American power was checked by the Soviet Union" (Applebaum 2005: 32).

By contrast, core countries in the West, especially France and Germany, saw the European project in some ways as a means of separating themselves from the United States. In particular, they disagreed with some aspects of US foreign policy, and they also did not buy into the same economic model of low taxes, privatization, and small government. Whereas Thatcher and

Reagan had forged a strong bond in pursuing American-style capitalism, most of the other member states rejected this approach in favor of upholding European values of social democracy (Applebaum 2005: 27–29). By pursuing EU integration according to their western vision, Europe could become an international actor to reckon with. But this involved concern that the addition of eastern countries into the EU would dilute the West's mission. Thus, the argument is that this intensifying sense of divide holds the key to understanding why European countries took the Iraq crisis so seriously. Essentially, it symbolically represented the larger power struggle between East and West, and the concern each side felt as they came closer to binding their fates together. The nature of these tensions will be discussed more fully later in the chapter.

Overall, this perspective, perhaps unlike the other two, requires a more nuanced understanding to put it into context. As this chapter will show, the crisis narrative was largely centered on East–West tensions, and yet, I argue that these tensions did not *cause* the crisis for Europe. Importantly, at the outset of the crisis, the real dividing lines were not simply East–West. The leaders in several major, western European member states – such as the UK, Spain, and Italy – were alongside many CEECs in supporting US action in Iraq (see Table 3.1). Meanwhile, numerous other countries from all over the map of Europe were vehemently opposed to the invasion, such as Austria, Belgium, France, Germany, Greece, Slovenia, and Sweden. Quite simply, and of key importance to our understanding of this process, the western member states were just as significantly divided among themselves as they were from the new member states. Indeed, the UK, Italy, and Spain are generally seen as the three main member states that initially led the pro-military side, while France and Germany are seen as having led the anti-military side (Tiriteu 2012: 219). All five are, of course, western European powers.

TABLE 3.1 *European Involvement in the Iraq War Coalition*

	Original Member States	New Member States
Contributors	Denmark, Italy, the Netherlands, Portugal, Spain, the UK	Czech Republic, Estonia, Hungary, Latvia, Lithuania, Poland, Slovakia
Non-contributors	Austria, Belgium, Finland, France, Germany, Greece, Ireland, Luxembourg, Sweden	Cyprus, Malta, Slovenia

As I will argue, despite the absence of a clear East–West divide in the creation of the crisis, once the crisis picked up steam, talk of East–West divisions became a kind of self-fulfilling prophecy, and these preexisting tensions rose to the surface. Indeed, at the height of the crisis, it was as if Iraq no longer had anything to do with the crisis because what was really at stake was the East–West relationship.

What's Missing?

All three of the preceding explanations emphasize structural explanations in different ways. It is certainly true that EU member states disagreed over whether or not to invade Iraq and support the United States. They had a variety of reasons for their stances, and while there were no clear "blocs," the divisions among member states were mostly portrayed this way. Again, the core "pro-invasion" states were Britain, Spain, and Italy, and the core "anti-invasion" states were Germany and France. Yet, even within these camps, leaders disagreed in significant ways, often just as much as they did with those in the "opposing" camp. But the larger point is that these differences do not in and of themselves explain how Iraq became a European crisis of such strong intensity. Member states had long struggled to speak with one voice, and at this stage they were only scratching the surface of having the ability to follow up their words with action at the European level.

Thus, the three perspectives outlined earlier certainly shed light on aspects of this crisis, but they are not sufficient to explain how the crisis put both European integration and enlargement at stake. Disparities in strategic culture and national interest were no more severe during the Iraq crisis than at other times. However, by the time the crisis reached its height in January–February 2003, the crisis narrative became self-fulfilling: the EU was seemingly on the brink of breakdown. The crisis threatened to undo the progress that had been made on CFSP, as well as to derail the impending enlargement to include the ten new Central and Eastern European member states. If these two things had happened, the EU would have ceased to exist as the actor it had grown to become.

I argue that we must pay attention to social narratives about this crisis – especially coming from the media and elites – to show how the Iraq conflict quickly transformed into an existential crisis for the EU. The socially constructed nature of this crisis deserves special attention in the story of its origins. The degree of confrontational and emotional language among elites, and the negative media frenzy surrounding these disputes, explains why this relatively routine disagreement over foreign policy escalated into a full-blown crisis for Europe. In Chapter 2, I explained why media narratives – especially in the leading international papers – have a strong and disproportionate effect on social narratives more generally, and how social narratives, in turn, are strongly indicative of what society generally believes to be true. In this case, media coverage extrapolated general problems with the EU from very specific disagreements on how to respond to Iraq. This quote from the *Financial Times* is representative of the kind of coverage that was typical in the early stages of the crisis:

The crisis over Iraq bears painful witness to a feeble Europe . . . Europe's malaise runs deeper than its failure to recalibrate and re-equip its armed forces after the Cold War. Power and prestige on the international stage are a measure of inner strength, of political self-confidence and of economic success. Europe can claim neither . . . The strategic benefits of EU enlargement are self-evident . . . You won't hear this from France's Jacques Chirac, Spain's Jose Maria Aznar, or Italy's Silvio Berlusconi. Nor, with one or two honorable exceptions, from any other EU leader. In place of a celebration of the new Europe there is almost universal foreboding. The promise made when the Berlin Wall came down is now cast as threat.

(Stephens 2002)

Writing as though disagreement over Iraq were symbolic of the enfeeblement of Europe as a whole and of the futility of the EU ever becoming a real actor on the international stage, the international media decided that this would be the main story, and not some other angle. There was disagreement among some leaders, to be sure, but one might step back and recognize that the conflict had actually brought European citizens together in an unprecedented way – something they openly displayed on February 15, 2003, when millions of people took to the streets all over Europe to protest the coming war. But as leaders ratcheted up the rhetoric, aggravating the sense of impending crisis, the media picked up certain tone-setting statements and amplified them, leading to new and unnecessary levels of intensity. Much of the remainder of the chapter delves into this process of crisis buildup in detail.

CONSTRUCTING THE CRISIS

The crisis trigger – President Bush's September 12, 2002, speech to the United Nations – was clearly external in origin as it stemmed from US foreign policy decisions in the wake of 9/11. But after Bush's speech, the buildup and consolidation of crisis narratives came with the interplay between media and elite rhetoric in Europe. This dynamic was crucial in construing this largely external event as a crisis for the EU. At the public level, there was actually little divisive tension over Iraq as European citizens across member states and candidate states were largely opposed to an invasion.

To be sure, the issue of how to respond to the supposed existence of WMDs had been discussed among European leaders prior to Bush's speech. During the summer of 2002, the seeds of the impending transatlantic crisis were planted. But as national positions on the issue solidified, a conflict that could have simply remained at the transatlantic level grew into a much more significant problem for Europe. Media coverage and elite statements forecasted from the outset that there was no possibility of agreement among European countries. As discussed in Chapter 2, key indicators of the social construction of crisis include exaggeration, extrapolation from the specific to the general, misconstruing significance, and negative forecasting. All of these indicators were present in the lead-up to the EU crisis over Iraq.

Media content analysis shows that the international media played a central role in construing European disagreement over Iraq as a major crisis for the EU through its sheer volume of coverage (Figure 3.1) and its lack of neutrality in tone (Figure 3.2).[11] The evidence was derived through reading *all* new stories that mention the keyword "Iraq," resulting in a total number of 465 articles across the four publications.

A barrage of negative media coverage, beginning in December 2002, defined this as a major European crisis and rapidly led to a heightened atmosphere of integrational panic, particularly among political leaders. Indeed, rather than simply reporting a divergence in foreign policy preferences, the content of the coverage preceding the crisis typically portrayed the Iraq issue as threatening the very legitimacy of the EU's integration process. When reflecting on the significance of the debate over Iraq, the media often "megasized" this into a policy failure with larger and long-term implications, frequently misinterpreting the nature of events as they unfolded. Representative examples of the kinds of statements made in the international press in the early stages of this conflict were as follows:

The Europeans may be constructing their architecture of a common foreign policy, with constitutional conventions, high representatives, Euro-armies and so on. But the ground on which this complex structure rests is made of sand. (Baker 2002)

---

[11] For details on the methodology of this media content analysis, see Chapter 2.

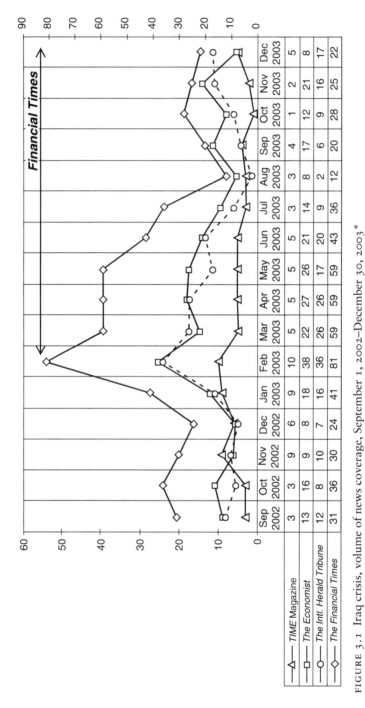

FIGURE 3.1 Iraq crisis, volume of news coverage, September 1, 2002–December 30, 2003*
* In this figure, the right side Y-axis pertains to the *Financial Times*, while the left side Y-axis pertains to the other three media outlets. The *FT* publishes more stories in general as well as those related to the European region.

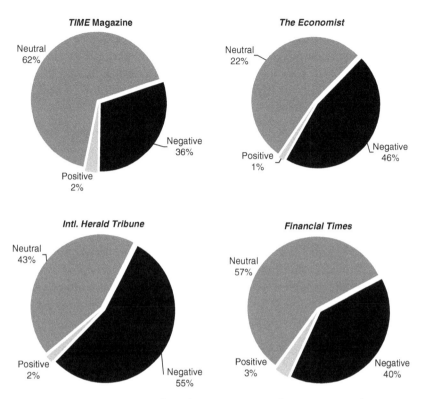

FIGURE 3.2 Iraq crisis, neutrality of coverage, September 12, 2002–February 15, 2003*
* The neutrality of an article is counted as *negative* when the anticipated consequences of the crisis for the EU's continued viability are depicted as negative, *positive* when the EU is portrayed as being able to overcome current challenges, and *neutral* if the story expresses no judgment about outlook.

Until 1948, Europe was geography. It has since been a number of things, without clearly identifying what it really wants to become. First it was divided into an East and a West … With Eastern and Western Europe reunited since 1989, Europe now intends to become a group with 25 members. But members of what? (Pfaff 2002)

The grandiose talk about the EU's new foreign policy continues to look silly whenever a real global crisis erupts, as it has done over Iraq.
(*The Economist*, "Testing, Testing," 2002)

Yet Europe's history is littered with discarded constitutions and failed conventions … But the Iraq crisis may leave a legacy of bitterness between different European leaders that could spill over into the constitutional negotiations.
(*The Economist*, "Philadelphia or Frankfurt," 2003)

In essence, the media turned a specific conflict into a generalized problem with the EU, and framed the debate over Iraq as a make-or-break issue for Europe.

While the media played a strong role in defining this as a European crisis, elite rhetoric also mattered greatly in constructing dominant narratives about the crisis, as I will return to in the next section. Anne-Marie Obajtek-Kirkwood writes:

The last step was illustrative of what had been developing throughout 2002 and even more during 2003, that is, a rift among pro- and antiwar European Union members. This divide between its members was at times forcefully promoted by Donald Rumsfeld or, in turn, initiated by Jacques Chirac's position against new pro-war European Union members like Poland. (Obajtek-Kirkwood 2006: 141)

The crisis soon took on a self-fulfilling prophecy dynamic. What started out as being mainly an issue of deciding whether or not to support the United States in its call to invade Iraq – that is, a transatlantic issue – morphed into an event threatening to derail Europe's future goals. Indeed, once the conflict was clearly defined as a crisis, the media continued to feed into the intensity of the crisis narrative through its negative forecasts for the future of Europe:

In practice, the chances of seeing a combined EU team all pulling in the same direction are slim. For all their fine talk about a common foreign and security policy, when it comes to a really divisive issue – particularly one in which the US is the most important operator – the EU partners cut and run in a host of different directions.   (Peel 2003a)

So much for a common European policy … To anyone outside Europe, the very idea of a common foreign policy must look like a fantasy. But it is worse. Most of those leaders are actively engaged in proposing ideas for strengthening their common actions. It stinks of hypocrisy.   (Peel 2003b)

The deep divide over Iraq between Britain and other pro-US members on the one hand and France and Germany on the other is turning the Union's ambitions for a common foreign and security policy into a sick joke.
          (*Financial Times*, "The Alliance Comes Apart at the Seams," 2003)

The divisions among Europe's leaders, especially over the prospect of war with Iraq, are deep and seemingly impossible to reconcile … France, together with Germany, has made much of the running of the EU's new constitution as well and has, in the past, been keen on a common European foreign and defence policy. The current split in the EU makes such ambitions appear laughable.
          (*The Economist*, "Old Europe's Last Gasp," 2003)

As with the two subsequent crises discussed in this book, the impression in the media at the height of the crisis was that this was a seriously negative turning point in EU integration that would forever be a stain on its history:

Even optimistic European diplomats insist the damage done to NATO – and to the prospects of unity among Europeans themselves – could be irreparable.
(*Financial Times,* " The Speech by the UN's Chief Weapons Inspector . . .," 2003)

It may be time to admit that there will never in fact be a common European foreign and security policy. Long before the crisis over Iraq erupted, momentum towards the creation of such a policy was quietly ebbing away. (Lieven 2003)

The image of the EU as a haven of security, prosperity and European cultural identity is frequently darkened by worries about membership costs and fears of being swamped by foreign capital and influence. (Wagstyl 2003)

Torn apart by a deep and bitter split over Iraq . . . The decision to go to war has raised the question of who speaks for Europe . . . [and] has made a mockery of the efforts to forge a common foreign and defense [policy] for Europe.
(*International Herald Tribune,* "EU Leaders Hold Summit . . .," 2003)

The war with Iraq has exploded the myth of European unity and it intruded at every turn.
(*International Herald Tribune,* "Blair-Chirac Quarrel Rages . . .," 2003)

All this could be seen as nothing more than an honest, if deep, disagreement among friends. But the pitch of anger in this debate proves there is much more to it than that. (*The Economist,* "Dealing with Iraq," 2003)

While the EU issues anodyne and instantly forgettable common statements on Iraq, its members busily plot diplomatic ambushes for each other . . . . So the EU's ideal as a fraternal club presenting a united face to the rest of the world has given way to something that looks more like a 19th century tangle of alliances.
(*The Economist,* "Charlemagne: Place Your Bets," 2003)

This exaggeration, and oftentimes blatant misrepresentation, of what the Iraq question meant for Europe would have been an unthinkable portrayal just a few years before when Blair and Chirac met at Saint-Malo to lay the foundation for an operational EU foreign policy – the new European Security and Defence Policy. However, this case shows how the dynamics of integrational panic work when social narratives drive crises. It was not necessarily the case that disagreement on Iraq was inevitable, nor by extension, that this meant the derailment of the enlargement process and the end of existence for CFSP.

INTEGRATIONAL PANIC AND CATHARSIS

Once the question over whether or not to invade Iraq became defined as a crisis for Europe, the main crisis narratives centered on the preexisting tensions of the time: the UK–France–Germany (Big Three) leadership question and East–West differences. It is important to understand that these preexisting tensions, which were unrelated to Iraq, did not *cause* the crisis for Europe. But when the Iraq debate emerged on the political scene, the crisis environment became an excuse to voice these preexisting tensions openly and more honestly than before. This helped feed into a process of crisis buildup within Europe from late 2002 to early 2003 until eventually the crisis narrative began to dissipate, taking the sharpest of tensions with it, in favor of a more positive outlook toward the future of European security and foreign policy. Indeed, as the narrative shifted away from such strife, there was actually a sense of embarrassment over the unabashed and public airing of their "dirty laundry," so to speak. In response, Europeans turned this crisis into an opportunity to move forward with integration, particularly in the area of security and defense.

I begin this section by outlining the nature of the preexisting tensions and how they came to comprise the dominant crisis narratives. I argue that the divisions among the Big Three and between eastern and western member states were not necessarily the most obvious way to talk about the crisis – especially considering that the nature of the crisis was primarily US-driven, and that European publics largely stood together in their opposition to invasion. I then describe how, as these narratives began to intensify, the crisis itself started to become a self-fulfilling prophecy, with serious talk of rolling back both enlargement and integration. Finally, I show how European leaders were able to move past the crisis with significant new initiatives in the area of the Common Foreign and Security Policy. In the process, I argue that this went hand-in-hand with the sense of catharsis among elites that came with the release of tensions during the crisis. Overall, the Iraq case demonstrates that a relatively common breakdown on foreign policy within the EU can evolve into a situation of integrational panic, and in the end, European leaders can turn this into an opportunity to reach newfound consensus and further integration (in this case, far-reaching agreement on deepening CFSP).

Preexisting Tensions

The conflict over Iraq could have been talked about as an issue involving Iraq itself and whether or not the circumstances warranted invasion. This might have included questions such as whether this would be a just war; whether it would be in line with the principle of using force as a last resort, or would instead set a future precedent for preventive war; whether there was enough evidence to justify invasion; and so on. The conflict could have also been talked about as primarily a crisis in transatlantic relations, rather than as a crisis for Europe. Naturally, these discussions did come to the fore, but they were generally not as prominent as two preexisting sources of tension that were becoming increasingly palpable even before the Iraq conflict became an issue of concern, especially at the leadership level: (1) divisions among the Big Three and (2) divisions between eastern and western member states.

First, the question of whether the Big Three – France, the UK, and Germany – would lead this newly enlarged EU was paramount among elites at the time. To add to this, the leaders of the Big Three had also been fighting over agriculture subsidy policies before the Iraq crisis, further aggravating the relationship among them. And then there was the ongoing question of the future of Europe. French and German leaders had always been at the heart of the European project, but while the Germans wanted a *single* foreign policy determined through majority voting, the French were loathe to accept this. Meanwhile, French leaders were criticizing the Germans for not contributing more to European defense. The UK–French relationship was similarly strained. As Jolyon Howorth argues, during the pre-crisis period of 1998–2001, "the UK and France tended to define the opposite poles of the debate," surrounding the nature of ESDP and its relationship to NATO (Howorth 2003: 174).

Second, tensions between eastern and western member states at the elite level were also of growing concern. As described earlier in this chapter, since the fall of the Berlin Wall (and, of course, largely as a result of divergent histories before it), these two broad regions of Europe had different worldviews; however, in the immediate lead-up to the crisis, these tensions were getting more intense, making further cooperation under ESDP difficult. At the time, Europe was in the final stages of the enlargement process to bring in the ten Central and Eastern European countries (CEECs) that had been separated from Western Europe during the Cold War. At the leadership level, many existing member states were worried about what such a "big-bang enlargement" would mean for the integration project. Many leaders of Western European countries worried that this new enlargement round would detract from deepening integration. There was a sense that the CEECs would have different political cultures, attitudes on foreign policy, and relationships to NATO, among other things.

For their part, CEEC leaders were increasingly frustrated with how long the accession negotiations took to complete – thirteen years

(Applebaum 2005: 31). The tone of the accession negotiations had also created some ill will as western member states questioned whether the East should have access to the West's labor market, whether eastern farmers could partake in the Common Agricultural Policy, and whether they should receive their full share of structural funds. Understandably, the candidate countries were beginning to feel like they were being relegated to the status of second-class Europeans (Applebaum 2005: 32).

To add to the intensity of elite tensions, from 2001 to 2003 a series of elections put more conservative politicians in office. Anne Applebaum observes that "Europe in 2003, on the eve of the war with Iraq, suddenly looked much different than it had a few years earlier" (Applebaum 2005: 29). Many of these countries had been pursuing social democratic economic policies, but there was a shift in popular thinking toward moving closer to what they thought was US economic success. Relatedly, East–West tensions also grew in the wake of 9/11 amid the discovery that many of the hijackers had originated from Europe and had drawn benefits from the European welfare system (Applebaum 2005: 29). The new wave of more conservative politicians wanted to rethink immigration policies.

As Anand Menon writes, "During the Iraq crisis itself, bitter disagreements between member states served to undermine further progress on ESDP and exacerbated the latent tensions that had always existed concerning the Union's future as a security actor" (Menon 2004). When the crisis for Europe began to taper off in March 2003, one op-ed described it this way:

> Europeans are shocked by the scale of their own disarray over the Iraq crisis, and by the depth of the rifts that have opened up inside the European Union. The question is, what are they going to do about it? ... It is that the EU's vaunted Common Foreign and Security Policy is revealed not so much as hollow as non-existent ... The issue of whether it is right or even useful to attack Iraq is a catalyst that has brought to the surface long dormant divisions over the nature of European security.   (Merritt 2003)

Thus, as Iraq became defined as a crisis for Europe, these preexisting tensions increasingly formed the basis of the crisis narrative and were progressively providing momentum for integrational panic.

The Crisis Narrative

Media content analysis shows that during the crisis, these preexisting tensions among the Big Three and between eastern and western countries rose to the surface and were aired openly as the dominant crisis narrative (Figures 3.3 and 3.4). This became the dominant way in which Europeans – particularly at the elite, political level – talked about the crisis. As Jeffrey Lewis argues, "The run up to the Iraq war in March 2003 split open fissures amongst EU member states rarely displayed in such naked clarity: 'new' versus 'old,' 'Atlanticist' versus 'Europeanist,' and within the big state 'triumverate' of Britain, France, and Germany" (Lewis 2008: 1). Again, given the nature of the crisis and its external origins, it might be expected that news coverage about Iraq would focus mainly on other things, such as tensions between the United States and specific member states, or the fact that numerous European leaders directly defied popular opinion against the war.

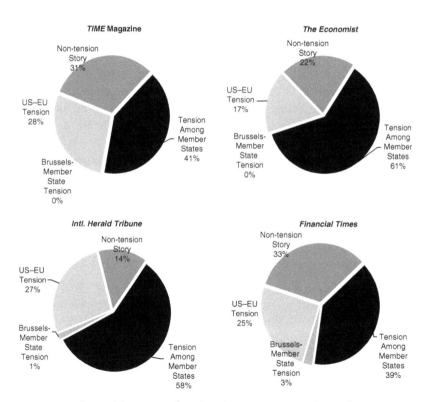

FIGURE 3.3 Iraq crisis, nature of tensions in news coverage, September 12, 2002–February 15, 2003[12]

---

[12] See Chapter 2 for an explanation of methodology.

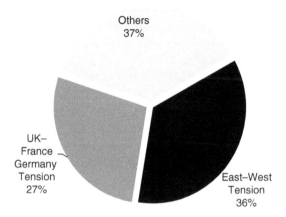

FIGURE 3.4 Iraq crisis, member state sub-tensions, September 12, 2002–February 15, 2003

Despite this, Figures 3.3 and 3.4 show that while around one-quarter of the news coverage addressed the transatlantic angle, much more of it was devoted to tensions among EU member states (Figure 3.3). Breaking this down further (Figure 3.4), two main tension-based media narratives emerge: Big Three and East–West.

With respect to the narrative about the Big Three, even though France and Germany were on the same "side" over Iraq, their differences in approach to security policy were amplified in the media, emphasizing that German leaders did not like the French determination to build up the EU to balance against the United States (Vinocur 2002a), among other things. Thus, even though both France and Germany opposed the Iraq war, their alliance was depicted in a very negative way. For example:

Jacques Chirac says that France and Germany's approach and vision concerning Iraq are 'identical and of the same nature' – an elastic, credulity-stretching description of unity across the Rhine.   (Vinocur 2003a)

France and Germany are trying to get back into the EU's driving seat ... yet, they differ about the Union's future shape.
(*The Economist*, "France, Germany and the EU," 2002)

Some coverage of this also made connections to broader issues that had little to do with debates over Iraq:

Open contradictions and rivalries exist between the two countries, notably on economic policy and their performance in the area of defense. Taken together,

they suggest that a perfect French-German embrace may be a wavering
prospect.   (Graham and Simonian 2003)

Fundamental differences between France's more inter-governmental approach
and Germany's federal leanings have been shelved, not resolved. Differences also
remain on the economic governance of the eurozone: German policymakers
remain tied to Bundesbank orthodoxy, while France wants to loosen the fiscal
constraints demanded by the stability pact . . . the question arises: can the Franco-
German axis be sustained? Are Mr Chirac and Mr Schroder making a mistake in
placing so much emphasis on a bipolar relationship in Europe when enlargement
increases the possibilities for multi-polar ties within the EU?   (Vinocur 2002a)

In addition to these Franco–German frictions, it was all too easy to play up
tensions between France and Germany on the one side, and the UK on the
other. More opinionated coverage in the American and British press
actually referred to France, Germany, and other anti-war countries as an
"axis of weasels" and a "chorus of cowards" (*Financial Times*, "Media
Deploy 'Old Europe' Hauteur to Counter Furor," 2003). It almost seemed
as if the media took delight in characterizing differences of opinion among
the Big Three in ways that bordered on insulting:

Welcome to the proxy war over Iraq, a spin-off of the traditional cross-channel
battle waged with brio for centuries between the United Kingdom and France.
                                         (*Time*, "Europe's Family Feud," 2003)

When it comes to foreign policy, Europeans rarely agree. Iraq has shown again
that Britain, France and Germany, Europe's three big powers, "nationalize"
foreign policy when hard choices confront them.   (Dempsey 2002: 3)

For all its aspirations to speak with one voice, Europe remains a vehicle for the
preoccupations and aspirations of its nation states. Mr. Chirac is not about to
give up France's self-chosen role as a voice robustly independent of the US.
Mr. Blair will not readily surrender Britain's place as Washington's best friend.
And Germany must live for a while yet with the demons of its past.
                                                            (Stephens 2003)

Among the early regional casualties has been unity within the European Union.
The impact will be not so much to disrupt the routine economic business that
meshes its members together, but inevitably to curtail the EU's foreign and defence
policy ambitions after so deep a split between its two protagonists, France and
Britain.   (*Financial Times*, "The Storms beyond the Azores," 2003)

With respect to East–West tensions, the divide was presented as though it
were clear-cut, even though, as previously mentioned, western countries
were just as divided among themselves as the new member states were
with them. For example:

Instead, in an EU expanding eastward to an increasingly pro-American membership of 25, there is incontrovertible evidence that neither the numbers nor instincts are there for a Europe ready to clasp a wavering, tentative French-German pair as its guide on the world stage, and toss out America as de facto leader and guarantor of its survival.   (Vinocur 2003c)

An indirect French-German warning enters here as a statement that a European core exists and will not easily accept a new environment and a new membership ready to disregard its convictions.

> (*International Herald Tribune*, "For Paris and Berlin, a Drive to Stay
> Important . . .," 2003)

While new entrants crowd into the Union, back in Brussels the finest minds at the European Commission are concentrating on a different problem: how to kick countries out ... The federalists have always been uneasy about letting poor Central Europeans in. How ironic if the EU found itself ushering in new members by the front door while inadvertently pushing some of Europe's richer and older democracies out by the back.

> (*The Economist*, "Charlemagne: The Perils of Penelope," 2002)

With 25 members, the EU will be a different place, and once they have their feet under the table, the new boys might turn out to be less grateful and compliant than has long been assumed.   (*The Economist*, "Now for the Hard Part," 2003)

Before the invasion of Iraq had even begun, what might have been discussed as a relatively routine foreign policy disagreement among member states – not unlike several similar cases that had happened in the past and several that would happen in the future – instead took on alarmist tones in the international press.

Beyond media coverage, EU leaders also used language to discuss Big Three and East–West tensions that under normal circumstances would have been considered confrontational. The leaders of the Big Three – Chirac, Blair, and Schroeder – contributed significantly to the sense of crisis. After a September 2002 meeting, an EU ambassador said, "The chemistry between all three leaders is far from good . . . The meeting fell apart because Blair, Chirac and Schroder simply do not get on" (*Financial Times*, "What to Do about Saddam Further Divides Europe's Big Three," 2002). At the EU summit in Brussels in October 2002, Chirac stormed over to Blair, and proceeded to attack him in front of the other EU heads of government and officials. He said, "You have been very rude and I have never been spoken to like this before" (*Financial Times*, "Chirac Blasts Blair in Summit Confrontation," 2002). Chirac then promptly canceled the upcoming Anglo-French summit.

The strife between the British and French leaders may have been understandable considering they held opposite views regarding the Iraq issue, but the tension between French and German leaders was just as sharp. A French diplomat said, "Germany does not share France's muscular view of Europe as a future counterweight to US hegemony on international security issues" (Graham and Simonian 2003). Another said, "There's a huge will to get a Franco-German agreement, but frankly we're struggling to find things to agree about" (*The Economist*, "Charlemagne: Wooing Marianne," 2002). German Foreign Minister Joschka Fischer said that the "Franco-German motor of Europe no longer exists" (*The Economist*, "Franco-German Relations: Spectacle or Substance?" 2003). And a high-ranking EU official said, "Frankly, people are getting fed up with this French-German axis" (Vincour 2003c). Naturally, the media took the opportunity to amplify these statements, adding fuel to the fire:

Whatever happens, France will be in a worse position that it was before the Iraqi crisis arose. Its relations with the US are awful and its position in the EU is being challenged by the countries of "young Europe."   (Heisbourg 2003)

As the crisis moved into 2003, various leaders' tone-setting statements provided more fodder for the press, and one in particular famously came from the other side of the Atlantic. On January 22, 2003, US Defense Secretary Donald Rumsfeld drew the East–West narrative into a maelstrom when he criticized the French–German axis:

Germany has been a problem and France has been a problem. But you look at vast numbers of other countries in Europe, they're not with France and Germany ... they're with the US ... You're thinking of Europe as Germany and France. I don't. I think that's old Europe ... If you look at the entire NATO Europe today, the center of gravity is shifting to the east.
                    (*BBC News*, "Outrage at 'Old Europe' Remarks," 2003)

Newspapers all over the world printed this famous quote, even though there was no reality to the claim that "old" and "new" Europe formed coherent and separate camps (Wood 2003). Some even hailed Rumsfeld's statement as accurate:

Though it was impolite of Donald Rumsfeld, America's defence secretary, to have dwelt with such high glee on the divisions between "old" and "new" Europe, he got it right. For many decades France and Germany gave the EU its sense of direction. But as only two countries in an EU that will soon number 25, they should not have pretended to speak for the rest.
(*The Economist*, "The Western Alliance in Disarray: How Deep Is the Rift?" 2003)

The very next week, on January 30, 2003, eight countries, comprising a mixture of western and eastern member states – Spain, Poland, Hungary, Czech Republic, Italy, Denmark, Portugal, and the UK – signed the so-called Letter of Eight, and published a major op-ed in the *Wall Street Journal* to show their support for the Bush administration's efforts to eliminate Saddam Hussein and his supposed weapons of mass destruction, as well as to "liberate" and democratize the people of Iraq (Levy 2005: xiv). As reported in the media:

> Friedbert Pfluger, a Christian Democrat foreign policy spokesman, said the chancellor's anti-war approach had "virtually provoked" eight European leaders to write a joint letter backing US policies towards Iraq ... Goran Persson, the Swedish prime minister, who was not asked to sign it, criticized the letter for splitting the EU, saying it "played into Iraq's hands."
>
> (Simonian and Bickerton 2003)

> The letter was meant to split Europe. It actually demonstrated that the split that exists is between politicians and public. While European governments do not have a common foreign policy, on some issues the European public does ... There is another split in Europe, a permanent one, between those who want Europe to be a united and autonomous actor in world affairs, and those who are frightened by the possibility that Europe might lose the Atlantic attachment. The latter is true for the former Communist countries, and some of the smaller West European states.
>
> (*International Herald Tribune*, "Why the U.S. Fears Europe Crushing German Dissent," 2003)

And then on February 6, 2003, the "Vilnius Ten" – comprised of Estonia, Latvia, Lithuania, Slovakia, Slovenia, Bulgaria, Romania, Albania, Croatia, and Macedonia (although Albania, Croatia, and Macedonia were not on the verge of joining the EU) – also expressed their open support for the United States in a letter (Gherghisan 2003).

Indeed, the crisis was becoming a self-fulfilling prophecy. The narrative about disagreement over Iraq had evolved into something that seemingly threatened the EU itself, even though there was little reason to interpret it this way. It was as if Rumsfeld's rather careless caricature of "new Europe" had become a reality overnight, even though as Levy et al. argue, the CEECs have actually resented being "lumped together" because they too have their own traditions (Levy, Pensky, and Torpey 2005: xxv). But after Rumsfeld's statement and the Vilnius letter, the media repeatedly referred to old and new Europe as if Europe were actually comprised of these competing blocs. For example: "Chirac Lashes Out at 'New Europe'" (*CNN World* 2003),

"Blair and Chirac Collide over 'New Europe'" (*Financial Times* 2003), "Old Europe's last gasp?" (*Time* 2003).

Later that month, Romano Prodi, European Commission president, warned that the "total lack of a European common foreign policy" was bringing the EU closer to disaster. At a February 2003 European Parliament meeting in Strasbourg, he said, "If Europe fails to pull together, all our nation states will disappear from the world scene ... Unless Europe speaks with a single voice, it will be impossible to continue working closely with the US on a longstanding basis while retaining our dignity" (*Financial Times*, "Summit Bar on EU Candidate Countries," 2003). The media reported on the same day:

There are no "old" or "new" Europeans, only bad Europeans ... Rivalry and mistrust remain basic patterns of European politics. For most EU member states, it is still unacceptable for one of their peers to gain influence and take the lead. Their main priority is therefore to hold one another on a leash and not to put at risk their protection by the United States. The fact that "new Europe" prepared its famous declaration of solidarity with the United States behind the back of "old Europe," just when the Franco-German bond had regained a certain dynamic, is a case in point.
(Schmitt 2003)

And this was followed the next day with the kind of statement that would come to define the buildup of the Eurozone crisis less than seven years later:

The Portuguese foreign minister said that what had earlier seemed a manageable crisis was now threatening to spiral out of control, affecting the security of countries like his. "Today the colors are of a darker shade of gray than they were yesterday," he said, "and they could become even darker."
(*International Herald Tribune*, "Blair Demands EU Back War in Iraq," 2003)

The crisis reached its high point on February 15, 2003, the day when major anti-war protests broke out across Europe. More Europeans took to the streets than at any time since World War II. For the duration of this crisis, European publics were largely homogeneous in their views opposed to the war, with little difference at all between eastern and western member states (see Table 3.2). Paris, Berlin, Rome, and Madrid took the lead in communicating this strong anti-war sentiment at the public level, and this narrative was emphasized during the peace rallies across Europe (Tiriteu 2012: 232). Indeed, the demonstration in the Italian capital on February 15 was the largest anti-war rally in the history of the world – most estimates put the crowd in Rome at around three million people – even though Italy was actually a member of the US coalition for war in Iraq (*Guinness Book of World Records* 2004).

TABLE 3.2 *Attitudes Toward Military Intervention in Iraq Question:*
"Do you consider that it would be justified or not that our country
participates in a military intervention in Iraq, if the United States intervenes
militarily in Iraq without a preliminary decision of the United Nations?"
(EOS Survey Gallup Europe 2003)

	Justified	Unjustified	Don't Know
EU-15			
Austria	8%	85%	6%
Belgium	13%	84%	4%
Denmark	13%	83%	4%
Finland	7%	89%	4%
France	13%	84%	3%
Germany	19%	89%	1%
Greece	9%	88%	3%
Ireland	13%	81%	6%
Italy	18%	81%	2%
Luxembourg	13%	84%	3%
Netherlands	13%	84%	3%
Portugal	16%	77%	7%
Spain	12%	78%	11%
Sweden	9%	85%	6%
UK	27%	68%	6%
CEECs			
Bulgaria	6%	81%	13%
Czech Republic	30%	65%	5%
Estonia	8%	85%	8%
Hungary	8%	76%	16%
Latvia	7%	85%	8%
Lithuania	12%	73%	15%
Poland	21%	72%	7%
Romania	16%	70%	13%
Slovakia	41%	59%	1%
Slovenia	8%	86%	6%

In the immediate wake of these peace protests, EU leaders renewed their effort to find a resolution to the crisis. To that end, they held a summit in Brussels on February 17, 2003, to try to craft a common reaction to the US stance on Iraq. Some leaders echoed Commission President Prodi's strong sentiments over what was at stake during this summit. Panos Beglitis, a Greek government official, said that the "EU will be plunged into a deep crisis" if it did not end the meeting with a common position (Fuller 2003). Things did not necessarily bode well, considering that the candidate countries from the East were not invited to attend (this was not required since they were not yet actual member states of the EU), and the media naturally forecasted a negative outcome from the summit before it had even begun. Few were ready to abandon the crisis narrative just yet:

[T]he political pressure of the crisis, coupled with simmering resentment between many of the leading figures, makes it one of the most combustible summits for years ... The differences over Iraq are so fundamental that it will be a small success if all 15 can conclude the one-day summit without rancor.
(*Financial Times*, "Tensions Hamper Hopes of Unity on Iraq," 2003)

Today's meeting in Brussels on the Iraq crisis has little prospect of reaching any fundamental agreement between the opposing factions.
(*Financial Times*, "Banging EU Heads," 2003)

EU member states were able to leave the meeting with a joint statement that "Iraq has a final opportunity to resolve the crisis peacefully" and that "inspections cannot continue indefinitely" (*The Economist*, "European Diplomacy over Iraq," 2003: 41). They agreed in principal that the use of force could come into play as a last resort. But in sharp contrast to this common stance, the media again put a negative spin on this. The *Economist*'s verdict on the summit was that Europeans were "[u]nited in theory, divided in practice" ("European Diplomacy over Iraq," *The Economist* 2003: 41). *Time* magazine further added to the negative bias, describing it as "Europe's Family Feud" (Graff 2003). The *Financial Times* argued that the summit was only successful insofar as member states "papered over" differences (*Financial Times*, "Blair and Chirac Collide over 'New Europe,'" 2003). The media's focus came back to East–West tensions, harkening back to Rumsfeld's words, and emphasizing the absence of "new Europe" at the summit:

The candidate countries have already had to accept the humiliation of being excluded by France and some other member states from attending Monday's special summit on Iraq ... They were then subjected to an extraordinary emotional outburst by France's President Jacques Chirac ... The French press corps could barely refrain from applauding. They said Mr. Chirac was simply saying out loud what other member states privately thought about the "disloyal" east and central European countries supporting such declarations.
(*Financial Times*, "Summit Outcome Leaves Future Members Reeling," 2003)

The new spirit of European unity was broken after less than 12 hours yesterday, after a successful EU summit on Iraq was overshadowed by a blazing new dispute between "old" and "new" Europe ... Just as EU diplomats were congratulating themselves on producing a joint declaration to give Saddam Hussein a "last chance" to avert war, the French president embarked on a tirade against "badly brought up" candidate countries. He cautioned the 10 candidate states due to join the EU next year ... that their stance could be "dangerous" as the decision to admit them had not yet been ratified.

(*Financial Times*, "Blair and Chirac Collide over 'New Europe,'" 2003)

After this summit, Chirac made another tone-setting statement when he openly called the EU candidate countries "not very well behaved and rather reckless" in regards to their signing the aforementioned letters of support for the US position, and that they had "missed a great opportunity to shut up" (*CNN World*, "Chirac Lashes out at 'New Europe,'" 2003). In response, Vladimir Lastuvka, chairman of the Czech parliamentary Committee for Foreign Affairs, compared Chirac's remarks to Rumsfeld's and complained that "such a tone is not customary in Europe" (Graff 2003). Latvian President Vaira Vike-Freiberga said, "Nowhere in the Copenhagen criteria does it say we cannot speak our minds" (Graff 2003). The Hungarian Prime Minister Peter Medgyessy said in perfect French that he was "too well brought up" to respond to the French president (*The Economist*, "Charlemagne: Jacques Chirac's Samson Option," 2003). Of course, the international media used these remarks as further fuel for the narrative about member states at logger-heads, and some EU leaders unfavorably compared Chirac to Rumsfeld. One Balkan diplomat went further, saying, "It was as if he was making us pay for our declarations. He might as well be Bush who said that any country that is not with us is against us" (*Financial Times*, "Summit Outcome Leaves Future Members Reeling," 2003). Chirac also threatened to veto these candidates' membership in the EU and made clear that the candidates had "reduced their chances of entering Europe" (Graham 2003). He said, "If they had tried to decrease their chances for getting in Europe, they couldn't have done a better job," and that these countries' views "can only reinforce an attitude of hostility" toward them (*International Herald Tribune*, "A Big Unhappy Family," 2003). He noted that Romania and Bulgaria, who were due to enter at a later date, were at particular risk of being rejected. In response, the Eastern European countries accepted the agreement that came out of the Brussels summit, but Romanian officials called Chirac's threats "irrational" and "undemo-cratic" (*International Herald Tribune*, "A Big Unhappy Family," 2003).

The media picked up this cantankerous exchange and amplified it:

Chirac's remarks have highlighted more than anything else that the EU has a long way to go before it lives up to its ideal of equality for all its members. Many people in the candidate countries have long been convinced that their countries won't be admitted to the EU as equals.

> (*International Herald Tribune*, "East European intellectuals are reluctant to take sides," 2003)

This expansion would end any possibility for a federal Europe, or even for a Europe of nations capable of an independent global role ... The old Europeans are now inclined to question, rethink or postpone expansion, or even to reformulate it so that the EU has first- and second-class members.

> (*International Herald Tribune*, "Winning a War and Losing the World: Washington's Folly," 2003)

Elite opinion makers also added to the heightened "end of Europe" atmosphere. Alain Duhamel, a French political commentator and Europhile opinion leader, called Spanish President Aznar "Washington's messenger boy," which in France is a strongly worded insult referring to a traitor willing to follow the orders of a sinister foreign power (Vinocur 2003b).

French leaders were not the only ones openly vocalizing East–West tensions. One of the most prominent disputes along these lines was between Germany and Poland. German outrage at Poland's active support of the Iraq invasion was highly visible in the crisis narrative, especially in light of the fact that Poland was given an occupation zone in Iraq (*Die Zeit*, "Polen hat keine Angst vor Europa," 2003). Many Germans felt that the Poles were no longer interested in being a part of the EU. For their part, the Poles tried to engage in damage control, reminding the others that "there is no contradiction between the support for the Iraq War, and the support for the Polish EU accession" (*Die Zeit*, "Polen hat keine Angst vor Europa," 2003). This statement was no doubt true, but in the crisis atmosphere of integrational panic, it fell on deaf ears. Poland's heightened prominence was reflected in the news coverage of the divide over Iraq, whereby the country was depicted as the representative of the applicant countries and the symbol of East–West tensions. In trying to placate the accusations, Polish President Alexander Kwasniewski insisted, "To say that we're a Trojan horse of the United States" in the EU "is unjust" (Vinocur 2002b). Poland had been describing itself as a bridge to understanding between the United States and Europe. Similarly, Roza Thun, the chairwoman of the Polish Schuman Foundation, told a gathering of journalists visiting from Brussels, "Here in Poland we love the United

States. We feel European, but we love America" (*The Economist*, "Polish Foreign Policy, 2003).

Nonetheless, the crisis had grown to such proportions that there was a strong fear within Europe that the Iraq issue could mean the failure of Europe's historic enlargement to include the ten Central and Eastern European countries (Fray 2003: 32). The media was not the only culprit. Influential commentators questioned whether the plans for enlargement to the East could be finalized given the serious divide over Iraq. Alain Duhamel wrote in an article that the goal of "European Europe" was seriously threatened by the prospects of enlargement given that the new member states would encircle Brussels with the "Europe of Washington" (*The Economist*, "France's High-Risk Diplomacy ...," 2003: 45). Such a failure was equated with a more general inability for the EU to move forward according to its own goals and values. Karel Lannoo, chief executive of the Brussels-based Centre for European Policy Studies, said, "Europe risks becoming the forgotten continent" (*Financial Times*, "EU Summit to Gloss over Economy," 2003). Several months of talk about the threat the Iraq crisis posed for enlargement involved French discussion of the creation of a Franco–German union that would be much tighter than the rest of the EU, and would naturally *exclude* the CEECs. This would involve a common foreign policy, diplomatic service, and army (*The Economist*, "All Aboard the Euro-train!" 2003). Another slightly more inclusive idea was that France and Germany could encourage the creation of an avant-garde group that would include Belgium and Luxembourg, among others, and would lead to political union. This narrative clearly emphasized the idea that the "new Europeans," or CEECs, would become second-class citizens in the EU (*The Economist*, "All Aboard the Euro-train!" 2003).

Again, all of this controversy occurred before military action had even begun in Iraq on March 20, 2003. Ironically, once it was confirmed that the United States would go forward with the invasion, media coverage of the European controversy surrounding this issue quickly declined after its peak in February. The narrative had finally shifted to how EU leaders would try to put the previous tensions behind them to find common ground once more. On March 19, 2003, a story in the *Financial Times* reflected on what had happened, calling this:

the end of a gruesome period of EU relations that has seen any semblance of a common foreign policy torn apart and knock-on effects spreading to other areas of European policy. "This is the most serious set of foreign policy differences the

EU has ever had," says one EU diplomat ... But in some ways it is too late: the tensions created by the build-up to war have already exposed the frailty of Europe's attempts to forge a common foreign policy and opened divisions among "old" and "new" Europe.

(*Financial Times*, "EU Summit Seeks to Mend Rifts Opened by Iraq Crisis," 2003)

And during a summit on the Iraq war in March 2003, the narrative had markedly changed from the previous month, especially in coverage of the event:

The scene was set for potentially the most divided and bitter EU summit for years. But by the time European leaders arrived in Brussels, it seemed that the spleen and vitriol over Iraq had been drained from them ... "It was surreal, almost ghostly," said Jean-Claude Junker, Luxembourg's prime minister, of the almost non-existent debate on the war on Thursday night.

(*Financial Times*, "Embittered Partners Look for a Reason ...," 2003)

This year's split between "New" and "Old" Europe, and the consequent bad-mouthing, blame, and bitterness, have torn through the web of trust that helps Europe's leaders to get along. However, the rift between the two Europe's may well heal.   (Grant 2003)

In a televised interview, Chirac had completely flipped in his attitude toward "new Europe," when he said, "I know Europe well. I'm perhaps one of those who knows best how it works. Once this crisis is over, it won't be divided at all. Europe's history is marked by a series of crises, from which, each time, it has emerged stronger" (*The Economist*, "France's Diplomacy: Against America?" 2003).

By May 2003 media coverage of the crisis was declining precipitously, and the tone of the coverage had softened. As if turning over a new leaf – and with it, an end to the crisis – on May 8, 2003, German Foreign Minister Joshka Fischer said, "The Iraq War is the past ... There is no point to continue discussions from yesterday" (*Die Zeit*, "Europa ist eine echte Macht," 2003). In line with the main argument of this book, crisis narratives born of integrational panic often dissipate as quickly as they appear. Because there is a socially constructed dynamic to them, when publics or elites lose interest or media coverage shifts its attention elsewhere, the sense of existential threat tends to go with it. This does not mean that all of the differences are eradicated – societies and institutions often deal with the aftermath of crisis for some time to come, and tensions of various sorts rarely disappear entirely – but the perception that Europe is no longer at the brink of breakdown signals resolution.

From Crisis to Opportunity

May 2003 marked the beginning of a backing down from existential crisis and a moving toward more EU integration. The German weekly newspaper, *Die Zeit*, expressed this newfound European cohesion profoundly:

The European governments have not yet given up their hopes for a new unity – on the contrary. After weeks of fighting over Iraq and the European role in it, after serious disputes about the proper actions towards the USA, and a lot of mistrust, the foreign ministers accomplished two little miracles on the island of Kastellorizo. Firstly, they tacitly decided not to continue making their disagreement about Iraq a public point of contention. Nobody wants to embarrass Europe in front of the world public anymore, as in the recent weeks in which the governments were insulting one another over the media. And secondly, they want to draw lessons from this foreign policy disaster. Concretely: in the following weeks a common security strategy is supposed to be designed. Optimists hope for a counterpart to the national security strategy of the USA.   (Pinzler 2003)

The common security strategy referred to in the article was signed into being as the European Security Strategy (ESS) on December 12, 2003. The ESS represented a major step forward in European plans for a common approach to foreign policy and defense. It put on display Europeans' strong common resolve for a "European Europe," one that would serve as a viable counterweight to the United States. The ESS stated:

As a union of 25 states with over 450 million people producing a quarter of the world's Gross National Product (GNP), and with a wide range of instruments at its disposal, the European Union is inevitably a global player ... The increasing convergence of European interests and the strengthening of mutual solidarity of the EU makes us a more credible and effective actor. Europe should be ready to share in the responsibility for global security and in building a better world.
                    (Solana and Institute for Security Studies 2003: 4)

The tone of this common statement could not have contrasted more sharply with the crisis narrative that had spilled across headlines only months before. Moreover, the ESS laid out actionable and concrete steps in other areas of common security, such as the role for the new European Defense Agency, which was established in July 2004. It also explicitly made the connection between internal and external security integration, and emphasized the importance of a multilateral approach. In strong defiance of the "end of Europe" narrative, the EU went on to rapidly make ESDP operational, launching 28 EU missions and operations across three continents in the span of a decade.

Also in May 2003, the influential philosophers Jürgen Habermas and Jacques Derrida published an important, tone-setting article arguing that in the end the Iraq crisis had enabled the birth of a new European identity and public sphere (Habermas and Derrida 2003: 291–297). They saw the potential for this transnational public sphere in the February 15, 2003, mass protests across Europe and emphasized the fact that Europeans of all backgrounds had come together across the continent to protest the war together. Indeed, earlier in March 2003, Dominique Strauss-Kahn wrote, "On Saturday, February 15, 2003, a nation was born on the streets. This nation is the European nation" (Strauss-Kahn 2003: xiv). According to Levy et al., Habermas and Derrida's essay could almost be described as a "European Declaration of Independence" from the United States (Levy, Pensky, and Torpey 2005: xvi).

On November 22, 2003, the cover of the *Economist* was entitled "When East Meets West" and featured numerous outstretched arms, eager to shake hands. The existential crisis that was fueled in part by these East–West tensions ultimately resulted in several major policy changes, bringing EU member states closer together. The more Europeanist side of the Atlanticist versus Europeanist theme had won out. Again, East–West tensions did not disappear entirely, but they were far weaker as a result of this post-crisis catharsis.

Describing Europe *before* the crisis, Charles Kupchan writes:

> EU members are struggling to come up with sufficient forces to handle conflicts in their own backyard; they are neither capable of, nor interested in, new commitments in distant lands … the EU must strengthen its ability to formulate and implement a common foreign and security policy. Similarly, the EU's prospective members in central Europe must realize that their future security, as well as their economic well being, rests with the EU. (Kupchan 2002)

After the crisis, the political will to change this was clearly present in force. The strengthened relationships among EU leaders, the broad-ranging goals of the European Security Strategy, the nearly thirty new missions and operations launched under the EU flag, and the emergence of a transnational public sphere all pointed to a new trajectory for the EU with much stronger consensus around the goal of shaping Europe into a meaningful foreign policy actor.

Catharsis

In 2004, the European Union was still standing, and it now had a membership of twenty-five. So, how did European leaders take the EU from the height of crisis toward new areas of consensus and integration?

First, there was a pivot that took place, from a focus on division within Europe to division across the Atlantic. In other words, catharsis involved contrasting what it meant to be European with what it meant to be American (Levy, Pensky, and Torpey 2005: xvi). Second, as Jeffrey Lewis argues, "[T]he lessons learned from the Iraq crisis include a new shared understanding among the EU foreign ministers on principled, substantive, and procedural grounds for concerted EU assistance to post-invasion Iraq" (Lewis 2008: 4). Indeed, as evidence of this, the EU had a strong common approach to reconstruction in Iraq.

But *why* was the EU able to move forward with more security integration immediately after having such a traumatic foreign policy breakdown? In this case study, as opposed to the Constitutional Treaty and Eurozone crises, the main tensions expressed – Big Three and East–West – were more at the level of the political leadership rather than the general public. Indeed, if anything, the Iraq crisis demonstrated solidarity across European publics. In short, this was an elite-level catharsis.

As evidence of this, comparing citizen attitudes across Big Three and East–West member states on the role of EU foreign policy and defense, it is clear that there was strong support for a significant EU role across the board. Collectively, this support grew stronger throughout the crisis as public opinion solidified around the notion that the EU should take a separate foreign policy path than the United States. As the Spring 2003 Eurobarometer report summarizes:

In the shed of the war on Iraq, the people of the candidate countries stand firmly behind common and articulated European presence on the world stage, as they support all the measures related to CFSP including the setting up of a European army and having a European Foreign minister. The acceptance of joint EU decision-making in defence matters increased significantly since the autumn of 2002 as well. In all of the candidate countries the European Union has much higher regard as than the US, and citizens believe that the EU foreign policy should be independent from that of the United States.

(European Commission, Eurobarometer CC-EB 2003)

The Eurobarometer did not include the CEECs in the standard survey until Spring 2004, but since 2001 it had conducted special surveys of candidate countries. Table 3.3 compares the 2001 and 2003 candidate Eurobarometer surveys, and demonstrates the strong support for the EU's role in defense and foreign policy. To the extent that there was a change after the crisis, it was actually toward even *more* support for the EU in this regard. Table 3.4 provides the closest comparison to the existing member states.

TABLE 3.3 *CEEC Support for EU Decision Making (Instead of Solely National Decision Making) on Defense and Foreign Policy* *

	Defense			Foreign Policy		
	Autumn 2001	Spring 2003	Autumn 2003	2001	Spring 2003	Autumn 2003
Bulgaria	47%	66%	51%	61%	67%	64%
Czech Republic	74%	69%	73%	70%	65%	68%
Estonia	62%	66%	69%	68%	63%	66%
Hungary	53%	50%	52%	56%	56%	56%
Latvia	72%	75%	77%	71%	71%	72%
Lithuania	53%	52%	55%	63%	64%	67%
Poland	67%	69%	64%	66%	68%	66%
Romania	58%	61%	70%	72%	69%	76%
Slovakia	71%	78%	78%	74%	79%	79%
Slovenia	66%	71%	79%	75%	77%	84%

* 2001 Candidate Eurobarometer (survey conducted in October 2001, published in March 2002): Annexes; 2003 Candidate Eurobarometer: Annexes.

Taking an even longer and broader view, in the Autumn 2004 Eurobarometer survey, the attitudes of Europeans toward their country's membership in the EU had actually spiked by eight percentage points, reaching the highest positive level since 1995. Fifty-six percent said they thought membership in the EU was a good thing, while only 13 percent thought it was a bad thing. Positive feelings about EU membership were particularly high within the original fifteen member states, with 85 percent of respondents from Luxembourg and 70 percent from Ireland, the Netherlands, Belgium, and Spain saying it was a good thing. This was significant particularly in light of the accession of ten new member states (European Commission, Eurobarometer Autumn 2004: 7–8). The same high numbers held also for the perceived benefits of membership, which also spiked in a positive direction, increasing by six points to 53 percent (with only 34 percent saying they did not benefit) since the previous poll six months before (European Commission, Eurobarometer Autumn 2004: 9). For both questions, the newer member states had somewhat less positive responses, but this was likely a result of the high level of "don't know" responses given their short-lived experience as part of the EU.

Opinion polls show that citizen attitudes toward security and defense were largely settled before and after this crisis. There was not a major

TABLE 3.4 *EU-15 Support for EU Decision Making (Instead of Solely National Decision Making) on Defense and Foreign Policy* *

	Defense			Foreign Policy		
	Autumn 2001	Spring 2003	Autumn 2003	Autumn 2001	Spring 2003	Autumn 2003
Austria	39%	37%	43%	66%	57%	64%
Belgium	61%	63%	63%	80%	80%	80%
Denmark	40%	37%	40%	58%	75%	60%
Finland	7%	6%	10%	61%	64%	63%
France	48%	47%	50%	72%	77%	78%
Germany	57%	59%	57%	74%	75%	74%
Greece	47%	46%	42%	73%	76%	75%
Ireland	30%	35%	34%	67%	71%	69%
Italy	58%	59%	62%	81%	80%	81%
Luxembourg	58%	68%	56%	78%	74%	65%
Netherlands	60%	58%	59%	73%	76%	75%
Portugal	32%	48%	50%	61%	68%	66%
Spain	57%	60%	57%	77%	78%	77%
Sweden	20%	20%	21%	60%	60%	56%
UK	38%	32%	31%	57%	58%	58%

* 2001 Autumn Standard Eurobarometer: Annex, pp. B.43–B.44; 2003 Spring Standard Eurobarometer 59, "Public Opinion in the European Union," field work March–April 2003, published July 2003, pp. 14–15; 2003 Autumn Standard Eurobarometer 60, "Public Opinion in the European Union," field work October–November 2003, published February 2004, pp. 83–84.

change, and support was generally very high for foreign policy, and a little lower for defense. Moreover, as described earlier in the chapter, citizen views in opposition to the Iraq invasion were relatively consistent across the board. By contrast, elites talked about the crisis in strong terms, and this is where we find the tensions and the catharsis.

At the elite level, there was a visible shift in attitudes toward European integration in the foreign and security policy area. There was a significant decline in the negative rhetoric surrounding the crisis at the same time as there was a flourishing of new dialogue among elites in the public sphere. As mentioned earlier, Habermas and Derrida's tone-setting essay created a new, cathartic narrative of moving forward after the Iraq crisis. It was at this point, in May 2003, that the transatlantic crisis became the main focus, and perhaps paradoxically, Europeans were brought closer together by defining themselves against the United States. The ability to overcome internal differences was helped along by the growing sense of transatlantic divide.

In the dialogue that ensued among elites, following the Habermas-Derrida essay, there was a "renewed effort to tackle the 'identity deficit,'" and go beyond just economic integration to achieve a common approach to security, defense, and foreign policy. They envisioned that a "core Europe" – Germany, France, and the Benelux countries – would be the engine for this innovation, rather than an impetus for a two-speed Europe. Joschka Fischer, the German foreign minister, agreed with the main thrust of this argument, also emphasizing the need to achieve political integration, but proposing a more inclusive approach than "core Europe." Timothy Garton Ash and Ralf Dahrendorf responded to Habermas and Derrida in a similar way, and Habermas reemphasized that the point was to achieve a faster pace of integration than had been the case in the past (Levy, Pensky, and Torpey 2005: xxii). The spirit of the discussion that Habermas spearheaded was to talk about the various ways in which European and national governments could take advantage of this newfound momentum in the wake of Iraq, and to try to come up with some workable solutions.

CONCLUSION

Looking back at the more than decade-long period following this crisis, some might jump to the conclusion that the EU has not really fulfilled the promise of the post-Iraq catharsis in which member states were able to agree to a range of policies in the area of CFSP. However, to the contrary, EU member states have no problem taking a common position on issues most of the time, especially in the context of the UN.[13] Since agreement on the European Security Strategy in 2003, security integration has proceeded in an incremental way, but with significant advancements in developing a common approach to security and defense, integrating defense industries, becoming interoperable, and engaging in joint actions, as compared to before the Iraq crisis. The internal side of security integration has proceeded much more quickly too, and with important spillover effects on the external side as well. EU member states understand well that they gain leverage from their collective weight, and that they share far

---

[13] Within the UN, the EU coordinates its votes and is unanimous as a block on nearly every single vote (97 percent), even on controversial issues involving the Middle East (European Commission, "The EU and How It Works at the UN").

more norms and worldviews than they do not share. This is true particularly in the areas of human rights, peaceful conflict resolution, and support for democracy. Naturally, if member states find themselves facing a situation in which agreement is difficult, they revert to national foreign policy stances and preferences, but this is accounted for in the treaties. A few high profile setbacks in the foreign policy area should not be equated with overall failure for the EU. Indeed, the 2009 Lisbon Treaty truly serves as a culmination of the successes that the EU has experienced since Iraq, with the advent of a "permanent" Council president, a new post equivalent to an EU foreign minister, an EU diplomatic service, permanent structured cooperation, a solidarity clause, mutual defense, and so on. Thus, the opportunities that came with the resolution of the Iraq crisis had longer-term significance. Even while member states still sometimes struggle to find common ground in facing new foreign policy challenges – such as with respect to Libya in 2011 and Ukraine in 2014 (see Chapter 6) – the EU's crisis over Iraq is long over.

In sum, this chapter makes the case that the question over whether to join the United States in invading Iraq did not necessarily have to be defined as an existential crisis for the EU. As stated at the outset, the EU has strived to create a common approach to foreign policy since its early founding as the European Coal and Steel Community of the 1950s. Over time, member states became more and more comfortable with the idea, but it was not until the 1990s that the first policy in support of this was signed into treaty. In the lead-up to Bush's request at the UN, CFSP was relatively new and had not truly become operational.

In order to really understand why a crisis in Iraq could come to be equated with a struggle for the very existence of the EU, it is necessary to examine the trajectory of social narratives at the time. Before the invasion of Iraq even took place, interpretations about the failure of the EU to speak with one voice became so dire and pessimistic that the EU's leadership and prospects for enlargement were thrown into question. Integrational panic among elites grew as the media exaggerated and amplified predictions of the end of Europe. Preexisting tensions among the Big Three and between eastern and western member states quickly became part and parcel of the intensifying crisis narrative. Much of this was socially constructed as there existed no clear divide in policy toward Iraq along East–West lines, but with the help of certain tone-setting statements from leaders at the time, urged on by the continued media spin, these articulated tensions grew into a self-fulfilling prophecy. Eastern member states started behaving as a bloc (as can be seen with the Vilnius letter), and the western member states began to do so as well (as can be seen with the February 2003 summit that purposefully excluded the candidate countries). Throughout this process, the consistent nature of the media coverage encouraged this narrative of division.

Integrational panic characterized the social construction of this crisis at the elite level. The threat to enlargement and integration in Europe over Iraq did not happen because of insurmountable problems with the CEECs or the development of CFSP. Indeed, at the level of the European public, in both East and West, there was widespread agreement that Europe was a good thing, and that CFSP was desirable. But the crisis served as a forum for airing preexisting tensions among leaders, and when everything was said and done, this allowed them to achieve a sense of catharsis. The crisis narrative dissolved almost as quickly as it had appeared, and the opportunity to move forward with the European project was strongly felt. Leaders expressed newfound consensus and political will to integrate further in a variety of ways, and in hindsight, they viewed the crisis as an unnecessary distraction, and almost an embarrassment. In the end, despite all of the prognostications of doom from seemingly every quarter, the EU emerged from this crisis stronger than it had begun.

References

Anderson, Jeffrey, John Ikenberry and Thomas Risse. 2008. *The End of the West? Crisis and Change in the Atlantic Order*, Ithaca: Cornell University Press.

Andrews, David. 2005. *The Atlantic Alliance Under Stress: US-European Relations After Iraq*, Cambridge University Press.

Applebaum, Anne. 2005. "'Old Europe' Versus 'New Europe'," in Tod Lindberg, *Beyond Paradise and Power: Europe, America and the Future of a Troubled Partnership*, New York and London: Routledge, pp. 27–29.

Baker, Gerard. 2002. "Europe's Three Ways of Dealing with Iraq." *Financial Times*, London edition, October 17.

BBC News. 2003. "Outrage at 'Old Europe' Remarks," world edition. January 23.

CNN World. 2003. "Chirac Lashes Out at 'New Europe.'" February 18.

Coicaud, Jean-Marc with Hélène Gandois and Lysette Rutgers, 2006. "Explaining France's Opposition to the War against Iraq." In *The Iraq Crisis and World Order: Structural, Institutional and Normative Challenges*, edited by Ramesh Thakur and Waheguru Pal Singh Sidhu. Tokyo, New York, Paris: United Nations University Press.

Cook, Robin. 2003. *The Point of Departure: Diaries from the Front Bench*. London: Pocket Books.

Cross, Mai'a. 2011. *Security Integration in Europe: How Knowledge-based Networks Are Transforming the European Union*. Ann Arbor: University of Michigan Press.

Davidson, Jason. 2011. *America's Allies and War: Kosovo, Afghanistan, and Iraq.* New York: Palgrave.

Dempsey, Judy. 2002. "What to Do about Saddam Further Divides Europe's Big Three," *Financial Times*, September 14–15, p. 3.

Dettke, Dieter. 2009. *Germany Says "No": The Iraq War and the Future of German Foreign and Security Policy.* Baltimore: Johns Hopkins University Press.

Die Zeit. 2003. "Europa ist eine echte Macht." Interview with Joschka Fischer. May 8. Translation by Molly Krasnodebska.

Die Zeit. "Polen hat keine Angst vor Europa." Interview with Adam Michnik, May 28.

Dumbrell, John. 2006. *A Special Relationship: Anglo-American Relations from the Cold War to Iraq.* Basingstoke: Palgrave Macmillan.

The Economist. 2003. "All Aboard the Euro-train! The European Union's Expansion Is Roaring Ahead, with Destination Unknown." April 5.

The Economist. 2003. "Charlemagne: Jacques Chirac's Samson Option." February 20.

The Economist. 2003. "Charlemagne: Philadelphia or Frankfurt?" March 6.

The Economist. 2003. "Charlemagne: Place Your Bets." February 13.

The Economist. 2002. "Charlemagne: The Perils of Penelope." December 12.

The Economist. 2002. "Charlemagne: Wooing Marianne." November 7.

The Economist. 2003. "Dealing with Iraq: Days of Reckoning," January 20.

The Economist. 2003. "Dealing with Iraq: When Squabbling Turns too Dangerous." February 13.

The Economist. 2003. "European Diplomacy over Iraq: United in Theory, Divided in Practice." February 22, p. 41.

The Economist. 2003. "France, Germany and the EU: The Old Motor Revs Up Again." December 5.

The Economist. 2003. "France's Diplomacy: Against America? Moi?" March 13.

The Economist. 2003. "France's High-Risk Diplomacy Is in Danger of Hurting France Itself." February 22, p. 45.

The Economist. 2003. "Franco-German Relations: Spectacle or Substance?" January 23.

The Economist. 2003. "Now for the Hard Part," March 3.

The Economist. 2003. "Old Europe's Last Gasp," February 13.

The Economist. 2003. "Polish Foreign Policy: Frosty for the French." February 27.

The Economist. 2002. "Testing, Testing." December 5.

The Economist. 2003. "The Western Alliance in Disarray: How Deep Is the Rift?" February 13.

EOS Gallup Europe. 2003. International Crisis Survey Report, 21–27 January, available at http://paks.uni-duesseldorf.de/Dokumente/International-Crisis-Survey_Rapport-Final.pdf [last accessed February 21, 2014].

European Commission. 2001. Autumn Standard Eurobarometer: Annex, pp. B.43–B.44

European Commission. 2003. Autumn Standard Eurobarometer 60, "Public Opinion in the European Union." Fieldwork October–November 2003. Published February 2004, pp. 83–84.

European Commission. 2003. Candidate Eurobarometer: Annexes.

European Commission. 2001. Candidate Eurobarometer: Annexes. Survey conducted in October 2001. Published in March 2002.

European Commission. 2003. Eurobarometer CC-EB, "Public Opinion in the Candidate Countries." Fieldwork May 2003. Published June.

European Commission. 2003. Spring Standard Eurobarometer 59, "Public Opinion in the European Union." Field work March–April 2003. Published July 2003, pp. 14–15.

European Commission. 2004. Autumn Standard Eurobarometer 62, "Public Opinion in the European Union." Fieldwork October–November 2004. Published December 2004.

European Commission. n.d. "The EU and How It Works at the UN," available at http://eu-un.europa.eu/documents/infopack/en/EU-UNBrochure-2_en.pdf.

Fawn, Richard and Raymond Hinnesbusch. 2006. *The Iraq War: Causes and Consequences*. London: Lynne Rienner.

Financial Times. 2003. "Banging EU Heads: Europe's Leaders Can at Least Agree How to Disagree," London edition. February 17.

Financial Times. 2003. "Blair and Chirac Collide over 'New Europe,'" London second edition, February 19.

Financial Times. 2002. "Chirac Blasts Blair in Summit Confrontation." October 28.

Financial Times. 2003. "Embittered Partners Look for a Reason to Believe in Reconciliation." London first edition. March 22.

Financial Times. 2003. "Europe's Torment: The EU Must Start to Pick Up the Pieces," London first edition. March 21.

Financial Times. 2003. "EU Summit Seeks to Mend Rifts Opened by Iraq Crisis," London first edition. March 19.

Financial Times. 2003. "EU Summit to Gloss over Economy," London first edition. March 20.

Financial Times. 2003. "Media Deploy 'Old Europe' Hauteur to Counter Furor: War of Words Europe," London edition. February 12.

Financial Times. 2003. "Summit Bar on EU Candidate Countries," London edition. February 13.

Financial Times. 2003. "Summit Outcome Leaves Future Members Reeling," London second edition. February 19.

Financial Times. 2003. "Tensions Hamper Hopes of Unity on Iraq," London edition. February 17.

Financial Times. 2003. "The Alliance Comes Apart at the Seams: The Iraq Crisis Is Causing Wider Collateral Damage to NATO," London edition. February 11.

Financial Times. 2003. "The Speech by the UN's Chief Weapons Inspector Today on Saddam Hussein's Compliance with Resolution 1441 Will Have Repercussions Far beyond Baghdad," London edition. February 14.

Financial Times. 2003. "The Storms beyond the Azores: The Diplomatic Crisis Will Reverberate Far beyond Iraq," London first edition. March 15.

Fray, Peter. 2003. "With Friends Like These, Who Needs Saddam?; Winds of War." *Sydney Morning Herald*, February 22, p. 32.

Fuller, Thomas. 2003. "A Divided EU to Hold Talks in Search for Unity on Iraq." *International Herald Tribune*, February 17.

Gherghisan, Mihaela. 2003. "Vilnius 10 Sign Letter on Iraq." *EUobserver*, February 6.

Gordon, Phillip and Jeremy Shapiro, 2004. *Allies at War: America, Europe, and the Crisis over Iraq.* New York: McGraw-Hill.

Graff, James. 2003. "Europe's Family Feud." *Time*, Paris, February 14.

Graham, Robert. 2003. "Chirac Vents Ire over Behavior of EU Candidates." *Financial Times*, London first edition, February 19.

Graham, Robert and Haig Simonian. 2003. "After 40 Years Together, France and Germany May Be Struggling to Keep the Spark in Their Close Relationship." *Financial Times*, London edition, January 20.

Grant, Charles. 2003. "Europe Will Pick Up the Pieces after the War." *International Herald Tribune*, March 24.

Guinness Book of World Records. 2004. Available at http://web.archive.org/web/20040904214302/http://www.guinnessworldrecords.com/content_pages/record.asp?recordid=54365.

Habermas, Jürgen and Jacques Derrida. 2003. "February 15, or What Binds Europeans Together: A Plea for a Common Foreign Policy, Beginning in the Core of Europe," *Constellations* 10(3): 291–297.

Heisbourg, François. 2003. "Do Not Expect France to Change Its Mind." *Financial Times*, London edition, February 7.

Howorth, Jolyon. 2004. "Discourse, Ideas, and Epistemic Communities in Epistemic Communities in European Security and Defence Policy," *West European Politics* 27(2): 211–234.

Howorth, Jolyon. 2003. "France, Britain and the Euro-Atlantic Crisis," *Survival* 45(4): 173–192.

Howorth, Jolyon. 2007. *Security and Defence Policy in the European Union.* Basingstoke: Palgrave.

International Herald Tribune. 2003. "A Big Unhappy Family." February 19.

International Herald Tribune. 2003. "Blair-Chirac Quarrel Rages on at EU Summit." March 22.

International Herald Tribune. 2003. "Blair Demands EU Back War in Iraq: Trans-Atlantic Rift Threatens to Grow as Briton Warns Time Is Running Out." February 14.

International Herald Tribune. "East European Intellectuals Are Reluctant to Take Sides." February 24.

International Herald Tribune. 2003. "EU Leaders Hold Summit Clouded by Split on Iraq." March 21.

International Herald Tribune. 2003. "For Paris and Berlin, a Drive to Stay Important in Europe." February 12.

International Herald Tribune. 2003. "Why the U.S. Fears Europe Crushing German Dissent." February 11.

International Herald Tribune. 2003. "Winning a War and Losing the World: Washington's Folly," February 27.

James, Barry. 2003. "Iraq Letter Splits Europe Action by 8 Countries Reveals Deep Breach." *International Herald Tribune*, February 1.

Jones, Seth. 2007. *The Rise of European Security Cooperation.* Cambridge and New York: Cambridge University Press.

Kupchan, Charles. 2002. "The Last Days of the Atlantic Alliance." *Financial Times*, London edition, November 18.

Levy, Daniel, Max Pensky, and John Torpey (eds.). 2005. *Old Europe, New Europe, Core Europe: Transatlantic Relations after the Iraq War*. London: Verso.

Lewis, Jeffrey. 2008. "EU Policy on Iraq: The Collapse and Reconstruction of Consensus-Based Foreign Policy," UCD Dublin European Institute, Working Paper 08–9, July.

Lieven, Anatol. 2003. "Europe Must Face Up to a Fractured Future." *Financial Times*, London edition, February 3.

Lindberg, Tod. 2005. *Beyond Paradise and Power: Europe, America, and the Future of a Troubled Partnership*. New York and London: Routledge.

Lindley-French, Julian. 2007. *A Chronology of European Security & Defence, 1945–2007*. New York: Oxford University Press.

Louis, William Roger and Hedley Bull (eds.). 1987. *The "Special Relationship" Anglo-American Relations since 1945*. Oxford: Oxford University Press.

Ludenstad, Geir. 2005. "Toward Transatlantic Drift?" In *The Atlantic Alliance Under Stress*, edited by David M. Andrews. Cambridge: Cambridge University Press.

Menon, Anand. 2004. "From Crisis to Catharasis: ESDP after Iraq," *International Affairs* 80(4): 631–648.

Mérand, Frédéric. 2010. "Pierre Bourdieu and the Birth of European Defense," *Security Studies* 19(2): 342–372.

Merritt, Giles. 2003. "The EU in Disarray on Iraq: Bickering Europe Needs a New Security Doctrine." *International Herald Tribune*, March 14.

Meyer, Christoph. 2006. *The Quest for a European Strategic Culture: Changing Norms on Security and Defence in the European Union*. Basingstoke: Palgrave.

Müller, Harald. 2006. "Iraq and World Order: A German Perspective." In *The Iraq Crisis and World Order*, edited by Amesh Thakur and Waheguru Pal Singh Sidhu. Tokyo, New York, Paris: United Nations University Press.

Nau, Henry. 2008. "Iraq and Previous Transatlantic Crises." In *The End of the West? Crisis and Change in the Atlantic Order*, edited by Jeffrey Anderson, G. John Ikenberry, and Thomas Risse. Ithaca, NY, and London: Cornell University Press.

Nikolaev, Alexander and Ernest Hakanen. 2006. *Leading to the 2003 Iraq War: The Global Media Debate*. New York: Palgrave Macmillan.

Obajtek-Kirkwood, Anne-Marie. 2006. "*Le Monde* on a 'Likely' Iraq War." In *Leading to the 2003 Iraq War: The Global Media Debate*, edited by Alexander G. Nikolaev and Ernest A. Hakanen. New York: Palgrave.

Peel, Quentin. 2003a. "The President Who Speaks for Europe." *Financial Times*, Japan edition/London edition, February 4.

Peel, Quentin. 2003b. "Why Europe Needs a United Foreign Policy." *Financial Times*, London edition, January 7.

Peterson, John and Mark A. Pollack. 2003. *Europe, America, Bush: Transatlantic Relations in the Twenty-First Century*. London: Routledge.

Pfaff, William. 2002. "A Constitution for Europe 'An Acceptable Word.'" *International Herald Tribune*, November 4.

Pinzler, Petra. 2003. "Europäische Eintracht." *Die Zeit*, May 1. Translation by Molly Krasnodebska.

Pond, Elizabeth. 2005. "The Dynamics of the Feud over Iraq." In *The Atlantic Alliance under Stress*. Cambridge: Cambridge University Press.

Rees, Wyn. 2006. *Transatlantic Counter-Terrorism Cooperation: A New Imperative*. London and New York: Routledge.

Rees, Wyn. 2011. *The US-EU Security Relationship: The Tensions between a European and a Global Agenda*. New York: Palgrave.

Schmitt, Burkard. 2003. "Disunity Holds the EU Back from a Major Global Role." *International Herald Tribune*, February 13.

Simonian, Haig and Ian Bickerton. 2003. "Schroder's Anti-war Approach Blamed for 'Isolating' Germany." *Financial Times*, London edition, January 31.

Smith, Michael. 2004. *Europe's Foreign and Security Policy*. Cambridge and New York: Cambridge University Press.

Solana, Javier and Institute for Security Studies. 2003. *A Secure Europe in a Better World: European Security Strategy*. Paris: European Union Institute for Security Studies. Available at www.iss.europa.eu/uploads/media/solanae .pdf.

Soutou, Georges-Henri. 2005. "Three Rights, Two Reconciliations: Franco-American Relations during the Fifth Republic." In *The Atlantic Alliance under Stress*, edited by David M. Andrews. Cambridge: Cambridge University Press.

Stephens, Philip. 2003. "Europe's Nations Are Bound Together Despite Everything." *Financial Times*, Japan edition/London edition, February 15.

Stephens, Philip. 2002. "The Real Weakness of Europe." *Financial Times*, September 20.

Stephens, Philip. 2004. *Tony Blair: The Making of a World Leader*. New York: Viking.

Stockholm International Peace Research Institute. (nd). Armstrade.sipri.org (last accessed February 6, 2014).

Strauss-Kahn, Dominique. 2003. "Die Geburt einer Nation." *Frankfurter Rundschau*, March 11, as quoted in Levy, Pensky, and Torpey, *Old Europe, New Europe, Core Europe*.

Time. 2003. "Article Title." February 13.

Tiriteu, Ioana. 2012. *The EU Member States' Iraq Policy of 2002–3 at the United Nations Security Council*. Hamburg: Verlag.

Treaty on European Union. 1992. Article J, Official Journal, C 191, July 29.

Vinocur, John. 2003a. "For Berlin and Paris, a Façade." *International Herald Tribune*, January 16.

Vinocur, John. 2003b. "In Backing U.S. on Iraq, Spain Charts Its Own Global Role." *International Herald Tribune*, February 28.

Vinocur, John. 2002a. "In EU, France Now Leads and Germany Follows." *International Herald Tribune*, December 18.

Vinocur, John. 2003c. "Outcome of German Ballot Douses Flame of Anti-war Alliance." *International Herald Tribune*, February 4.

Vinocur, John. 2002b. "The Big Winner in the EU Expansion: Washington." *International Herald Tribune*, December 9.

Wagstyl, Stefan. 2003. "EU Accession States Woo the Voters: Support for Membership in Most Candidate Countries Is Wide, but There Are Pockets of Skepticism." *Financial Times*, Europe edition/London edition, January 10.

Wallace, William and Tim Oliver. 2005. "A Bridge Too Far: The United Kingdom and the Transatlantic Relationship." In *The Atlantic Alliance under Stress*, edited by David M. Andrews. Cambridge: Cambridge University Press.

Wood, Barry D. 2003. "There Is No Clear Line between 'Old' and 'New' Europe, Spring." Available at www.europeaninstitute.org/200303023 51/Spring-2003/th ere-is-no-clear-line-between-qoldq-and-qnewq-europe.html (last accessed on November 21, 2013).

4

The Constitutional Treaty Crisis

INTRODUCTION

At the time, the 2004 Treaty establishing a Constitution for Europe – more commonly known as the Constitutional Treaty – was the latest step in a series of treaties signed by member states since the founding Treaty of Rome to advance the European integration project. As a document, the Constitutional Treaty was not as controversial as its name might imply. The use of the term "constitution" was in many ways symbolic, as early European Court of Justice (ECJ) rulings in the 1960s had already made clear that the Treaties of Rome had "direct effect" on individual citizens and supremacy over national law.[1] The EU's legal system had essentially interpreted the Treaties of Rome, and every subsequent EU treaty, as having the status of an evolving de facto constitution.[2] Moreover, the Constitutional Treaty itself was at most ambiguous as to whether it actually constituted something of a different, more "constitutional" nature compared to the EU treaties that had come before (Fossum and Menéndez 2011).

The process of crafting a draft Constitutional Treaty began with German Foreign Minister Joschka Fischer's speech at Humboldt University in 2000, when he called for a more democratic EU that would continue moving forward with integration in the political realm (Fischer 2000). After the speech, political elites were inspired to begin

---

[1] See European Court of Justice decisions *Van Gend en Loos* 1963 and *Costa v. Enel* 1964.

[2] See Weiler (1999). The body of EU treaties is treated as an evolving constitution even though the actual method and process of agreeing to them is still typical of international treaties. See D'Atena (2012).

work on a Constitutional Treaty for Europe. They launched the new treaty process with the 2001 Laeken Declaration and continued the discussions during the 2002–3 Convention on the Future of Europe. Former French President Valéry Giscard d'Estaing, well known for his pro-integration stance, chaired the convention and set the procedures for writing a single text of the Constitutional Treaty. The treaty-making process eventually culminated in a formal Intergovernmental Conference in June 2004.

As with many of the previous treaties, the spirit of the Constitutional Treaty was to improve the democratic legitimacy of the EU and to enable a larger membership of states to function effectively within its institutional structures. To the extent that it was more constitution-like, it would replace the increasingly unwieldy body of previous treaties with a *single* treaty. But beyond this, the Constitutional Treaty represented only incremental change in terms of how the EU would impact the daily lives of European citizens. It was mainly geared toward streamlining and clarifying the evolving system, not changing it in any fundamental way. For example, among its most noteworthy innovations to governance were increasing the policy areas subject to qualified majority voting (QMV), especially in the field of Justice and Home Affairs (JHA), and creating a more efficient mechanism – known as *passerelle* – to enable the transfer of more areas from unanimity to QMV going forward. This aspect also included dismantling the outdated pillar system of the Maastricht Treaty, which artificially separated JHA from the rest of the community policies. In addition, the treaty created a clearer double majority voting system in the Council, and made co-decision the main legislative decision-making procedure for the EU, thereby increasing the power of the European Parliament. The treaty allowed for the number of European Commissioners to reflect the number of member states and explicitly incorporated the European Charter of Fundamental Rights. The most significant innovations were actually in the area of foreign policy – the advent of a European foreign minister, diplomatic service, and "permanent" president – but even these more far-reaching provisions did not meet with any significant controversy. A strong majority of EU citizens have consistently supported a stronger European security and defense policy for decades (Howorth 2007: 59).

How then did such a seemingly uncontroversial document morph into an existential crisis for the EU? Of the three main crisis cases considered in this book, this is the only one in which the crisis trigger was internal in origin. Specifically, it was the launch of the ratification process for the

Constitutional Treaty. On October 29, 2004, all twenty-five heads of government signed the new treaty. The next stage was for each member state to follow its own ratification procedures, which had to result in unanimous approval for the treaty to be implemented. A few months before, on April 20, 2004, British Prime Minister Tony Blair had unexpectedly promised a referendum on the Constitutional Treaty (a procedure he had previously rejected), which would make it much more difficult to approve. Then, another nine member states – Denmark, France, Ireland, Luxembourg, the Netherlands, Poland, Czech Republic, Spain, and Portugal – followed Blair's lead and also announced that they would hold referenda (Nielson 2008: 457).[3] The fact that so many member states had promised referenda provided the seeds for a crisis narrative to grow.

Just like every treaty ratification process since the Treaties of Rome, the Constitutional Treaty faced a long and complicated process of approval, both in national parliaments and through popular referenda. Most accounts of the constitutional crisis treat the actual negative referenda as the cause of the crisis, but the analysis here describes how the crisis atmosphere actually emerged at the *beginning* of the ratification process, and not at the point that it failed. Indeed, the crisis narrative was already strong and widespread by the time the French and Dutch voted "no" in their referenda, and by this point, the doomsday narrative had already reached its height of intensity. As will be described in detail later in this chapter, journalists continually alluded to the "death of Europe," and elites repeatedly lamented that the end of the road for EU integration had come, describing this as Europe's "greatest crisis." The perception that there "is no plan B," and that Europe faced the threat of "political cataclysm" or "political breakdown" was widespread. But as I will show, the French and Dutch "no" were actually the *result* of crisis buildup rather than the cause. Opinion polls indicated strong support for a constitutional treaty until just before the referenda took place (e.g., 73 percent of the Dutch and 70 percent of the French were in favor in autumn 2004) (Qvortrup 2006: 91). But the overblown narrative of failure, especially in the media, had become a self-fulfilling prophecy, and this plunged Europe into an even deeper crisis. The negative referenda marked the height of the crisis, and shortly after the negative results, the sense of existential crisis

---

[3] This was an unusually high number of member states planning referenda on an EU treaty. Beyond these ten, several other member states had considered holding referenda. Belgium actually announced that it would have a referendum but then backed down from this decision.

started to diminish. This led to a "reflection period," which was followed eventually by the successful ratification of the Lisbon Treaty.

The central puzzle here is: considering that the Constitutional Treaty was relatively modest in its aims, especially with regard to its impact on the European public, why did even the *possibility* of failed referenda grow into a seeming existential crisis for Europe? After all, nearly every major EU/EC treaty that had come before, except for the founding treaties, had resulted in initially negative referenda, including the 1986 Single European Act, the 1992 Maastricht Treaty, and the 2001 Nice Treaty, among others (see Table 4.1) (Vassallo 2008: 411–429).[4] In addition, other referenda over issues such as accession or adopting the euro had also resulted in narrow or negative results. A failed ratification process was, of course, undesirable for Europe's leaders, but the mere threat of negative referenda did not necessarily have to translate into a full-scale EU crisis. In the past, it had not done so, so what was different now?

I argue in this chapter that the exaggerated crisis narrative, especially in the media and among elites, led to integrational panic that became widespread and intensified over time. The European public also used this crisis context to voice preexisting public–elite tensions, both toward national and supranational leaders. Once the negative referenda exacerbated the crisis, driving it to its height of intensity, a sense of catharsis was achieved. I argue that this catharsis eventually enabled an unprecedented breakthrough in integration in the form of societal-level politicization (Statham and Trenz 2013: 3).[5] Thus, the kind of integration that was achieved post-crisis did not just come in the form of the Lisbon Treaty, which is often described as more modest than the Constitutional Treaty; it mainly came in the form of the Europeanization of national public spheres and the resulting engagement in European issues, creating a far more robust *European* public sphere (Statham and Trenz 2013). This kind of societal-level integration is arguably just as significant as formal treaties and agreements since public engagement ultimately serves as the backbone of the European project.

This chapter first discusses the main debates surrounding the causes of the constitutional crisis. I conclude from this review of the literature that the

---

[4] Francesca Vassallo (2008) shows the deep similarities between the French referenda over the 1992 Maastricht Treaty and the 2005 Constitutional Treaty.

[5] As Statham and Trenz note, public contestation over EU issues had been on the rise throughout Europe since the 1990s, but the constitutional crisis was a critical juncture, during which there was a "decisive and substantive step forward."

TABLE 4.1 *Major EU Treaties Since Founding and the Process of Ratification**

	Referenda?	Ratification Process	Entry into Force
1965 Merger Treaty	No	Signature of heads of government	1967
1986 Single European Act	Denmark, Ireland	Danish parliament rejected, accepted in referendum; Irish referendum accepted	1987
1992 Maastricht Treaty	Denmark, France, Ireland	First Danish referendum failed; French referendum narrowly passed; UK parliament divided, but narrowly passed it; approved through Irish referendum	1993
1997 Amsterdam Treaty	Denmark, Ireland	Referenda passed	1999
2001 Nice Treaty	Ireland	Irish first rejected it, then accepted it in a second referendum	2003

* Compiled by author. For a full listing of referenda on EU issues, see Nielson (2008).

negative vote neither stemmed from the actual terms of the treaty nor from a growing tide of Euroskepticism. I then explain how a narratives approach is valuable in understanding the socially constructed nature of this crisis. To shed light on this, the second section of the chapter traces the role of the media in contributing to a sense of impending crisis with its amplification of conflict among elites, predictions of referenda failure, and exaggerated claims about the consequences of a negative vote. The third section then delves into the nature of the crisis narrative within European society, which centered on public–elite tensions of various sorts. Finally, I argue that the open expression of these tensions enabled European society to experience a period of catharsis, which eventually led to increased societal integration and much greater public engagement with the EU.

THE CAUSES OF THE CONSTITUTIONAL CRISIS

Most analyses of the constitutional crisis focus on two specific dimensions: why the French and Dutch voted "no" and the significance of the treaty's failure for EU legitimacy and democracy. One argument is that the treaty represented more integration than the European public was willing to accept. This perspective recognizes that EU leaders wanted the treaty (that is why they signed it), but gives various reasons for how, why, and when it became a systemic crisis for Europe. Another argument is that the public was actually indifferent to the treaty and did not really understand its terms, so individual voters did not really know what their votes determined when they cast them. And a third perspective is that the public was easily co-opted by the "no" side and thus used the referendum as an excuse for a protest vote. There is naturally some overlap in these explanations, but they can also be regarded as distinct rationales for the crisis. I address each of these in turn and argue that while they all offer reasons for why the treaty failed to pass muster, most do not offer a specific explanation for why this event grew into such a severe crisis for Europe. I argue that a closer examination of the crisis narrative at the time shows that the way Europeans talked about the crisis was indicative of integrational panic.

First Perspective: The Treaty Went Too Far, Too Fast

Perhaps the most straightforward explanation for this crisis is that the European public simply did not want a "constitution" for Europe. In general, this perspective makes the case that political elites liked the idea of a constitutional treaty, formed consensus around it, and rapidly came up with a text, but they failed to pay enough attention to the popular mood. This argument has been made either directly (the public did not like the constitution) or indirectly (the public did not like EU integration and therefore did not like the constitution).

The *direct* argument from this perspective is that European leaders pushed things too far with this treaty. As Larry Siedentop writes, since the late 1980s, "[t]he EU ceased to be about limited institutional changes and began to threaten national identities ... When those promoting the EU ignore hostile opinion, they play a dangerous game" (Siedentop 2005). In particular, an oft-mentioned problem with the Constitutional Treaty from this perspective was its symbolism and language. The treaty makes reference to the nationlike symbols of the EU anthem, flag, currency, motto ("United in Diversity"), and Europe Day. The argument is that in referring explicitly to nationlike symbols (even though these symbols – except for the motto – had existed long before), leaders inadvertently framed the EU as in competition with nation-states, and the "no" campaigns were able to successfully exploit this (Zowislo-Grünewald 2008).

In short, this direct perspective argues that the rejection of the Constitutional Treaty in two founding member states was a serious blow to European cohesion precisely because citizens did not approve of the issues at stake. Naturally, if EU citizens thought that the treaty went too far, then this would also indicate that they were not in favor of how the European project was evolving in general. The treaty's failure thus meant a true legitimacy crisis for Europe that confirmed the existence of a democratic deficit, with serious implications for EU integration. Without somehow finding a new way forward, it was expected that the constitutional crisis would cause the EU to stall or fall apart because it had been fundamentally discredited. This perspective is in contrast to many other studies of the ratification process, discussed in the next section, that instead find that much of the public deliberation hinged on domestic politics rather than anything specifically to do with the Constitutional Treaty itself.

A more *indirect* argument from this perspective is that when the majority of French and Dutch voters said "no," they were actually opposed to the progress of EU integration at the time and the role of the EU more generally. That is, voters made their decisions based on what they thought of European integration, rather than the specific attributes of the constitution itself (Glencross and Treschsel 2011: 755–772). As Ben Crum writes, "[T]hese votes cannot be brushed aside as a mere expression of discontent about national politics. The 'no' votes say something substantial about the appreciation of European affairs" (Crum 2012: 144–145). In France and Luxembourg, for example, motivations for voting against the treaty were about "the impact of further European integration on the domestic employment and economic situation" (Crum 2012: 144). The French were worried that the perceived neoliberal quality of the treaty would negatively impact their domestic-level concerns.

Thus, the argument here is that citizens felt that they were losing their say in European policy making, both at the national and EU levels, and that the twin processes of integration and enlargement were taking their toll on economic growth, jobs, and immigration issues (Pusca 2009: 4). Some worried that the EU in general needed to pay closer attention to social priorities instead of liberal, market-oriented aims. Without enough emphasis on these social dimensions, citizens feared that they would lose their national, cultural identity (Lubbers 2008: 59–86). Philippe Legrain acknowledges this perspective but also derides it: "Many French people rejected the constitution because they regard Brussels as the handmaiden of 'ultra-liberal' Anglo-Saxon capitalism, intent on deregulating markets and opening up the French economy to competition ... This is mostly nonsense" (Legrain 2005).

Even though the purpose of the Constitutional Treaty was to help alleviate these concerns, especially in terms of complaints about the democratic deficit, the argument from this "indirect" perspective is that EU citizens were not convinced of this. Gilles Ivaldi argues that the vote in France most significantly hinged on a "retrospective performance evaluation vote on the EU model of social and economic governance" (Ivaldi 2006: 59). In other words, some EU citizens just wanted to say no to Europe, and this was their chance. Thus, the crisis had little to do with the treaty but much to do with a knowledge-deficit that was leaving citizens behind, and the inability of elites to "sell Europe" effectively to the public.

While at first glance this argument might seem compelling, opinion poll data works against this account of why the Constitutional Treaty failed. As will be discussed in more detail later in this chapter, post-referenda surveys indicate that in France, the Netherlands, and Ireland, citizens actually did not vote based on a desire to reject the EU or the provisions of the Constitutional Treaty. Moreover, before the referenda, a Eurobarometer poll asking about the primary reasons for opposing the Constitutional Treaty found that only 11 percent of respondents said that the treaty was going too far, too quickly (European Commission 2005).

Second Perspective: Grand Constitution Making Was Not Necessary

Some argue that the 2001 Nice Treaty was already sufficient to keep the EU going on a stable path; thus, inviting controversy over such a seemingly high-profile treaty was neither a smart nor desirable move. In addition, according to this view, the constitutional crisis emerged because of the symbolism of the treaty rather than its substance. In this case, the argument is that EU leaders did *not* push things too far with the treaty, but their mistake was being too loose with how they presented the treaty process to citizens who did not necessarily want to devote effort to understanding its actual provisions. As Andrew Moravcsik writes,

Far from demonstrating that the EU is in decline or disarray, the crisis demonstrates its essential stability and legitimacy. The central error of the

European constitutional framers was one of style and symbolism rather than substance. The constitution contained a set of modest reforms, very much in line with European popular preferences. Yet European leaders upset the emerging pragmatic settlement by dressing up the reforms as a grand scheme for constitutional revision.   (Moravcsik 2005)

Moravcsik argues that the Constitutional Treaty was unnecessary since there was no democratic deficit that needed to be corrected in the first place. He argues that EU issues are only of secondary importance to European citizens, and EU competences are already embedded in a system of checks and balances (Moravcsik 2006: 219–241). Moreover, the sorts of pragmatic reforms put forward in the Constitutional Treaty could have been achieved incrementally over the same period of time, without the need for the huge amount of hype that surrounded the treaty ratification processes (Moravcsik 2006: 219–220). Even if elites were engaging with the public – in what has frequently been described as the most democratic and open treaty-making process in EU history – the public was not interested. Moravcsik argues, "One is forced to conclude that this document became controversial not because its content was objectionable, but because its content was so innocuous that citizens saw a chance to cast an inexpensive protest vote" (Moravcsik 2005).

Thus, according to this perspective, questions surrounding the ratification process grew into a crisis for Europe because elites did not seem to recognize the high level of public apathy, and instead continued widening the gap between their goals and the public will (Crum 2008: 1–22). Ben Crum describes the treaty as "the most dramatic demonstration of a mismatch between the European decision-making process and the will of the European people" (Crum 2008: 1). And Gráinne de Búrca writes of "[t]he lack of citizen identification with the European Union as a political entity which helps to account for the lack of broad public engagement with the constitutional process and the absence of evidence of popular enthusiasm for a European constitution" (Búrca 2006: 206).

In support of this view, the pre-referendum Eurobarometer poll found that 33 percent of respondents had never heard of the draft European Constitution, and 35 percent were not sure whether they supported it or not (European Commission: 2005: 3–4). Leaders did make some efforts to inform the citizenry of the substance of the treaty. Berlusconi's office sent out 400,000 copies of the document on CD-ROM to small and medium-sized businesses. And just a week before the French referendum, the government sent out 46 million copies (all 191 pages) to citizens. But, in the end, this did not help clarify the nature of what was at stake in voting for the Constitutional Treaty. From this perspective, it is important to pay attention to the more general pattern in Western democracies, which is that citizens tend to only pay attention to a small handful of issues, and even if they do debate issues, they tend not to do so intensively or in an informed way (Moravcsik 2006: 226–227).

Third Perspective: Referenda Do Not Serve Their Purpose

A third major argument is that treaty reform and referenda are an important part of the democratic process in Europe, but referenda are often a flawed form of gauging citizens' preferences (Duff 2005: 187). This is because the public often fails to understand the nature of what is being proposed, especially if it is not about a single issue. Indeed, it has been shown that referenda are more likely to be flawed if they reduce complicated issues into a single, simple question with a yes or no answer. Moreover, the public is often swayed by whichever political party is more effective at (or has more money for) marketing its messages. In some cases, national politicians do not engage with the public about the issues at stake. And many times the public uses an upcoming referendum as an opportunity to voice their dissatisfaction with the government in power, regardless of the issue at hand. This is why referenda can be risky or faulty, and unreliable in terms of serving their purpose in contributing to the democratic process. Indeed, in the case of the Constitutional Treaty, numerous distortions detracted from the ability of the ratification process to function as an exercise in democracy (Paris-Dobozy 2008: 504).

Taking this into account, scholars from this perspective have approached the constitutional crisis with the question: did the outcome reflect a strong tide of Euroskepticism, unhappiness with domestic politics, or the impact of the yes versus no campaigns (Hobolt and Brouard 2011: 309–322)? None of these issues had anything to do with the actual terms of the Constitutional Treaty, although Euroskepticism could be argued to have been a precipitating factor in leading Europe into crisis. Right away, however, we can eliminate Euroskepticism as an explanation for the "no" votes. Eurobarometer polls show that a strong majority of "no" voters were actually "favorable to the pursuit of the European construction" and two-thirds believed that a European constitution was necessary for this.[6] Also,

---

[6] Also, three-quarters of those polled overall said that they believed the Constitution is or was of crucial importance to European construction (Flash Eurobarometer 171, May 30–31, 2005).

those who registered "yes" votes tended to vote based on their views of Europe's desired role in the world (Dehousse 2006: 153).

So what about the second part? Did domestic politics determine the outcome of the referenda (Crum 2006: 63)? European elections are often described as "second-order elections" compared to elections at the national level, and the same holds true for referenda (Dehousse 2006: 151–164). This means that voters will choose how to vote based on whether they want to empower or punish domestic political actors (i.e., political parties and the government), instead of on how they feel about the actual issue at hand. Governments and political parties may encourage the electorate to do this by framing a referendum – on any issue – as a test for the government in power (Crum 2006: 64). There is strong evidence for this argument as exit polls indicate that many French and Dutch voters who voted against the treaty were punishing their very unpopular govern- ments (Dehousse 2006: 152). Colette Mazzucelli argues that the treaty failed in France because societal perceptions of the treaty were closely tied to French notions of leadership and authority, rather than the substance of the treaty or even opinions about the EU. She writes, "Chirac's call for the popular referendum is a quest for legitimacy and the personal identifica- tion of each French citizen with a great project of national significance" (Mazzucelli 2008: 166–167). The problem with this was that the French public was not sure that Chirac actually represented the national interest or that he still possessed personal legitimacy as a leader.

Thus, it was a kind of "sanction-vote effect" instead of a true sign that publics were against the European political order. Some research has also analyzed the correlation between political party membership and how the electorate decided to vote. Matt Qvortrup argues that in both the French and Dutch cases, center-left electorates went against what they perceived to be a center-right document, and they saw the treaty as part of the center-right's larger goal of threatening the existence of the welfare state (Qvortrup 2006).

What, then, about the third part of this perspective's approach? Did the yes versus no campaigns matter in determining the vote? Campaigns can, of course, set the agenda for voters through defining issue salience and priming audiences for the vote. In both France and the Netherlands, those who campaigned against the Constitutional Treaty devoted far more time and resources to dissuading the population from voting in favor of it than their opponents on the "yes" side did in encouraging support of the treaty. Sara Hobolt and Sylvain Brouard argue, for example, that the "no" campaigns were effective in convincing Europeans – who overwhelmingly favored EU integration and membership – that they wanted a different Europe than the one embodied in the Constitutional Treaty. This involved opposition from both ends of the political spectrum, as they find that the far-right campaign framed the Constitutional Treaty as a "cultural threat" to France, while those on the left labeled it as a "social threat" (Hobolt and Brouard 2011: 312). They argue that the campaigns themselves made a difference in this outcome because the French debate in the lead-up to the referendum was "long and impassioned" and focused on economic and social issues. And while the Dutch campaign was "shorter and less intense" and focused on procedural issues (Hobolt and Brouard 2011: 319), in both cases societal views on Europe nevertheless became intertwined with traditional domestic issues.

Nicolas Jabko provides a good summary of this perspective: "the fact that the treaty did not pass the test of national referenda only proves that the means of its ratification method was perhaps ill suited to the contents of the treaty. It does not at all prove that the use of a constitutional repertoire was politically misguided in the constitutional drafting phase" (2007, as cited in Mazzucelli 2008: 168).

What's Missing?

The question still remains, why did the developments surrounding the Constitutional Treaty grow into a full-blown existential crisis for Europe? As the preceding analysis indicates, there is much debate over why the majority of voters in France and the Netherlands went against the treaty: from it being too ambitious, to voter apathy, to protest voting over domestic politics. And yet, given that several similar treaties before had resulted in initially negative referenda without then throwing the future of the European project into peril, I argue that the failed votes in the 2005 constitutional case do not alone explain why this grew into an existential crisis.

Of these various explanations, perhaps the ones that most connect the failed referenda to a crisis for Europe are those based on either direct opposition to the terms of the treaty or on growing Euroskepticism (even if unrelated to the treaty). These explanations have the potential to bridge the gap between popular rejection of the treaty and the creation of significant problems for the EU. However, as we have seen, the existing literature makes clear that the substance of the Constitutional Treaty itself was not very controversial. Moravcsik (2006) observes that citizens were generally not that concerned with the issues embodied in the treaty (even if they had knowledge of what it contained). Moreover, the treaty's provisions were incremental, and the changes that affected the public served to enhance avenues of participation in decision making as well as make the EU's institutional structures more transparent and efficient. One of the main points of the European Constitution was to help resolve any existing democratic deficit and narrow the gap between the public and the elites. As Francesca Vassallo puts it, with respect to the negative vote in France, "the European Constitution itself was not responsible for the final result. Any other document in the same national consultation at that time would likely have produced the same outcome" (Vassallo 2008: 426).

It is also quite obvious that European citizens had been given an opportunity to participate. A year before the Constitutional Convention,[7] a public debate on the future of Europe took place, and this continued on until the end of the convention in 2004. The convention itself was open and gave citizens the possibility of participating in the discussions and even attending the plenaries (Lu 2008).[8] There was a four-month "listening phase" at the beginning, online discussion forums were established, documents and records were displayed on the convention website, and contact information for each participant was made publicly available. The convention organizers also wrote directly to all of the major presses throughout Europe asking them explicitly to launch public debates about the Constitutional Treaty. EU citizens were thus encouraged in multiple ways to participate and to communicate their concerns. It cannot be emphasized enough that the entire process of creating this treaty, as well as the end result, was to enhance democracy, to bring EU institutions closer to EU citizens, and to encourage citizens to participate more fully in the construction of Europe (Paris-Dobozy 2008: 499–508; Přibáň 2011: 71). David Phinnemore calls it "the most open and transparent process of treaty reform in the history of the EU" (Phinnemore 2013: 3–4). Thus, it is reasonable to conclude that the convention and subsequent treaty had little to do with the eventual negative outcome. Indeed, the reasons why citizens voted "no" were not even brought up by the public as concerns during the convention despite the fact that large-scale opportunities for deliberation and participation had taken place.

---

[7] For national-level media content analysis for the period of the Constitutional Convention and Intergovernmental Conference (IGC), see Vetters (2009).

[8] For more on the nature of the convention, see Fossum and Menéndez (2011: 132–142).

Moreover, on several measures of public attitudes toward the EU and the Constitutional Treaty, citizens were clearly positive. Vast majorities supported the need for a Constitutional Treaty, the belief that membership in the EU was a good thing, and the desire to continue with integration (Standard Eurobarometer 61 2004: 76). So the puzzle is why strong support for the treaty at the outset turned negative as the referenda drew closer. Such an explanation could not be based on longer-term, structural reasons because all of the evidence indicates that the fate of the treaty was determined in just the last few weeks or even days before the vote. Instead, we must look to developments that happened in the final lead-up to the negative votes, such as elite input, media coverage, and the nature and content of the respective campaigns.

With several arguments ruled out, the remaining explanations – public apathy and domestic politics – still do not directly tell us why the "no" was equated with an existential crisis for Europe. In his list of ten recommendations for Europe after the referenda, Michael Maclay writes, "People were simply not convinced by the proposal that was put to them. They had their reasons, some intelligible, some less so. Don't read too much into their verdict, nor too little. It is not a failure of democracy when people say no" (Maclay 2005). And after the negative outcomes in France and the Netherlands, surveys suggest that if the "yes" campaigns had been better organized, the referenda could have easily gone the other way (Pusca 2009: 3). This does not suggest that there was some kind of deep malaise or disgruntlement toward EU integration on the scale necessary to create a crisis of the proportions experienced. The negative results do not in and of themselves provide enough of a rationale for the buildup of an intense, existential crisis in Europe. Therefore, we are still left with a gap in explaining the root cause of the crisis.

In order to help explain this, I argue in the next section of this chapter that the media and elites played a strong role in construing the ratification process as a crisis for Europe through their negative predictions and framing of the issues. This initial stage in which opinion shapers defined the crisis as such was somewhat more complex than the initial stages of the crisis over Iraq because ratification of the treaty quickly became imbued with so many other issues, whether they were related to the actual Constitutional Treaty or not. Then, once the public started getting involved in the debate, the crisis narrative started to revolve around preexisting public–elite tensions. This was followed by a ratcheting up of the crisis narrative to its peak, which culminated in the "no" votes, thus marking a self-fulfilling prophecy dynamic.

CONSTRUCTING THE CRISIS

In considering narratives as indications of rising integrational panic, it becomes evident that the launch of the national ratification procedures on October 29, 2004 – the day heads of state signed the treaty – served as the crisis trigger. From that point, the crisis narrative began to build, quickly taking on an overblown tenor until it reached its height with the failed referenda in late May and early June 2005. The media played a significant role in the rapid buildup of this crisis with a dramatic spike in coverage both at the international and national levels. The volume of international media coverage (Figure 4.1) and negative spin (Figure 4.2) were significant factors in framing this episode as a crisis for the EU's very survival in the months *before* the referenda were to take place.[9] This happened at the national level as well, as *Le Monde* in France published nearly 600 articles about the Constitutional Treaty in the second quarter of 2005 alone. In the Netherlands, *De Telegraaf* published more than 100 articles on the treaty as the Constitutional Convention wrapped up, and *NRC Handelsblad* featured the treaty in more than 200 articles in the month before the referendum. Even in Germany, where there was no referendum, newspapers noticeably increased coverage of the Constitutional Treaty's ratification process (Crum 2012: 139).

It is important to point out that the European Convention, and the Intergovernmental Conference that followed, had actually devised a plan for what would happen in the event that the Constitutional Treaty failed to pass ratification and required revision. The plan was that if by two years after the signifying of the treaty (October 30, 2006), four-fifths of the member states had ratified it and "one or more Member States have encountered difficulties in proceeding with ratification, the matter will be referred to the European Council" (Declaration No. 30 Article IC-443.4 as cited in Duff 2005). Thus, there was a plan B in place from the outset, a clearly articulated procedure in case the treaty encountered difficulties, and the idea was to continue with ratification *even if* some member states rejected it. A threshold was created such that ratification would proceed unless as many as six states failed to ratify it. This adds weight to the socially constructed aspect of this crisis, as it is clear that

---

[9] See Chapter 2 for methodology. The evidence was derived through reading *all* new stories that mention the keyword "constitution" during the relevant crisis time period in The *International Herald Tribune, Financial Times, Economist,* and *Time* magazine. The total number of articles was 266 for the constitutional crisis.

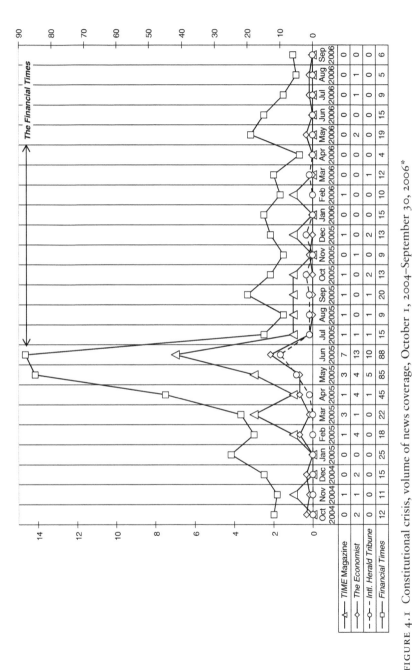

FIGURE 4.1 Constitutional crisis, volume of news coverage, October 1, 2004–September 30, 2006*

* In this figure, the right side Y-axis pertains to the *Financial Times*, whereas the left side Y-axis pertains to the other three media outlets. The *FT* publishes more stories in general as well as those related to the European region.

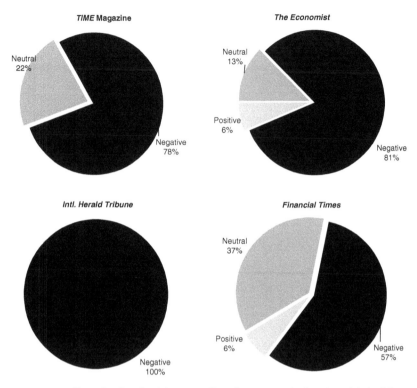

FIGURE 4.2 Constitutional crisis, neutrality of coverage during the crisis buildup, October 29, 2004–May 28, 2005

a scenario in which the treaty was not successful in a few states during the ratification process was not entirely unexpected, and was certainly not considered a trigger for an existential crisis about the future of the entire European project.

Nonetheless, beyond the sheer volume of coverage, throughout this period the international media continually published negative forecasts about the fate of the impending referenda, even as opinion polls on the treaty continued to show a positive majority in all member states except the UK. These passages are representative of such coverage:

The bandwagon against the European constitutional treaty is rolling ... The chances that the constitutional treaty will be ratified in all 25 EU countries are not high ... Given the realistic prospect of a No vote in France and the Netherlands, it is worth asking whether there is such a thing as Plan B.

(Munchau 2004)

Vote early and often: that seems to be the strategy of European governments that are fast-tracking national referendums on the EU constitution. They hope to win passage quickly – before a lethal cocktail of ignorance, apathy and low turnout produces a potentially fatal no vote. ("Winner Takes All" 2005)

The race to ratify the European Union constitution is like a steeplechase in which the hurdles become progressively higher and more intimidating ... Most analysts see this as a bid to stop the no campaign gaining steam as it capitalises on a variety of sentiments, from the unpopularity of the government to hostility to Turkish entry into the EU. ("Europe: Vote Early" 2005)

There is also the ever-present danger that the voters will choose to answer a different question, treating the referendum as a chance to lodge a protest against the government ... more Europe could now mean less France. (Stephens 2005b)

Mr Chirac appears to believe that, by railing against the commission and labeling "ultra-liberalism" as the new communism, he will demonstrate France's political prowess in Europe and seduce disaffected left-leaning voters into the yes camp. Equally Mr Blair labours under the delusion that he can talk British voters into backing the constitution by stressing the "red lines" he has protected from unwanted incursions by Brussels and claiming that he is winning the argument in Europe. (*The Economist*, "Leaders: Outlook: Gloomy" 2005)

Referring to a kind of contagion effect, one editorial stated that if the outcome were negative in France, "it would be a profound shock to the European body politic. It could well trigger a No vote in other countries holding referendums, including the Netherlands ... It could also bring EU policymaking to a standstill" (Peel 2005a).

From the start, elites also contributed to this narrative of failure, providing dramatic fodder for the press. For example, former president of the European Commission, Jacques Delors, anticipated a negative outcome in November 2004 and argued that "[t]o say 'No' would be a great historic mistake for France" (Thornhill 2004). Similarly, European Commissioner Franco Frattini warned that even if only one country rejected the treaty, it would be a "complete disaster" and would only serve to increase the gap between EU institutions and European citizens. He also argued that it would make future enlargement difficult (Buttiglione 2004). In the Netherlands, Lousewies van der Laan, a leftist Dutch politician said, "I am seriously worried the Dutch will vote No. A French No or a Dutch No means the treaty is dead" (Bickerton 2005c). In the lead-up to the Dutch vote, *Elsevier* – a weekly Dutch magazine – published a nine-page article entitled "Why No Is Better than Yes." In reaction to this, a senior Dutch official said, "If France is the only country that says No, France has a problem. If there is more than one country that says No, then Europe has a problem" (Bickerton 2005b). The Dutch finance minister added to this, saying that "the lights would go out" if there were a no vote (*Financial Times*, "After the Votes," 2005). And Luxembourg Prime Minister Jean-Claude Juncker, the newly appointed president of the Eurogroup, jumped on the bandwagon, saying that it would be a "catastrophe" if the results were negative (*Financial Times*, "After the Votes," 2005). Spanish Prime Minister José Zapatero added his warning too, saying to the French, "Voting yes for the European constitution is a step forward; voting no is a step backward toward crisis" (*Time*, "A Party Divided," 2004).

In opposition to EU leaders – who obviously supported the treaty despite their dire warnings – were the well-funded "no" campaigners who emerged out of the woodwork in several member states. They were passionate in their attempts to advance a broad variety of arguments against the treaty. For example, in France, these campaigners blatantly connected the treaty to the issue of Turkish accession, trying to stir up anti-Islamic feelings among the population, even though the two issues were completely unrelated. The "no" campaigners in Spain actually wanted to reject the constitution because they said that the new treaty did not go far enough in moving integration forward. Other "no" campaigners argued that the treaty fundamentally threatened national sovereignty.

Some leaders tried to counter these "no" campaigners. For example, Denis MacShane, the British Minister of State for Europe, put forward an eighteen-month plan for Labour to "put the facts about the benefits of EU membership to the British people" (Adams 2004). He warned that a "no" vote from the UK would mean the country's isolation in Europe. The pro-EU lobby group, Britain in Europe, pleaded with the UK chancellor to stop "playing to the gallery" by referring repeatedly to the EU's shortcomings. British Labour politician Jack Straw, then Secretary of State for Foreign and Commonwealth Affairs, described the "myths, exaggerations and distortions" about Europe that these "no" campaigners were proliferating (*Financial Times*, "Straw Warns on Rejection" 2004). In general, however, leaders were not particularly good at informing their electorate of the purpose of the treaty. As Philip Stephens put it in an op-ed, "many of today's leaders close their eyes and stand perfectly still" (Stephens 2004).

Significantly, only 2 percent of major international media coverage actually dealt with the substantive terms of the constitution itself (see Figure 4.4). Thus, articles that put the constitution in a negative light, but did not go into detail about what was actually problematic about it, were common. Typical of this tone is a *Financial Times* article that declares, "Britain and other EU member states should steer clear of a constitution that promises little benefit and much hardship" (Epstein 2004). Indeed, EU citizens were not very well informed at all about what the treaty contained. One study cited in *Time* magazine indicated that only 11 percent of those polled knew the substance of the constitution, 56 percent said they knew little, and 33 percent said they had not even heard of it (*Time*, "Winner Takes All" 2005). A similar European Commission poll had even worse results with only a third of EU citizens saying they had heard of the constitutional treaty, and again, only 11 percent indicating that they "broadly knew its content" (European Commission 2005). In the UK (the only country for which pre-referendum polls indicated a negative result), a whopping 94 percent of citizens said they knew little or nothing about the treaty. Their opinions were clearly not based on the actual treaty itself.

To make matters worse, many leaders blatantly misrepresented what the constitution actually entailed. For example, Czech President Vaclav Klaus said,

The new EU based on its constitution will in fact be a new European state with all essential features of a state, in which the existing member countries will be reduced to regions or provinces and in which the formal agreement to sub-ordinate to the superior entity will lead us to the abandonment of our national democracy, sovereignty and political independence. (Gloom 2004)

Similarly, Ole Krarup, a Danish politician and European parliamentarian from the People's Movement against the EU, said that the treaty was "the final step to a militarized EU superstate aiming to control Denmark down to the tiniest detail" (*Financial Times*, "Danes Set Date for EU Constitution Vote" 2005). Pia Kjaersgaard, leader of the Danish People's Party, derided the treaty as "an elitist project" and said that she was "convinced that the Danish people do not want to be a part of an EU state" (*Financial Times*, "Danes Set Date for EU Constitution Vote" 2005). In the UK, there was open talk among the leadership of the Constitutional Treaty representing a threat to British sovereignty because it would turn the EU into a superstate complete with a European army. Of course, the treaty itself did not contain any such measures and actually served to clarify the distinction between national and European decision-making power, as well as reinforcing the importance of national parliaments.

Perhaps unsurprisingly, the standard metanarrative of the EU being too complicated to understand was also plainly visible:

Trying to explain the European Union to outsiders – or insiders, for that matter – sometimes feels like trying to describe an elephant to a man from Mars. You can describe what it looks like, but it is still well nigh impossible to demonstrate how it works, or quite what it is for.   (Peel 2005c)

By contrast, the ongoing approval process of the treaty received relatively little international media attention. Spain was one of the first member states to approve the treaty in its February 2005 popular referendum with an overwhelming majority, but there was little mention of this in news coverage outside of Spain. Germany also quietly and easily ratified the treaty in May 2005 through a parliamentary vote that received little attention. The German citizens were not that interested in the treaty (politicians did not engage them in the discussion) until the "no" vote in France at the end of that month. Indeed, by the time the French cast their vote, twelve member states had already approved the treaty through either parliamentary vote or referendum: Austria, Belgium, Bulgaria, Germany, Greece, Hungary, Italy, Lithuania, Romania, Slovakia, Slovenia, and Spain. This represented nearly half of the EU's population. However, there was very little coverage of this positive process compared to the ubiquitous predictions of doom and gloom. As a result, the crisis narrative steadily gained momentum. In short, the media's negative framing, combined with amplification of elite exaggerations and misstatements, was essential in turning a relatively standard treaty ratification process into a period of integrational panic and existential crisis for Europe.

INTEGRATIONAL PANIC AND CATHARSIS

As the crisis narrative strengthened and became widespread, the main feature of it was the emergence of a focus on public–elite divisions. To be sure, the tension between European publics and leaders (at both the national and EU levels) had been growing for some time before the crisis. As discussed in Chapter 3, the Iraq crisis had left a legacy of integration and assimilation of the new member states into Europe. In 2004, most of the CEECs had formally joined the EU (there was a three-year delay for Romania and Bulgaria), and it was now a union of twenty-five. As part of the post-Iraq crisis catharsis, member states shared the view that the EU needed a stronger international presence as a coherent actor, and to achieve the right balance between Atlanticist and

Europeanist orientations they had to shift toward the latter. However, this left room for new, unresolved tensions to build in the lead-up to the 2005 constitutional crisis.

In this section, I briefly describe the nature of these preexisting public–elite tensions, and explain how they came to characterize the dominant crisis narrative. I argue that the public–elite divide was not necessarily how Europeans had to talk about the crisis, especially since the purpose of the Constitutional Treaty was actually to bring Europe closer to the people, and to better delineate the relationship between national and European institutions. I then advance the argument that the "no" votes were actually the product of a kind of self-fulfilling prophecy in light of intensifying "end of Europe" rhetoric. Finally, I explain how this crisis ultimately resulted in a renewed European consensus, particularly at the societal level. The eventual achievement of the Lisbon Treaty represented a strong effort on the part of European leaders to move past the crisis, but the most significant aspect of recovery from this crisis was the emergence of a stronger European public sphere. Citizens increased their engagement with EU issues transnationally and demonstrated significant, new levels of transnational politicization. I argue that this was a result of the catharsis that came with the release of public–elite tensions during the crisis period. In effect, Europeans turned the crisis into an opportunity to enhance their engagement with Europe, and to bolster subsequent EU integration with a stronger sense of popular legitimacy.

Preexisting Tensions

In the 1990s, the era of the "permissive consensus," defined as support for the European project needing to rely merely on tacit public consent, came to an end. With the implementation of the 1992 Maastricht Treaty – which created a clear political dimension to the EU, significant areas of social and internal security policy, and the advent of monetary union – the effects of EU integration began to be felt directly by regular European citizens. They became more and more aware of the existence of the EU and of its impact on their daily lives (Risse 2010).

Around the same time, Brussels officials started to engage in significant efforts to democratize EU processes, striving to make their institutions more transparent, legitimate, open, and with due respect to subsidiarity.[10]

---

[10] For example, with each new treaty, the European Parliament gained more power.

However, despite having an electorate that was increasingly aware and affected by EU issues, national elites continued to use the EU as a scapegoat for their own failures and to campaign on exclusively national issues. The media also seriously downplayed any coverage of EU achievements, especially in terms of substance (Sutton 2005: 9). Brussels seemed increasingly remote and difficult to understand for regular people, indicating a mounting knowledge deficit alongside a perceived democratic deficit.

In short, public–elite tensions led to a nascent, but growing sense that decision makers were out of touch with their publics, that the EU was too remote to be democratic, and that citizens were not as important as member-state leaders. It was in this climate that European leaders put the Constitutional Treaty to referenda.

The Crisis Narrative

Media content analysis shows that preexisting public–elite tensions came to the surface, were openly aired, and were then amplified in the media, marking the growth of integrational panic. Figure 4.3 provides an indication of the tone and tenor of this coverage.[11] At the same time, one cannot assume a priori that the divide between the public and elite levels would necessarily be the primary way that Europeans would talk about the Constitutional Treaty ratification process. As described previously, treaty ratification processes are regular events that happen every few years, and there was nothing about this particular treaty that somehow violated citizens' preferences or signaled the opening of a new void between elites and publics. Indeed, besides accommodating the recent enlargement of membership to include the Central and Eastern European countries, the Constitutional Treaty was intended specifically to *alleviate* the perceived democratic deficit. Moreover, the changes it introduced were for the most part merely incremental.

One could argue that it is actually paradoxical that the main crisis narrative here centered on public–elite tensions because the level of transparency, openness, and public engagement surrounding the treaty-drafting process was wholly unprecedented in the evolution of the EU. Moreover, the very country that spearheaded the momentum behind the Convention on the Future of Europe – France – was the one that ultimately produced the first "no" vote. Indeed, these seemingly counterintuitive developments may

---

[11] See Chapter 2 for methodology.

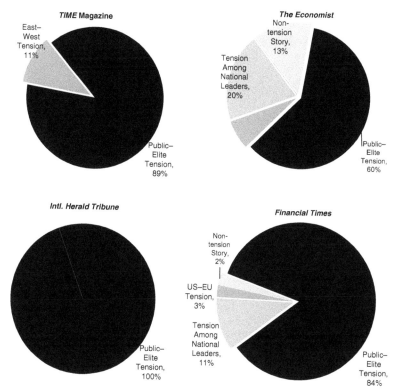

FIGURE 4.3 Constitutional crisis, nature of tensions in news coverage, October 29, 2004–May 28, 2005

help account for why previous attempts to explain the crisis and its causes have fallen short of the mark. After all, it would have arguably made more sense for the narrative to be about the actual terms of the treaty, and about whether or not these terms improved the functioning and accountability of the EU. But as we have seen, this was not the case, and thus this crisis can only be fully understood by taking into account its socially constructed nature, which put public–elite tensions at the heart of the crisis narrative surrounding the treaty-ratification process.

As far as media coverage is concerned, these public–elite tensions took several forms, depending on whether the focus was on national or EU elites. At the national level, these tensions often involved the fear of losing national identity and sovereignty, citizens' unhappiness with the current government, unemployment concerns, and the role of migrant workers. These tensions were particularly dominant in coverage involving the

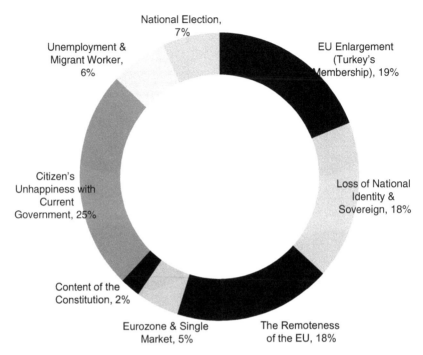

FIGURE 4.4 Constitutional crisis, public–elite sub-tensions, October 29, 2004–May 28, 2005

French, Dutch, and British publics. At the European level, public–elite tensions often reflected a feeling that the EU was remote, that the Eurozone and single market would take precedence over citizens' rights, and that citizens feared what future enlargements would bring. Media content analysis shows that the predominant source of these tensions covered in the international press came from national elites rather than EU elites (Figure 4.4).[12] As far as the latter were concerned, one major issue dominated – Turkey's application for EU membership – and this was not even part of the Constitutional Treaty. Notably, only 18 percent of international media coverage of public–elite tensions surrounding the treaty was related to public dissatisfaction with the European project, specifically a feeling of remoteness on the part of the EU.

---

[12] The chart in Figure 4.4 further breaks down the public–elite tensions depicted in Figure 4.3.

Some representative examples of the media narrative surrounding public–elite tensions include the following:

Perhaps the biggest problem for the EU is that the European project, now approaching its 50th anniversary, still suffers from such a marked lack of enthusiasm among ordinary people. To most voters, Brussels, with its preposterous farm subsidies, overpaid bureaucrats and incomprehensible institutions, remains remote and apparently unaccountable.
(*The Economist*, "Books and Arts: An Optimist's View ...," 2005)

But the confusion of the constitutional treaty in a melee of issues and emotions highlights a wider divide between rulers and ruled in Europe. Put bluntly, the policies, practices and ideas that constitute the EU are failing to deliver what people want.   (*Financial Times*, "Chirac Does Battle ...," 2005)

The opinion polls show that the vibrancy of the No campaign had little to do with the specific defects of the treaty, establishing new rules for the expanded European Union. Rather, it reflects voters' frustration with the failings of their national leadership.   (*Financial Times*, "France's Fears" 2005)

The no campaign is about a lot more than incoherent resentment of the ruling class, however. The no campaign points out that the same elite that signed up to the euro and allowed mass immigration with little public discussion is now lining up behind the EU constitution.
(*The Economist*, "Europe: Putting the Clog In," 2005)

Dominique Moisi, a think tank expert, said, "The young, who are pro-European, are not mobilizing because the cause of Europe is being represented by people they don't like. It is a leadership problem from Barroso to Chirac" (Hollinger and Thornhill 2005). Francesca Vassallo describes the discussions in both France and the Netherlands as "intense, emotional, popular and constant" (Vassallo 2008: 419).

A closer look at France shows that at least some portion of the citizenry was interested in the chance to weigh in on their country's role in Europe, and there were even numerous pamphlets and best-selling books on the topic of the Constitutional Treaty (Fossum and Menéndez 2011: 146). But rather than debating the content of the treaty, much of the discussion instead firmly connected the referendum to a wide variety of domestic social issues.[13] Many saw this as a referendum on French President Jacques Chirac's government, and the upcoming 2007 presidential elections became strongly intertwined with this vote. As one *Economist* article describes it:

---

[13] For good overviews of this, see Mazzucelli (2008); Vassallo (2008); and Paris-Dobozy (2008).

What might have been an arcane question about constitutional arrangements has morphed into a battle over the future of France. There are three elements. The first is about France's place in the world. The second is about the failure of its economy to create jobs. And the third is about the nature of its political elite.

(*The Economist*, "France and the EU . . .," 2005)

Some of the unhappiness with the Chirac government came from the socialists who were still incensed that they had to vote for Chirac in 2002 to avoid a government led by the far-right National Front Party leader Jean-Marie Le Pen. To add insult to injury, two months before the referendum a scandal erupted causing the finance minister to resign when it was discovered that the government was paying €14,000 per month for his apartment in Paris, even though he owned five other properties (Thornhill 2005a).

Besides dissatisfaction with the government in power, many French citizens had grievances with specific domestic policies. They worried about a range of issues such as unemployment rising above 10 percent, immigration's effect on public services, inflows of cheap labor from the east, and the declining effectiveness of the French social model. Many believed that these were symptoms of low economic growth, reflecting a lack of innovation, reliance on off-shoring, and mounting public debt. Moreover, there was a growing sense that this economic and political malaise was manifesting itself in societal fragmentation and violence. To add to this, Philippe de Villiers, a right-wing, anticonstitution politician, drew connections between the Constitutional Treaty and the unrelated Services Directive. He said of this directive, "Every aspect of French daily life will be shaken up: wages, social protection, unfair competition, legal insecurity and outsourcing. The only way of rejecting the directive is to vote No to the European constitution" (Thornhill 2005b). Even the composition of those who opposed the treaty – described in one article as "a motley collection of Trotskyists, disaffected socialists, hardline Gaullists and fascistic nationalists" (Thornhill 2005d: 8) – indicated that the treaty was an excuse to bring preexisting tensions to the surface. There was little else holding the "no" camp together. Ultimately, as one expert put it, "Few if any of the electorate could indicate with any degree of precision the precise way in which the Constitution itself caused, contributed to or aggravated any of these phenomena" (Sutton 2005: 6).

To the extent that French voters did see the referendum as having to do with Europe, a variety of tensions still unrelated to the treaty itself rose to the surface to become reasons for voting "no." Many voted based on fears that Turkey would join the EU, and that this would threaten their national identity. Of course, as we have seen, the issue of Turkish membership was not a part of the constitution at all. But Le Pen was happy to draw connections between Turkey's candidacy and the argument that the EU was neglecting its social model. Some became convinced that new EU member states such as Poland and Slovakia were too different from the rich countries of the West, and that they therefore posed a threat to France's approach to governance. The famous "Polish plumbers" campaign was symbolic of the fear many citizens had that Europeans from the East would take their jobs because they were willing to work for less pay. Politicians on both sides of the political spectrum also had the tendency to blame Brussels for domestic problems. They were in the habit of using the EU as a scapegoat, and as a result, voters were becoming increasingly disillusioned with elites at both levels. In sum, the French public was answering a different question on May 29 than the one printed on the referendum ballot (Vassallo 2008: 416). And this had greater consequences, as one observer pointed out: "The No camp . . . is merely venting its frustration with the state of France to the detriment of Europe" (Thornhill 2005d: 8).

In the case of the Netherlands, many in the Dutch electorate also voted based on public–elite tensions, specifically unhappiness with their current government and fear of a threat to national identity. At the time, the government was comprised of an awkward three-part coalition that only had a public approval rate of around 20 percent (Bernstein 2005). The Dutch "no" camp also made spurious links between the Constitutional Treaty and Turkey's bid for EU membership, as well as the threat to national sovereignty. Others focused on the economic cost of the EU and the Euro. In 1990, the Dutch realized that they had become the highest per capita contributor to the EU budget (Wolinetz 2008: 182). Even though the Dutch contribution to this budget amounts to less than 1 percent of GDP, a majority felt that the Netherlands was paying too much to the EU. The issue of Muslim immigrants and assimilation into European society was also a major issue, bringing up feelings that the Dutch way of life was under attack. "No" campaigners were effective at raising alarm over what they described as too much immigration. Just like in France, many voters failed to realize that none of these issues were actually at stake in voting for or against the Constitutional Treaty.

To make matters worse, Dutch Prime Minister Jan Peter Balkenende was so confident that the outcome of the referendum would be positive that he made little effort to explain the treaty to the public and garner their support. This was perhaps understandable considering that numerous polls showed that Dutch attitudes toward a constitution for Europe were highly positive. The Dutch people were happy with the final draft and felt that it struck the right balance between integration and member-state sovereignty (Wolinetz 2008: 186). There was no feeling that they had to compromise too much at the Constitutional Convention. Moreover, all of the major political parties supported the treaty (including the three in the governing coalition), as did 85 percent of the lower house of Parliament. The "yes" side was justifiably confident. But this also prompted them to not go out of their way to craft a coherent message in favor of the treaty, leaving the stage open for the rather passionate "no" camp (Wolinetz 2008: 187). And again, as in France, the negative narrative that the "no" camp constructed around the treaty did not have much grounding in the actual content of the treaty itself.

The debates in France and the Netherlands – because they were the most visible – did have some impact in other EU member states. For example, in Germany, which did not hold a referendum, some of the same issues involving Turkey's candidacy, enlargement in general, economic liberalization, and complaints with the current government emerged in public debates. All of the major political parties supported the treaty, and opposition voices only came from more fringe antiglobalization groups, the far left, and a few neo-Nazis. Daniel Cohn-Bendit, a European parliamentarian from Germany, said, "The feeling of the people is that we want to say no to what exists to prove that we exist" (Bernstein 2005). Thus, the national-level debates about the new treaty were in a sense hijacked by a vocal minority, and this contributed to increasing expressions of public–elite tensions, despite the fact that these issues had nothing at all to do with the terms of the treaty.

As the dates of the referenda approached, the anticipation of failure became ever more acute, so much so that European Commission President Barroso warned French leaders that they were fueling Euroskepticism. He said, "I have to tell you frankly that I am sometimes amazed by the French debate, with all due respect to French democracy. The debate is to a certain extent biased and skewed, giving excuses to europhobes and eurosceptics. The political situation in France as far as Europe is concerned is poisoned" (Parker and Buck 2005). Opinion polls showed that French attitudes were intensifying as the date of the referendum drew near. The public was becoming less satisfied with their government, more worried about their economy, and concerned about the liberal path the EU seemed to be taking. Dutch Prime Minister Balkenende also criticized opponents in his country, saying they were making up false "horror stories," when in fact the treaty was a "unique chance for a better Europe" (*Financial Times*, "Dutch Premier Hits at Treaty Opponents," 2005).

In the month before the referenda, international media coverage underlined an ever-increasing sense of threat – not just to the treaty, but also to the EU and the integration process more generally. This coverage bolstered mounting integrational panic in Europe, equating the fate of the treaty to the fate of Europe. For example, an op-ed in the *Financial Times* entitled, "France's Electorate Could End European integration," expressed the following:

> By voting No, French voters would throw their own country and the EU into a protracted political crisis and thereby create the worst possible political climate for economic reform ... In its epic battle against the libertarian Anglo-Saxon model, the French No campaign hopes that a No vote will strengthen "social Europe" through the formation of a core Europe with its own special brand of integration. This is nonsense. A No vote will merely put at risk the integration Europe has achieved so far, and will not strengthen anyone.   (Munchau 2005)

Other articles conveyed a similar, alarmist sentiment:

> "There is no plan B" may be the most hackneyed phrase in the Brussels lexicon, trotted out whenever any EU scheme runs into trouble ... But there is a worse possibility: that the EU might begin to break down. National governments, many of them in serious economic difficulty, might be tempted to seize on the unpopularity of the EU and ignore inconvenient edicts from Brussels.
> (*The Economist*, "Europe: The Great Unraveling" 2005)

> This row exposes many of the political fault lines in modern France and helps explain why a seemingly technical debate about the functionality of the EU has erupted into an existential crisis over the country's identity and Europe's destiny.
> (Thornhill 2005c)

It did not help that during this last month, elite rhetoric also reached a new level of integrational panic: Former Commission President Romano Prodi equated France's potential rejection of the treaty with the end of Europe, saying, "There would be no more Europe. We will pass through a long period of crisis. The problem will not only be a catastrophe for France but the fall of Europe" (Thornhill 2005e). Similarly, France's foreign minister, Michel Barnier, said it would lead to "political breakdown in the European Union" (Thornhill and Parker 2005). Jacques Delors also repeated his sentiment that a potential "no" vote would amount to a "political cataclysm" (Jones 2005). Think tank expert Charles Grant supported this view in a Center for European Reform paper, writing that a British "no" vote would "throw the Union into a political crisis, sparking off a chain reaction that could lead to the end of the EU as we know it" (Grant 2005). All of these statements were repeated and amplified in media coverage all across Europe. Any sense of proportion, including the fact that the European Convention and Intergovernmental Conference had taken into account the possibility of some member states voting "no" and had prepared a mechanism for dealing with this, had gone out the window. In the press, many countries were thrown into the limelight at various times as potentially causing a negative outcome, including Poland, the Czech Republic, France, and the Netherlands.

The signals that this crisis had become a self-fulfilling prophecy also came through in media coverage at the time:

> The public anger expressed in the opinion polls has thrown France's political elite into a panic and dismayed the country's European partners. How could France – described recently by Jose Manuel Barroso, the European Commission president, as one of Europe's "indispensable" countries – threaten to smother its own political creation? ... When President Jacques Chirac announced on July 14 last year that he was to hold a referendum to approve the constitution, pro-European sentiment was strong ... events have since conspired against him.
>
> (Thornhill April 6, 2005f)

> The grassroots are about to have their revenge on the establishment, in the shape of two presidents: Jacques Chirac, the incumbent, and Valery Giscard d'Estaing, the principal architect of the treaty. The EU has become the surrogate target for the revolt.
>
> (Peel 2005b)

Self-fulfilling prophecies mark the culmination of crises that have a socially constructed dynamic to them. In other words, strong expectations of failure were leading to actual failure. Opinion polls that had revealed robust support for the treaty just a few months earlier were starting to go the other way. Indeed, one opinion poll three weeks before the vote in France showed an even split (*Le Figaro* 2005). And as the vote got closer, the polls increasingly seemed to indicate that a negative result was likely. In a last effort, Chirac held a few public debates, his government even recruited famous actor Gerard Depardieu to try to persuade more citizens to vote "yes" and promised the French people that they would have the chance for a separate referendum on Turkish accession – to distinguish it from the Constitutional Treaty vote. Nicolas Sarkozy, head of the ruling center-right UMP Party, gave a major speech defending the "European dream" to promote the "Yes" campaign. Then, two days before the vote, President Chirac himself addressed the nation on television, explaining how the treaty would make Europe better and arguing that "[r]ejection will be seen as a No to Europe. Europe will break down." François Hollande, Socialist Party secretary at the time, also chimed in at the eleventh hour saying, "Our conviction is that Europe should not be the victim of the mistakes of the government and the president of the republic" (Thornhill 2005g). The Dutch government did less, but as opinion polls began to turn against the "yes" side, some ministers scrambled to make positive public statements about the Constitutional Treaty in the immediate lead-up to the vote.

Crisis Height

Many accounts of this crisis assume that it began with the failed referendum votes in France and the Netherlands in May and June 2005. But as the previous analysis clearly shows, the growth of the crisis was constructed through public–elite tension narratives well before this. Indeed, the crisis actually reached its *height*, after a culmination of months of buildup, with the failed referenda. The French voted "no" on May 29, 2005, with 55 percent opposed and 45 percent in favor, with a high voter turnout of 70 percent.[14] A Flash Eurobarometer poll immediately following the vote indicated that lack of information about the treaty did not influence whether citizens voted for or against it.[15] Sixty percent of voters knew how they would vote either when the referendum was announced or shortly after that. But this means that nearly 40 percent of voters made up their minds only in the last few weeks, and many of them at the last minute.[16] It was only in the final few weeks of the campaign that the fate of the treaty was determined. Thus, the data indicates that the "no" campaigns, media coverage, and public debate on this issue did matter in the outcome of the vote. In line with the dominant crisis narrative, the top two reasons given for voting against the treaty in France were national or social reasons, rather than European considerations. Specifically, "no" voters were worried about unemployment (31 percent) and economic growth (26 percent) in France. This was followed by the impression that the treaty was too liberal (19 percent), and a desire to oppose the current French government (18 percent) (Flash Eurobarometer June 2005: 7).

---

[14] The question they were asked was: *Approuvez-vous le projet de loi qui autorise la ratification du traité établissant une Constitution pour l'Europe?* (Do you approve of the Bill authorizing the ratification of the Treaty establishing a Constitution for Europe?)

[15] More than half of those who chose not to participate in the vote did so because they felt they did not have sufficient information about the treaty.

[16] The timing of this decision did not affect whether they ultimately voted "yes" or "no."

"Yes" voters, by contrast, voted in favor of the treaty mainly based on European issues and predominantly because they thought it was essential for the building of the European project.[17]

Just three days after the French referendum, on June 1, 2005, 61 percent of Dutch voters said "no" compared to 39 percent who voted "yes." Voter turnout was relatively high in the Netherlands as well, with 62 percent of the population participating in the referendum. According to a Flash Eurobarometer poll taken after the Dutch vote, 67 percent of respondents complained that the debate on the treaty began too late and as a result, 56 percent of those who voted felt that they did not have enough information (Flash Eurobarometer June 2005: 7). As in France, around half of those who abstained did so because of this perception that they had not been provided with enough information. Even more significant than in France, fully one-third of Dutch voters made up their minds on how to vote in just the last few *days* before the referendum took place (i.e., after they realized that the French had voted "no"). After the Dutch vote, exit polls showed that much of the "no" voters' rationale was tied directly to public–elite tensions, rather than the contents of treaty itself. They feared Turkey's application for membership, were concerned about the ostensible growth of the EU as some sort of imagined superstate, or wanted to express displeasure with the Balkenende administration. Many voted against the treaty because they did not like politics, and around one-third were opposed to the euro (even though, again, the treaty had nothing to do with the future of the common currency) (Bickerton 2005a). In the Flash Eurobarometer poll, the top reason given by those who opposed the treaty was that they felt they had a lack of information (32 percent). This was followed by fear of a loss of national sovereignty (19 percent) and opposition to the current government (14 percent) (Flash Eurobarometer June 2005: 15). The crisis narrative had focused on these tensions with little discussion of what the treaty really entailed, and this was clearly evident in the referendum's result.

The scenario that everyone had feared had come to pass. Faced with the reality of the "no" votes, the integrational-panic floodgates opened. In the words of one former EU official, with decades of experience in Brussels, the negative referenda represented "without a shadow of a doubt, a turning point in European integration" (Sutton 2005: 2). The *Economist* embraced "end of Europe" rhetoric. "The Europe That Died" was on

---

[17] Fifty-two percent of "yes" voters did so for European reasons, while 47 percent of "no" voters did so for national reasons.

the cover of the June 4–10, 2005, issue, and the article itself stated, "The EU should move in the direction of being a looser, less federalist and more decentralized club ... the club must pass more powers back to its members" (*The Economist*, "The Europe That Died" 2005). Later that month, the *Economist* published a cover image of a garbage can with the title "Where to File Europe's New Constitution" (June 19, 2003). In the United States, the cover of the June 13, 2005, issue of *Time* described the constitutional crisis as "The Great Crackup," and the article stated, "In Brussels, there is still a reluctance to admit the obvious: that the constitution is dead." The French paper *Liberation* described the failed referendum as "a masterpiece of masochism," and *Le Figaro* stated that it "turned everything upside down" (as cited in Lu 2008: 431). And not to be outdone, the *Financial Times* called the result the moment of the EU's "greatest crisis" (Parker 2005b).

Journalists and commentators, especially those of the antifederalist persuasion, argued that the EU had reached the end of the road for integration and enlargement. They described the EU as at an impasse and said that it would become a lot less effective, even possibly leading to the departure of some member states. Among other things, they insisted that the EU must become looser and that there would not be a more integrated core, as some federalists had suggested. They talked about ceding back some of the sovereignty pooled in Brussels to the member states. There was a sense that the "no" votes were a sign that the EU should focus more on economic liberalization and growth, not on social or political Europe, which for all intents and purposes was "dead" (*The Economist*, "The Europe That Died ...," 2005). Representative examples of the tone and tenor of this narrative include:

In light of the fact that Germany had approved the treaty just two days before: Ideas of a core Europe or a Franco-German union now seem all but dead.
                    (*The Economist*, "A Tale of Two Couples," 2005)

France's rejection of the European Union constitution is, in lots of ways, a triumph for Britain ... Britain is still in the European club, but political union is dead ... Better still, French fingerprints are all over the murder weapon.
                    (*The Economist*, "Europe: The Triumph of Perfidious Albion" 2005)

That dream is now dead. Though there were many reasons for the votes against the constitution, it is not unreasonable to say that they had in common a fear of the future.   (Elliot 2005)

The rejection of the treaty by two of the original six members raises profound questions about the future of Europe and, above all, about the monetary union.

A rising tide of integrationist ambition swept the single currency on the European shore in the 1990s. Now, it is in danger of becoming a beached whale.

(Wolf 2005)[18]

With respect to Europe and its future, the analogy to death was widespread.

At this height of the crisis, public–elite tensions were visible everywhere. The cover of the June 6, 2005, *Der Spiegel* had the title, "Dictatorship of Bureaucrats," with an image of the European Parliament in the background and the mythological woman, Europa, holding the EU flag with a red X painted across it. Andrew Gamble captures the essence of the dominant public–elite narrative in Europe at the time:

The failure of the Constitutional Treaty prompted much questioning about the future of the EU – whether further integration would now be possible, whether enlargement would proceed and even whether the EU could survive in the long term, or would lapse into a condition of increasing disunion. It was widely seen as a watershed moment in the development of the EU. There had always been tension between two different bases of EU legitimacy – one deriving from treaties between states and the other deriving from democracy and citizenship – but never before had the collision between them been so serious.   (Gamble 2006: 35)

Expressed more simply, as one French "no" voter put it, "We have had this constitution imposed on us. I don't know what it is for, they sent us the text a week before and we are supposed to decide" (Arnold, Hollinger, and Thornhill 2005). From the perspective of the public, the narrative was that "it would be fatal if the leaders went on in the same way as of now" (Klingst 2005).[19] In the words of one *Die Zeit* article:

In all this Poles, Slovaks and Baltics push into our job market, while the old EU states, such as Germany, France and the Netherlands have not even managed to integrate their long residing minorities from North Africa and Turkey ... In Berlin, Amsterdam and Marseille a big dispute is taking place whether Muslim immigrants are even willing or able to adapt European values and live the European everyday life.   (Klingst 2005)[20]

The *International Herald Tribune* put it this way:

It wasn't the constitution itself voters were rejecting. Polls reveal they were articulating a broader malaise. The highest "no" votes came from the most vulnerable ... The "no" campaign united the fearful right ... with the fearful left ... Influenced by anxiety about the future, every faction across the political spectrum found something to feel menaced by ... The only commonality was fear

---

[18] In this quote, we can even observe the preexisting tensions that would characterize the next major crisis for Europe.
[19] Translation by Molly Krasnodebska.   [20] Translation by Molly Krasnodebska.

itself, the desire to hang on to what they have in the face of change and tumult all around.   (*International Herald Tribune*, "Fear and Rejection," 2005)

And the *Financial Times* had a similar take:

Europe in the guise of the EU does not matter. Old Europe is dying ... France and Germany are better left to sink into their self-dug economic mire ... It embraces all the insecurities that have led to the disenchantment of voters: from unemployment and strained welfare systems to immigration and cultural cohesion ... Europe's leaders have lost the Union's narrative.   (Stephens 2005a)

And the *Economist* drew upon the standard metanarrative that the EU was simply too difficult for regular people to understand:

The complexity of its laws and institutions helped, by blurring popular understanding of what the Union did, and thus allowing both admirers and critics to make exaggerated claims about its power. Now the daylight is streaming in on Europe, and the magic has gone ... This is the trend that used to be called, disparagingly, "Europe a la carte", meaning the freedom for countries to pick and choose between the projects they wanted to join and the commitments they wanted to make within the Union. Once countries were allowed to diverge in some things, the argument went, they would diverge in all things, and the Union would break up altogether.
                    (*The Economist*, "Survey: Meet the Neighbours," 2005)

Even though the media had already amplified the sense of impending failure in the lead-up to ratification, political elites were still relatively shocked when it actually became a reality, especially because the "no" came from two founding-member countries (Lu 2008: 431). In frustration, European Commission President Barroso said to EU leaders, "If you attack Brussels six days of the week, can you really expect citizens to support it on Sunday?" (Minder 2005). He added that the outcome now risked "a permanent crisis and paralysis" of the EU (Parker 2005a). Leaders across Europe became serious about addressing the root cause of what they saw as an unexpected outcome. In many EU member states, but especially Germany, France, and the Netherlands, there was a tendency to turn inward and to reflect on the problems within, such as the economy, the aging population, the decline of the welfare state, and the negative effects of globalization. As the *Economist* reported:

The French have many reasons to reject the constitution, but underlying their defiance was a simple point: times are hard, jobs are scarce, nothing changes, promises go unkept, we are fed up, and you – the political class – refuse to listen.
                    (*The Economist*, "It's Chirac, Stupid," 2005)

Thus, both elites and the public asked themselves: What is Europe? Who is Europe? Where is Europe going? Admitting to a sense of helplessness was part of this discourse (Schmit 2005).

In conclusion, the socially constructed aspect of this crisis is clearly visible in the paradoxical fact that the majority of EU citizens – including those in France and the Netherlands – initially supported the Constitutional Treaty. The rationale behind the eventual French and Dutch "no" had little to do with the treaty's actual substance. Instead, the negative outcome was the result of an intensifying crisis narrative predicting failure, alongside the sharpening of preexisting public–elite tensions. In effect, the negative referenda were a direct result of the self-fulfilling prophecy dynamic of integrational panic.

From Crisis to Opportunity

The end of June 2005 marked the decline of the crisis and the beginning of a period of crisis resolution. The intensity of the crisis narrative weakened precipitously shortly after the initial reaction. After all, it rapidly became clear that this was not to be the "end of Europe" that so many had foreseen. The expectation had been that a rejection would plunge the EU into the biggest crisis it had faced since its founding. As Maurizio Carbone put it, the "predicted lethal effects, however, failed to materialize" (Carbone 2009: 44 as cited in Phinnemore 2013: 18). Despite the strong crisis narrative that had consolidated around the ratification process of the Constitutional Treaty, the mood shortly after the height of the crisis could be summed up as "life goes on." Around this time, German Chancellor Gerhard Schröder said that the French "no" was "a blow for the constitutional process, but not the end of it. It is also not the end of the German-French partnership in and for Europe" (Sciolino 2005). Juncker, Barroso, and European Parliament President Josep Borrell together issued a joint statement that "Europe has known difficult moments before and each time it has emerged stronger" (Parker and Dombey 2005). In France, Chirac stayed in office but replaced Prime Minister Jean-Pierre Raffarin with Dominique de Villepin. He also gave Villepin's previous position as Minister of the Interior to Nicolas Sarkozy. But essentially, the main leadership cadre was still intact after the crisis. At the EU level, there was ultimately little impact at all. It was still business as usual, although at first there was a sense of enlargement fatigue, treaty fatigue, and a feeling that the integration process had to be reevaluated (Paris-Dobozy 2008: 509).

On June 16–17, 2005, member states agreed at the European Council on a *Declaration by the Heads of State or Government of the Member States of the European Union on the Ratification of the Treaty Establishing a Constitution for Europe*, calling for a period of reflection during which a broad debate could take place. The ratification process even continued for some time after the failed French and Dutch referenda, and the subsequent decline of integrational panic. In total, eighteen member states actually ratified the Constitutional Treaty. In the end, only France and the Netherlands rejected it, as the remaining five member states had suspended their ratification processes.

There are two main ways in which Europeans found new consensus, and even renewed will for integration, in the wake of the constitutional crisis: (1) the signing of the Lisbon Treaty and (2) the strengthening of the European public sphere. And although the former implemented most of the changes that had originally been part of the Constitutional Treaty, it was the latter development that was perhaps the more significant of the two.

During the so-called reflection period, EU leaders resolved to craft a new plan for a treaty that would be very similar to the failed constitution, but would not replace all existing treaties. This decision is significant because at that point it would have been easy and even understandable for them to abandon the ideas put forth in the Constitutional Treaty. Instead, European leaders used this failure and the crisis surrounding it to find a way to move the EU toward more integration. The determination to move forward also reflects the fact that the negative referenda were not based on any significant or real problems with the treaty itself. The result was the Reform Treaty, later renamed the Lisbon Treaty, which was signed in December 2007 and implemented in December 2009.

On the surface, it may seem that more integration was *not* achieved. After all, the Lisbon Treaty dropped the language of statehood, such as "minister" or "ministries," as well as references to some of the symbols of statehood, such as a European anthem, flag, and national holiday. But aside from this, the innovations of the Lisbon Treaty were nearly identical to those of the Constitutional Treaty, demonstrating the renewed desire for consensus and further integration post-crisis.[21] The biggest steps forward in terms of integration were in the foreign policy area.

---

[21] For a detailed overview of what is entailed in the Lisbon Treaty, see Craig (2010); Blanke and Mangiameli (2012); and Phinnemore (2013).

Some of the provisions included the creation of a post equivalent to EU foreign minister, who would be in charge of a new, supranational diplomatic service, with around 140 embassies around the world. The Lisbon Treaty scrapped the system of the rotating presidency in favor of a "permanent president" of the European Council with a five-year term. It contained a mutual defense clause and solidarity clause, and it enabled groups of member states that desired even more integration to engage in permanent structured cooperation. It got rid of the old pillar system of the Maastricht Treaty and brought Justice and Home Affairs fully into the area of supranationalism. In terms of effect on the regular public, the treaty formalized a Charter of Fundamental Rights, guaranteed European citizenship, and created a Citizen's Initiative, which allows one million citizens to bring policy proposals to the Commission. Thus, newfound consensus enabled all of these provisions, among others, to be launched even after the failure of the Constitutional Treaty. As I describe in Chapter 2, this did not necessarily have to happen. Leaders may have just as easily chosen to roll back or freeze integration. But the integrational panic, existential crisis, release of tensions, and catharsis that followed paved the way for the success of the Lisbon Treaty.

Despite these major advances, the most significant area of renewed integration was not actually at the formal treaty level, but at the societal level. It is important to recognize that at the start of the treaty-making process – the 2001 Laeken Declaration – EU citizens were not very interested in integration or the policy-making processes happening in Brussels. This apathy was so apparent that it was largely what motivated leaders to hold a Constitutional Convention in the first place. As I will elaborate upon in the next section on catharsis, by the time Europe entered its post-referenda reflection period in mid-2005, the European public had transformed: it was politically engaged, EU issues were increasingly visible and salient, and average citizens were far more involved in debating EU issues as part of domestic politics (Statham and Trenz 2013).[22] Moreover, since 2006, it is clear that the European Parliament and Commission have purposefully worked toward encouraging more public engagement through various new policies.

---

[22] It is true that some scholars have been less ready to see this as a true flourishing of democratic participation. Thomas Christiansen, for example, argues that it did not become the "deliberative forum" that leaders had hoped to create, but still, "the political class within member states did become engaged in an unprecedented way" (Christiansen 2005: 16–33).

In short, the EU came out of this crisis more integrated than ever, and the tensions characterizing the divide between the elites and general citizenry became far less prominent. Representing newfound consensus across Europe, there was a sense that the Lisbon Treaty would serve Europe well for some time to come. And yet, the main integrational effect of the crisis was at the societal level, a product of post-crisis catharsis.

Catharsis

The process of airing public–elite tensions – openly and far more frankly than ever before – enabled Europeans to renew their will for continued integration. If catharsis did indeed occur as a result of the constitutional crisis, we would expect to see a diminution in public–elite tensions. That is, the public should feel more positive about national and European leaders post-crisis.

Most scholars' assessments of the EU after this crisis argue that the public remained disgruntled and continued to see elites as out of touch, particularly since the 2009 Lisbon Treaty was approved and entered into force without much formal public participation. Fossum and Menéndez write, "The whole undertaking reeked of cloning of a legal kind because the new draft was close to a replica of the Constitutional Treaty . . . largely the same substance but in the form of a nonconstitutional treaty in a secretive process of intergovernmental negotiations" (Fossum and Menéndez 2011: 6–7). Vivien Schmidt describes increasing EU decision-making authority during this period as making "policy without politics" (Schmidt 2006: 5).

Of course, catharsis is not synonymous with democratization. As explained in Chapter 2, it is about moving forward after releasing societal tensions. The direction of that forward movement is not predetermined, but it should reflect in this case a sense that public–elite tensions were less severe after the crisis than they were before it began. The question of democracy is related to this but is not the same. Thus, the focus here is more on whether the public felt more at ease with what elites were doing post-crisis rather than whether elites were *actually* taking greater democratic steps. The latter approach would be, after all, analyzing a much more complex issue that extends beyond the effect of the crisis itself.

One aspect of post-crisis catharsis is paradoxical in that it stemmed from the actual failure to pass the Constitutional Treaty. As Fossum and Menéndez write, "[I]t *affirmed in the negative*, the democratic character of the procedure of treaty reform" (Fossum and Menéndez 2011: 159). Paul Statham and Hans-Jörg Trenz similarly argue that "the emergence of a public dissensus over integration is not damaging but potentially enhancing for democratic legitimacy, because it transforms debates over Europe into the stuff of 'normal politics'" (Statham and Trenz 2013: 80). Thus, the negative referenda should not be interpreted solely as a failure for Europe. If the "no" votes are taken at face value, the message is that a bottom-up approach to democracy in the EU is increasingly necessary. A democratic process occurred in which the result could have gone either way, and the outcome showed that the people had spoken. This is desirable when it comes to legitimizing the European construction. Anca Pusca writes, "EU citizens became increasingly aware of their democratic power" as a result of the constitutional crisis (Pusca 2009: 3).

As mentioned previously, another important aspect of post-crisis catharsis stems from the debate over the impact of the failed Constitutional Treaty. Statham and Trenz argue that the crisis (i.e., the failed votes) served as a catalyst for the genesis of European politicization (Statham and Treanz 2013). They find that there was a constriction of European public spheres during the ratification phase, and in the immediate wake of the negative referenda (i.e., when member states began to look inward). But as the crisis atmosphere began to dissipate, the European public became much more aware of the EU's many dimensions. And elites, for their part, realized that public acceptance of new reforms (even with the Lisbon Treaty, which was initially rejected in the Irish referendum) could not be counted upon as automatic.

Numerous studies show that there was an emerging public sphere even before the constitutional crisis – enabled significantly by the 2003 Iraq crisis for Europe (see Chapter 3) – but it was not one that had developed enough for citizens to start building a shared value system in a sustained way.[23] Chien-Yi Lu argues, for example, that even though the Constitutional Convention featured one of the most large-scale and sustained efforts to involve the public in open deliberations, this dialogue ultimately did not achieve its goals because of the lack of a true European public sphere (Lu 2008: 431–451). Lu finds that information about the EU was "flat" in that details about the treaty were certainly disseminated, but there is little evidence that these communications were received and then

---

[23] For more on the nature of the European public sphere, see Eriksen and Fossum (2000); Risse (2000); Trenz and Eder (2004).

debated in a way that transcended national borders. Indeed, before and during the buildup of the constitutional crisis, Lu argues, there was still a level of apathy on the part of EU citizens toward the EU. To the extent that discussions were taking place, it was mostly at the elite level.

However, there was a visible strengthening of the European public sphere during the period after the negative referenda (Risse 2010; Statham and Trenz 2013). Some described this as "the great debate," which would include citizens, parliaments, political parties, social groups, and civil society in reflections on the future of Europe as well as the sources of tension that rose to the surface during the Constitutional Treaty ratification process (Duff 2005: 191). Despite the conflict that the constitutional crisis sparked, European citizens and leaders were debating the future of Europe across national boundaries, and this was ultimately a positive development for the EU's legitimacy. Right after the negative referenda, the vast majority of voters in France and the Netherlands believed that the treaty could be renegotiated as it was. In France, 83 percent of "no" voters and 62 percent of the overall population believed this to be a possibility, and in the Netherlands, 71 percent of "no" voters and 66 percent of the total population concurred (Flash Eurobarometer 171: 25–26; Flash Eurobarometer 172: 23–24).

The crisis also provided a new impetus for enhancing and strengthening the Europeanization of national public spheres. In France, citizens were clearly now more politicized when it came to European issues as a result of the referendum experience, and the main political parties were now bringing EU policies much more into national debates (Paris-Dobozy 2008: 515). Similarly, in other member states, European issues significantly increased in debates among national political parties (Hooghe and Marks 2009). Liesbet Hooghe and Gary Marks find that Europe became much more salient among citizens than it was in the past, and that European publics seemed to have gained a deeper knowledge of EU issues (Hooghe and Marks 2009). At the European level, the Parliament and Commission also emphasized the need to bring the EU into national debates on a far wider scale than in the past. Statham and Trenz argue that more links emerged between political elites and the general public, especially through mass communication processes (Statham and Trenz 2013: 149). The Commission launched plan D (for Democracy, Dialogue, and Debate) in October 2005 to encourage this process. Considering that one significant aspect of the "no" votes was citizens' lack of understanding of the real purpose of the Constitutional Treaty, such a flourishing of public dialogue about the EU is indicative of a kind of post-crisis catharsis.

TABLE 4.2 *Trends in Attitudes Toward the EU*

	Satisfaction with EU Democracy	Your Country's Membership in the EU Is a "Good Thing"	Your Country Has Benefited from EU Membership
Spring 2004	43%	48%	47%
Spring 2005	49%	54%	55%
Spring 2006	50%	55%	54%
Autumn 2009	54%	53%	57%

If citizens had a better understanding of the substance of the Lisbon Treaty compared to the Constitutional Treaty, the effect can be seen as even stronger.

What about public–elite tensions? Did they diminish post-crisis? Eurobarometer polls show that satisfaction with EU democracy from spring 2004 to autumn 2009 steadily increased across Europe. This was demonstrably so even in the countries where the constitutional referendum had failed. In the Netherlands, those who responded that they were satisfied with EU democracy started at 36 percent in spring 2004, rose to 47 percent in spring 2006, and increased even further to 53 percent in autumn 2009, when the Lisbon Treaty went into effect. In France, public views on whether EU membership was a good thing started at 43 percent in spring 2004 and rose to 60 percent in autumn 2007. In the Netherlands, spring 2004 polls showed 64 percent saying EU membership was a good thing, and this number reached 79 percent in autumn 2007. In response to the question of whether their country has benefited from EU membership, 46 percent were affirmative in France in spring 2004 and 57 percent felt this way in autumn 2007. In the Netherlands, polls on the same question were 55 percent affirmative in spring 2004 and 74 percent in autumn 2007. And as Table 4.2 indicates, these sorts of steadily increasingly positive responses can be seen across the whole EU. Autumn 2009 is also included in this table as it provides a longer-term perspective, and because this was the period during which the Lisbon Treaty was approved.

Another important question to consider in opinion polls is support or lack of support for the *idea* of a European constitution (Table 4.3). This question was asked in a more concentrated period of time. The autumn 2005 Eurobarometer poll, which was conducted across all of Europe after

TABLE 4.3 *Support for the* Idea *of a European Constitution**

	Spring 2004	Autumn 2004	Spring 2005	Autumn 2005
Austria	60%	67%	47%	49%
Belgium	72%	81%	76%	77%
Cyprus	69%	74%	73%	72%
Czech Republic	48%	63%	44%	50%
Denmark	37%	44%	42%	45%
Estonia	54%	64%	52%	49%
Finland	52%	58%	47%	49%
France	62%	70%	60%	67%
Germany	68%	79%	68%	74%
Greece	66%	69%	60%	68%
Hungary	75%	62%	78%	76%
Ireland	59%	61%	54%	58%
Italy	78%	73%	74%	70%
Latvia	57%	61%	56%	57%
Lithuania	52%	73%	64%	65%
Luxembourg	75%	77%	63%	69%
Malta	59%	56%	50%	60%
Netherlands	70%	73%	53%	62%
Poland	65%	73%	61%	60%
Portugal	57%	61%	59%	63%
Slovakia	65%	71%	60%	64%
Slovenia	68%	80%	76%	74%
Spain	70%	72%	63%	62%
Sweden	53%	50%	38%	44%
UK	42%	49%	43%	46%
EU-25	63%	68%	61%	63%

* Standard Eurobarometer 61, 62, 63, and Candidate Countries Eurobarometer 2004.1.
It is important to note that there was a relatively high number of "don't know" responses, and so it should not be assumed that the remaining percentages were opposed to the idea of a constitution. Although not displayed in this table, the figure for Spring 2006 was 61 percent in support.

the failed French and Dutch referenda, showed strong support for the *idea* of a European constitution: 63 percent compared to 21 percent who opposed the idea (Standard Eurobarometer Autumn 2005: 23). Moreover, at the time, this poll showed that "support for the idea of a constitution is now more widespread in France and the Netherlands than it was in Spring 2005." Indeed, just a few months after the negative vote in France, support for the EU constitution in France actually exceeded the EU's already high average (Standard Eurobarometer Autumn 2005: 24).

This suggests that the catharsis effect was relatively strong in France, and also lends weight to the argument that the outcome of the referendum in France was based on short-term concerns that became prominent in the crisis narrative, rather than any longer-term structural cause or dissatisfaction with the EU or the process of further integration. Francesca Vassallo concludes that "support for Europe in France in 2005 seemed to be hijacked by temporary concerns, misplaced interpretations and a short-term amnesia of what voters were really assessing with the popular consultation" (Vassallo 2008: 421–422). In the Spring 2006 Eurobarometer, support for each country's membership in the EU went up by an average of 5 percent, while in all but three of the countries in the union – Finland (26 percent), the UK (25 percent), and Austria (24 percent) – the negative response came in at 20 percent or below (Standard Eurobarometer First Results Spring 2006: 9).

CONCLUSION

As we have seen, the Constitutional Treaty did not necessarily have to become a full-blown crisis for Europe. More often than not, EU treaties do not go through a smooth ratification process. Nearly all have suffered from failed referenda before they were eventually approved, even the Lisbon Treaty itself. Any explanation of this crisis and its ramifications for the trajectory of European integration must include an examination of narratives at the time. In the case of the Constitutional Treaty, the narrative about the upcoming referenda had become so pessimistic, particularly in the media and among elites, that the stakes were perceived to be very high. In the process, the fate of this one treaty became interwoven with perceptions about the fate of the EU itself, equating the possibility of the former's failure with the downfall of the latter's very existence. Before the referenda in France and the Netherlands had even taken place, integrational panic had set in. Predictions were dire, which helped bring preexisting tensions to the surface. As a result, in the final days, as the French and Dutch were ready to take to the polls, a self-fulfilling prophecy of the treaty's rejection was all but inevitable. In general, we know that voters in referenda, as opposed to in elections, are not as certain about how they are going to vote and are less swayed by party affiliation (Hobolt and Brouard 2011: 309). In this crisis, voters by and large made up their minds at the last minute, in the midst of a vocal and sharply controversial narrative that swayed them rather suddenly in a more negative direction.

Indeed, the main crisis narrative and the reasons for how people voted had little to do with the terms of the treaty itself. Despite the negative result, overwhelming majorities in both countries still supported EU membership, and even the idea of a constitution. Thus, it is important to recognize the socially constructed nature of this crisis, especially at its height. The treaty did not fail because of anything inherent about its terms nor did it fail because of widespread agreement that more Europe was a bad thing. While French socialists argued that the constitution was too "Anglo-Saxon" and free-market oriented, British Euroskeptics criticized it for being too socialist, federalist, and "French." Neither of these two views reflected the substance of the treaty. The debate over the referenda became an excuse to air preexisting tensions between publics and elites, contributing to the buildup of integrational panic.

As the crisis narrative began to weaken in the wake of the failed referenda, there was a general sense of catharsis. In France, "[p]recisely because it *did* produce a sense of crisis and has required that serious political attention be paid to the voices of popular disaffection and alienation from the EU, the French 'no' vote provoked an acute sense of urgency about the European construction and started the interesting process of involving the citizens in the arena of European politics" (Paris-Dobozy 2008: 519). Thus, with crisis came opportunity. The ability to air public–elite tensions more bluntly than ever before enabled societal catharsis to take place. The newfound consensus that subsequently led to agreement on the Lisbon Treaty, as well as to the flourishing of the European public sphere, shows the extent to which the release of tensions during the crisis opened up a path to move forward. We must remember that crises like these do not necessarily have to end with more consensus and integration. Indeed, the narrative about the "death" of Europe had reached a peak at the height of the crisis and was even beginning to play a role as a self-fulfilling prophecy. And yet, as in the case of the Iraq crisis, the EU persisted and was in the end arguably stronger than ever.

References

Adams, Christopher. 2004. "MacShane Urges 'more Ministers for Europe.'" *Financial Times*, London first edition, November 17.

Arnold, Martin, Peggy Hollinger, and John Thornhill. 2005. "High Turnout Reflects Deeply Divided Electorate in France." *Financial Times*, London second edition, May 30.

Bernstein, Richard. 2005. "Charter for the European Union Meets Resistance." *International Herald Tribune*, New York, May 22.

Bickerton, Ian. 2005a. "Dutch Find 20 Reasons to Reject EU Treaty." *Financial Times*, London first edition, June 2.

Bickerton, Ian. 2005b. "Dutch to Launch Yes Vote Offensive." *Financial Times*, London first edition, April 19.

Bickerton, Ian. 2005c. "Fears Grow That Dutch Voters Will Turn Down EU Treaty Referendum on Constitution." *Financial Times*, London first edition, April 12.

Blanke, Hermann-Josef and Steilo Mangiameli. 2012. *The European Union after Lisbon: Constitutional Basis, Economic Order and External Action*. Berlin: Springer.

Búrca, Gráinne de. 2006. "The European Constitution Project after the Referenda," *Constellations* 13(2): 206.

Buttiglione, Rocco. 2004. "EU Vote Is an Attack on Berlusconi, Says Italy." *Financial Times*, London first edition, October 13.

Carbone, Maurizio. 2009. "From Paris to Dublin: Domestic Politics and the Treaty of Lisbon," *Journal of Contemporary European Research* 5(1): 43–60.

Christiansen, Thomas. 2005. "The EU Reform Process: From the European Constitution to the Lisbon Treaty." In *National Politics and European Integration: From the Constitution to the Lisbon Treaty*, edited by Maurizio Carbone. Northampton, MA: Edward Elgar, pp. 16–33.

Craig, Paul. 2010. *The Lisbon Treaty: Law, Politics, and Treaty Reform*. Oxford: Oxford University Press.

Crum, Ben. 2012. *Learning from the EU Constitutional Treaty: Democratic Constitutionalization beyond the Nation-State*. Milton Park, Abingdon, Oxon: Routledge.

Crum, Ben. 2006. "Party Stances in the Referendums on the EU Constitution: Causes and Consequences of Competition and Collusion," *European Union Politics* 8(1): 63.

Crum, Ben. 2008. *The EU Constitutional Process: A Failure of Political Representation?*. RECON Online Working Paper.

D'Atena, Antonio. 2012. "The European Constitution's Prospects." In *The European Union after Lisbon: Constitutional Basis, Economic Order and External Action*, edited by Hermann-Josef Blanke and Stelio Mangiameli. Heidelberg: New York, pp. 3–79.

Dehousse, Renaud. 2006. "The Unmaking of a Constitution: Lessons from the European Referenda," *Constellations* 13(2): 151–164.

Duff, Andrew. 2005. *The Struggle for Europe's Constitution*. London: I.B. Tauris.

The Economist. 2005. "A Tale of Two Couples." June 2.

The Economist. 2005. "Books and Arts: An Optimist's View; The European Union." February 26.

The Economist. 2005. "Europe: Putting the Clog In." May 21.

The Economist. 2005. "Europe: The Great Unraveling." April 23.

The Economist. 2005. "Europe: The Triumph of Perfidious Albion." June 2.

The Economist. 2005. "Europe: Vote Early, Vote Often; The European Union Constitution." February 26.

The Economist. 2005. "France and the EU: A Severe Crisis D'identité." May 26.

The Economist. 2005. "It's Chirac, Stupid." June 2.

The Economist. 2005. "Leaders: Outlook: Gloomy; The European Union." April 2.

The Economist. 2005. "Survey: Meet the Neighbours." June 25.

The Economist. 2005. "The Europe That Died: And the One That Should Live On." June 2.

Elliot, Michael. 2005. "The Decline and Fall of Rome." *Time*, June 5.

Epstein, Richard. 2004. "The Dangers of a Contradictory Constitution." *Financial Times*, London first edition, October 11.

Eriksen, Erik O. and John Erik Fossum. 2000. *Democracy in the European Union – Integration through Deliberation*. London: Routledge.

European Commission. 2005. *The Future Constitutional Treaty: First Result*. Report.

Financial Times. 2005. "After the Votes," London third edition. June 3.

Financial Times. 2005. "Chirac Does Battle for the Constitution," London first edition. April 12.

Financial Times. 2005. "Danes Set Date for EU Constitution Vote: September Referendum," London first edition. March 1.

Financial Times. 2005. "Dutch Premier Hits at Treaty Opponents," London first edition. April 29.

Financial Times. 2005. "France's Fears." April 18.

Financial Times. 2004. "Straw Warns on Rejection of EU Constitution Treaty," London third edition. December 8.

Fischer, Joschka. 2000. "From Confederacy to Federation – Thoughts on the Finality of European Integration." Speech, Humboldt University, Berlin, May 12.

Flash Eurobarometer 171. 2005. "The European Constitution Post-referendum Survey in France." May 30–31, Publication June.

Flash Eurobarometer 172. 2005. "The European Constitution: Post-referendum Survey in The Netherlands." June 2–4, Publication June.

Fossum, John E. and Agustín José Menéndez. 2011. "From Laeken to Lisbon: Moving Beyond Synthesis or Heightened Constitutional Ambiguity?" In *The Constitution's Gift: A Constitutional Theory for a Democratic European Union*. Lanham, MD: Rowman & Littlefield Publishers.

Fossum, John E. and Agustín José Menéndez. 2011. *The Constitution's Gift: A Constitutional Theory for a Democratic European Union*. Plymouth, UK: Rowman & Littlefield Publishers.

Fossum, John E. and Agustín José Menéndez. 2005. "The Constitution's Gift: A Deliberative Democratic Analysis of Constitution Making in the European Union," *European Law Journal* 11(4): 380–440.

Gamble, Andrew. 2006. "The European Disunion," *British Journal of Politics and International Relations* 8: 35.

Glencross, Andrew and Alexander Treschsel. 2011. "First or Second Order Referendums? Understanding the Votes on the EU Constitutional Treaty in Four EU Member States," *West European Politics* 34(4): 755–772.

Gloom, Brian. 2004. "Kohl Voices Fears over Turkey EU Entry." *Financial Times*, London third edition, November 22.

Grant, Charles. 2005. "What Happens if Britain Votes No?" *Center for European Reform*, March.

Hobolt, Sara B., and Sylvain Brouard. 2011. "Contesting the European Union? Why the Dutch and the French Rejected the European Constitution," *Political Research Quarterly* 6(2): 309–322.

Hollinger, Peggy and John Thornhill. 2005. "Chirac's Record on Europe Hampers Yes Campaign." *Financial Times*, London first edition, April 15.

Hooghe, Liesbet and Gary Marks. 2009. "A Postfunctionalist Theory of European Integration: From Permissive Consensus to Constraining Dissensus," *British Journal of Political Science* 39(1): 1–23.

Howorth, Jolyon. 2007. *Security and Defence Policy in the European Union.* Houndmills: Palgrave.

International Herald Tribune. 2005. "Fear and Rejection," June 2.

Ivaldi, Gilles. 2006. "Beyond France's 2005 Referendum on the European Constitutional Treaty: Second-order Model, Anti-establishment Attitudes and the End of the Alternative European Utopia," *West European Politics* 29(1): 59.

Jabko, Nicolas. 2007. "The Constitution as a Repertoire: The Power and Limits of Symbolic Politics." Paper, Dalhousie University, Halifax, Canada, May 22.

Jones, Adam. 2005. "Polls Give Ray of Hope to French Yes Campaigners." *Financial Times*, London first edition, May 2.

Klingst, Martin. 2005. "Wer Auf Das Volk Nicht Hört." *Die Zeit*, June 2. Translated by Molly Krasnodebska.

Le Figaro. 2005. "Opinion Poll," May 10.

Legrain, Philippe. 2005. "French Myth-making." *Prospect*, July.

Lu, Chien-Yi. 2008. "Constitution-making and the Search for a European Public Sphere." In *The Rise and Fall of the EU's Constitutional Treaty*, edited by Finn Laursen. Leiden: Martinus Nijhoff Publishers, pp. 431–452.

Lubbers, Marcel. 2008. "Regarding the Dutch 'Nee' to the European Constitution: A Test of the Identity, Utilitarian, and Political Approaches to Voting 'No,'" *European Union Politics* 9(1): 59–86.

Maclay, Michael. 2005. "Hints for the Elite." *Prospect*, July.

Mazzucelli, Colette. 2008. "The French Rejection of the Constitutional Treaty." In *The Rise and Fall of the EU's Constitutional Treaty*, edited by Finn Laursen. Leiden and Boston: Martinus Nijhoff Publications, pp. 161–180.

Minder, Raphael. 2005. "MEPs Hit 'pause' Button on Out-of-tune Treaty." *Financial Times*, London second edition, June 9.

Moravcsik, Andrew. 2005. "Europe without Illusions: A Category Error." *Prospect*, July.

Moravcsik, Andrew. 2006. "What Can We Learn from the Collapse of the European Constitutional Project?" *Politische Vierteljahresschrift* 47(2): 219–241.

Munchau, Wolfgang. 2004. "An a La Carte Europe Is Likely to Split." *Financial Times*, London first edition, October 4.

Munchau, Wolfgang. 2005. "France's Electorate Could End European Integration." *Financial Times*, London first edition, April 11.

Nielson, Ramous L. 2008. "Everything Shall Now Be Popular: Explaining Elite Behaviour in the Constitutional Treaty Referenda." In *The Rise and Fall of the EU's Constitutional Treaty*, edited by Finn Laursen. Leiden and Boston: Martinus Nijhoff Publishers, pp. 453–477.

Paris-Dobozy, Marie-L. 2008. "The Implications of the 'No' Vote in France: Making the Most of a Wasted Opportunity." In *The Rise and Fall of the EU's Constitutional Treaty*, edited by Finn Laursen. Leiden: Martinus Nijhoff Publishers, pp. 497–523.

Parker, George. 2005a. "Budget Deadlock Fears Deepen Crisis Mood." *Financial Times*, London first edition, June 16.

Parker, George. 2005b. "Leader on a Mission to Resuscitate EU Dream." *Financial Times*, London first edition, June 6.

Parker, George, and Tobias Buck. 2005. "Brussels Fears Growing French Euroscepticism." *Financial Times*, London first edition, March 18.

Parker, George and Daniel Dombey. 2005. "EU Dreams Collide with French Antipathy, Brussels Reaction." *Financial Times*, London second edition, May 30.

Peel, Quentin. 2005a. "Britain Has Obligations to Europe." *Financial Times*, London second edition, May 5.

Peel, Quentin. 2005b. "France Cannot Have the Last Word." *Financial Times*, London first edition, May 26.

Peel, Quentin. 2005c. "The World Has a Distorted View of Europe." *Financial Times*, London first edition, January 27.

Phinnemore, David. 2013. *The Treaty of Lisbon: Origins and Negotiation.* New York: Palgrave.

Přibáň, Jiří. 2011. "Desiring a Democratic European Polity: The European Union Between the Constitutional Failure and the Lisbon Treaty." In *The European Union after Lisbon: Constitutional Basis, Economic Order, and External Action*, edited by Hermann-Josef Blanke and Steilo Mangiameli. Berlin: Springer, pp. 71–92.

Pusca, Anca M. 2009. *Rejecting the EU Constitution?: From the Constitutional Treaty to the Treaty of Lisbon.* New York: IDEBATE Press.

Qvortrup, Matt. 2006. "The Three Referendums on the European Constitution Treaty in 2005," *The Political Quarterly* 77(1): 89–97.

Risse, Thomas. 2010. *A Community of Europeans?: Transnational Identities and Public Spheres.* Ithaca, NY: Cornell University Press.

Risse, Thomas. 2000. "'Let's Argue!' Communicative Action in World Politics," *International Organization* 54(1): 1–39.

Schmidt, Vivien A. 2006. *Democracy in Europe: The EU and National Polities.* Oxford: Oxford University Press.

Schmit, Helmut. 2005. "Wir Brauchen Mut." *Die Zeit*, June 9.

Sciolino, Elaine. 2005. "French Voters Soundly Reject European Union Constitution." *International Herald Tribune*, New York, May 31.

Siedentop, Larry. 2005. "A Crisis of Legitimacy." *Prospect*, July.

Standard Eurobarometer 61, Spring. 2004. "Public Opinion in the European Union." Fieldwork February–March 2004. Published July 2004.

Standard Eurobarometer 62, Autumn. 2004. "Public Opinion in the European Union." Fieldwork October–November 2004. Published December 2004.

Standard Eurobarometer 63, Spring. 2005. "Public Opinion in the European Union." Fieldwork May–June 2005. Published July 2005.

Standard Eurobarometer 64, Autumn. 2005. "Public Opinion in the European Union." Fieldwork October–November 2005. Published December 2005.

Standard Eurobarometer 67, Spring. 2006. "Public Opinion in the European Union." Fieldwork May–June 2006. Published July 2006.

Statham, Paul, and Hans-Jörg Trenz. 2013. *The Politicization of Europe: Contesting the Constitution in the Mass Media.* Abingdon, Oxon: Routledge.

Stephens, Philip. 2005a. "Europe Cannot Afford to Retreat From the World." *Financial,* London first edition, June 10.

Stephens, Philip. 2004. "Europe Must Open Its Eyes and Look to the Future." *Financial Times,* London third edition, December 11.

Stephens, Philip. 2005b. "France Begins to Question the Rationale for Europe." *Financial Times,* London first edition, March 18.

Sutton, Alastair. 2005. "Treaty Establishing a Constitution for Europe: Impact of Negative Votes in the French and Dutch Referenda." *White paper,* White & Case.

Thornhill, John. 2004. "French Socialists Fight to Sway EU Future." *Financial Times,* London first edition, November 12.

Thornhill, John. 2005a. "Corruption Trial Deals Blow to Chirac Campaign." *Financial Times,* London second edition, March 22.

Thornhill, John. 2005b. "Draft Law Row Could Hit French Treaty Vote." *Financial Times,* London first edition, January 27.

Thornhill, John. 2005c. "France Grapples with Ghosts over the Referendum Vote." *Financial Times,* London first edition, April 30.

Thornhill, John. 2005d. "French No Campaigners Say Love for Europe Is Their Principal Driving Force." *Financial Times,* London third edition, April 15.

Thornhill, John. 2005e. "French No Would Lead to Fall of Europe, Says Prodi." *Financial Times,* London first edition, April 25.

Thornhill, John. 2005f. "Many Voters in Next Month's Referendum Are Disenchanted with Their Leaders." *Financial Times,* London first edition, April 6.

Thornhill, John. 2005g. "Rejection of Treaty Would Cause Break Down, Chirac Warns." *Financial Times,* London second edition, May 27.

Thornhill, John. 2005h. "The Yes Camp Looks Frailer than in 1992." *Financial Times,* London first edition, May 26.

Thornhill, John, and George Parker. 2005. "An Unhappy Union." *Financial Times,* London first edition, April 27.

Time. 2004. "A Party Divided." November 28.

Time. 2005. "Winner Takes All." February 27.

Trenz, Hans-J. and Klaus Eder. 2004. "The Democratizing Dynamics of a European Public Sphere," *European Journal of Social Theory* 7(1): 5–25.

Vassallo, Francesca. 2008. "The Failed EU Constitution Referendums: The French Case in Perspective, 1992–2005." In *The Rise and Fall of the EU's Constitutional Treaty,* edited by Finn Laursen. Leiden and Boston: Martinus Nijhoff Publishers, pp. 411–430.

Vetters, Regina. 2009. "Just Another Missed Opportunity in the Development of a European Public Sphere: The European Constitutional Debate in German, British, and French Broadsheets." In *Media, Democracy, and European Culture,* edited by Ib Bondebjerg and Peter Madsen. Bristol, UK: Intellect, pp. 157–176.

Weiler, Joseph. 1999. *The Constitution for Europe.* Cambridge: Cambridge University Press.

Wolf, Martin. 2005. "The Crushing Reality of Making the Eurozone Work." *Financial Times*, London first edition, June 8.

Wolinetz, Steven B. 2008. "Trimming the Sails: The Dutch and the EU Constitution after the Referendum." In *The Rise and Fall of the EU's Constitutional Treaty*, edited by Finn Laursen. Leiden and Boston: Martinus Nijhoff Publishers, pp. 181–200.

Zowislo-Grünewald, Natascha. 2008. "On Europe's Representation: A Symbolic Interpretation of Rejecting the Constitution." *PS: Political Science & Politics* 41(30): 551–555.

5

The Eurozone Crisis

INTRODUCTION

EU member states have spent many decades crafting an "ever closer union," particularly in the economic and monetary area.[1] They have largely followed a strategy of gradualism, creating close targets, and maintaining flexibility in achieving them (Dinan 2013). Indeed, there had long been little reason for an urgent pace of integration as this measured approach had worked well going back to the 1957 launch of the European Economic Community, a precursor to the EU. The 1992 Maastricht Treaty marked an important step in this gradual consolidation as it created both a monetary union and an economic union. The former meant the establishment of an independent European Central Bank, with a mandate to ensure price stability. The latter was purposefully left less developed as EU leaders planned to strengthen the fledgling economic union over time. The Stability and Growth Pact was a key component of this and was further codified in 1997 when member states agreed to a ceiling of 3 percent fiscal public deficit and 60 percent public debt to GDP. Essentially, in keeping with their gradual pace of integration, EU member states launched a monetary union before "completing" their economic union.

The reason for this overarching gradualist strategy, instead of the wholesale establishment of a federalist economic union at the outset, was that there were certain obstacles in the way of completing the goal

---

[1] The phrase "ever closer union" comes from the preamble to the 1957 Treaty of Rome, which established the European Economic Community. Its meaning alludes to the idea that member states agree to achieve progressive political integration.

of a truly single market, and EU leaders knew that these would have to be overcome in stages. The remaining obstacles mainly boiled down to differences in the nature of Eurozone member states' economies, and attitudes toward the role of the EU and the single market. However, well aware of the remaining work to be done, those leaders who were committed to achieving monetary stability anticipated that economic growth and opportunity, alongside continued integration, would lead to convergence and eventual socialization toward similar attitudes.

In the years following the 1992 Maastricht Treaty, EU financial integration continued apace, unemployment fell, and the EU successfully achieved eastern enlargement. In 1999, when the euro began its existence as an accounting currency in world markets, EU leaders knew that it was still "unfinished business," and intended to stay on the path of their gradualist strategy (Alphandéry 2012; James 2012).[2] Indeed, they knowingly went forward with the common currency – formally launching it into circulation in 2002 – without full economic integration because they expected that the establishment of the euro would give a strong boost to commercial and economic exchange within the common market, and in turn, to economic growth (Marsh 2012: 3). This was no doubt true, and the euro performed well from 1999 to 2009, with stable price levels, a strong value on the foreign exchange, and favorable economic growth across the Eurozone (Alphandéry 2012: 3; Mayer 2012: 4). This growth was comparable to that of the United States during this period, averaging 2.1 percent per year (Buti, Deroose, Gaspar, and Martins 2010).[3]

When the global financial crisis of 2008–9 arrived on European shores, the EU's gradualist strategy, as well as the decade-long solid record for the euro and the single market, came under threat. The global financial crisis is obviously the context in which the Eurozone crisis occurred, but the emphasis in this chapter is on how this externally driven event influenced Europe. Specifically, the question I address is: why did the global financial crisis become an existential crisis for the EU?[4]

---

[2] Some have suggested that the monetary union could have worked as it was when it was originally launched, but they are generally in a minority. They might have been correct if it had not been for the global financial crisis, but it is difficult to know.

[3] The growth rate of GDP per capita over this period was more or less the same for the Eurozone and United States.

[4] Many scholars have correctly pointed out that beyond the financial dimension of the Eurozone crisis, there have been implications for the institutional and constitutional dimensions (Fossum 2014). The crisis has also affected the relationship between Eurozone and non-Eurozone member states. For the purposes of this chapter, I confine

This chapter begins with an analysis of the main perspectives on the origins of the Eurozone crisis, pointing out their strengths and limitations. The remainder of the chapter is then divided into two parts. In the first part, building on the existing debate, I argue that the Eurozone crisis cannot be fully understood without taking into account the socially constructed nature of it, and especially the role of the media in amplifying fears and contributing to a sense of integrational panic. In the lead-up to the global financial crisis, the only country that really had a serious solvency problem was Greece, and it only accounted for 2 percent of the entire Eurozone economy. Thus, there was no immediate reason why a liquidity crisis in a small country should give rise to a full-blown European crisis. Although the global financial crisis exposed the structural weaknesses in the monetary union, it is important to put this into perspective: all economies have their vulnerabilities, and as this chapter shows, the Eurozone was no worse than anyone else in this regard.

In the second part of this chapter, I explain how Europeans were able to turn this crisis into an opportunity to achieve major steps forward in integration and in the functioning of the common market. In the process, I show how the dominant crisis narrative during 2010–12 centered on preexisting North–South tensions in European society. These tensions, stemming mainly from differences in economic culture, had been present for decades, but for a variety of reasons intensified in the lead-up to the crisis. Although these tensions did not *cause* the crisis, the crisis became an excuse to speak openly about them in far more harsh terms. In resolving the crisis, the sense of catharsis that came with the open expression of these tensions ultimately underpinned EU leaders' ability to move forward with far-reaching agreements in economic integration. Several key steps, from increased Commission oversight to the creation of a banking union to a vastly more powerful European Central Bank, were a direct result of this crisis and would have been extremely difficult to achieve so quickly in the absence of crisis. I will argue that societal catharsis played no small role in enabling these innovations to be agreed upon as the worst of the crisis came to an end. Indeed, as will be shown, a clear convergence in North–South attitudes toward the EU provided some degree of legitimacy to this process, allowing it to go forward despite ongoing resistance to integration in some sectors of society.

my analysis to the core financial aspect of the Eurozone crisis and its impact on Eurozone member states.

Thus, the conclusion of this chapter is that the crisis enabled member states to overcome obstacles to integration that had existed previously. Of course, the effects of the Eurozone crisis will be felt for some time to come, given its widespread impact and severity, but the integrational panic and existential threat of the crisis significantly diminished in 2012. In that year, Europe stepped away from the brink. The North–South tensions that rose to the surface through the crisis narrative will also not go away entirely. But with catharsis, the punitive nature of these tensions is also much diminished. At the same time, post-crisis, the common governance of the euro has never been stronger. In some respects, as I will argue, the Eurozone economy is now even more integrated than that of the United States. And through all of the talk of the "end of Europe," EU industries as well as its commercial and financial sectors have remained highly competitive.

THE CAUSES OF THE EUROZONE CRISIS

Dozens of books, articles, and opinion pieces have been published about the buildup, intensification, and contagion effect of the Eurozone crisis. There is much debate over the precise causes of the crisis, and also sometimes a tendency to gloss over them. As Jason Manolopoulos argues, "We spend much time analyzing the fallout of economic crises, and devote insufficient attention to understanding the causes" (Manolopoulos 2011). Pradumna Rana also suggests that some analysts have found it difficult to distinguish between the symptoms of the crisis and the origins of it (Rana 2012). But failing to understand this can result in serious misjudgments about the causes of the crisis as well as faulty policy prescriptions, as happened in the Asian financial crisis of the late 1990s (Sachs 1997; Krugman 1998). In Asia, the International Monetary Fund (IMF) prescribed austerity when it should have injected liquidity, and this plunged the region into a deeper recession. Indeed, a similar miscalculation occurred in Europe some ten years later. This is why, on a broader level, it is important to fully understand the various dimensions of how the crisis came about.

With the benefit of hindsight, the debate surrounding the causes of the Eurozone crisis has ranged from big-picture to more specific explanations. One argument is that the global financial system with its emphasis on market fundamentalism is inherently flawed, and this is what made the financial crisis in Europe possible. A second argument is that the euro itself was a bad idea from the beginning and was inevitably heading toward crisis. And a third argument is that although the central economic problems were really centered on Greece, the crisis picked up momentum when a variety of other weaknesses rose to the surface in other member states, thus creating a general crisis of confidence in the European economy. These three perspectives are generally competing explanations, but it is not uncommon to find elements of all three in some accounts, with an emphasis on one or another. In outlining these three perspectives in some detail, I will explain how they are important, but still ultimately fall short in providing the full story. Nearly every explanation is structural in some way, and while scholars and experts have recognized that this was a crisis of confidence, there is little understanding of the process by which confidence was lost. After summarizing these various perspectives, I will shed light on this issue, and argue that an examination of crisis narratives is key. The effects of international media coverage, in particular, served to amplify a sense of integrational panic, leading to a contagion effect, which eventually threatened the viability of the entire Eurozone.

First Perspective: The Fundamental Flaws
of the Global Financial System

Some argue that the global financial system itself was deeply flawed and, by extension, the European monetary union has been vulnerable to this (Kouvelakis 2012). The argument is that the nature of the financial system has been deeply problematic since the Reagan–Thatcher era of the 1980s in which market fundamentalism – the belief that markets are naturally efficient if governments do not interfere – became the central philosophy guiding economic policy (Soros 2012: vii). This meant that any regulatory and supervisory structures that had been in place at the systemic level were gradually being dismantled. The US repeal of key elements of the 1933 Glass-Steagall Act was a significant part of this process in the 1990s, eliminating legal barriers between commercial banks, investment banks, securities firms, and insurance companies.[5] The Asian crisis of the late 1990s should have served as a warning cry for the problems with this ideology. As Pradumna Rana argues, "The root cause of the Asian crisis was the weaknesses of domestic banking sectors, which had recently been liberalized and encouraged to borrow from abroad" (Rana 2012).

---

[5] As a result of the Great Depression of the 1930s, these barriers were put up to prevent investment banks from gambling with the money depositors had put into commercial banks for safekeeping.

Without a strong regulatory framework in place, it then became possible for banks and investors to take on more risk, even without realizing it. In some cases, of course, big banks such as Goldman Sachs were well aware of the risk but structured their investments and rewards in such a way as to capitalize on it. Big bonuses to top bankers rewarded them for making risky choices. The name of the game became short-term profit, and the ability to take advantage of credit rating agencies – they were essentially paid to award specific rates – meant that exposure was high. Despite all of the signals, rating agencies were shockingly wrong in their predictions and had been relying on faulty models to come up with their ratings (Silver 2012: 20–23). In the absence of regulation and with the lack of effective rating-agency surveillance, banks made little effort to manage risk. In the end, there was widespread underpricing of risk, which led to low interest rates across the board, and increasing indebtedness.

Macroeconomic monetary policies around the world were also influenced by this lack of regulation and supervision, especially in the decade before the failure of Lehman Brothers. The availability of cheap credit from surplus-running countries and regions such as China, Russia, and the Middle East led to high levels of consumption in other places, especially in the real estate sector. Costas Lapavitsas et al. also describe a trend of *financialization* during the three decades before the financial crisis (Lapavitsas et al. 2012). This meant that large corporations across the globe became increasingly entrenched in financial markets, rather than using traditional banks as is more typical with smaller companies.

In short, this perspective argues that neoliberalism was the problem. The fundamental flaws in the global financial system eventually manifested themselves in the United States, the biggest culprit in advancing this ideology. The US quickly built up the largest current account deficit in the world (Central Intelligence Agency 2015). The culmination of such market fundamentalism was the buildup and collapse of the US mortgage market (Paulo 2011). Banks irresponsibly sold and repackaged subprime mortgages – loans given to home buyers not financially eligible for regular mortgages or primes – without labeling them as risky investments. The banks packaged these risky loans into "securities" so that the risk associated with default would be diluted by spreading it across many banks. But when the housing bubble burst and at the same time home buyers started to default on their mortgages, these securities served to do the opposite of their original intention: they spread this increased risk across multiple creditors, turning what had been meant as immunization into contagion, which put the entire financial system in danger. Next, trust among banks declined, so they reduced loans to each other and had to sell off assets, which led to falling prices of these assets, low liquidity, and eventually the threat of bankruptcy (Paulo 2011: 3–4). The US government ultimately bailed out several big banks and mortgage agencies, but in late 2008, it drew a line when it came to Lehman Brothers. This marked the point at which the US financial crisis brought global markets down with it.

According to this perspective, the domino effect just described constitutes the root causes of the Eurozone crisis. While some European banks with considerable transnational ties (such as Dexia and Fortis), were directly exposed to US subprime toxic assets, there were also multiple other channels through which many other banks were affected. The global financial and economic crisis impacted Europe as a kind of exogenous shock. The globalization of US problems meant that the US credit crunch spread throughout the world. With less credit available, small and medium enterprises suffered the consequences immediately. Global demand declined, harming export-oriented countries. The 2009 global contraction caused a significant collapse in governmental revenue in Eurozone countries – as it did in nearly all other countries around the world. With the need to uphold welfare commitments and other public responsibilities, governments had no choice but to increase public debt. This caused all of the members of the Eurozone to have to violate the Stability and Growth Pact at the same time.

While this argument is undoubtedly an accurate assessment of the big picture, and of the context and beginnings of what would become the Eurozone crisis, it does not offer a convincing explanation for why these systemic problems seemingly threatened the very existence of the euro and the EU. In particular, as will be described, global markets subsequently punished Eurozone countries with far greater borrowing costs and downgraded outlooks than they did other sovereign countries in similar situations (de Grauwe and Ji 2013: 15–36). If market fundamentalism were the full explanation, then we might have seen certain Eurozone countries suffer in the way Japan did, for example. But instead, the situation in Europe became much more dire.

Second Perspective: The Euro Was Always a Bad Idea

A second perspective – common among economists, some political scientists, and even some politicians – is that the root cause of the crisis for Europe was that the euro as a currency was fundamentally flawed (Eichengreen 2009; Kirkegaard 2011; Van Overtveldt 2011; Ash 2012; Bergsten 2012). As EU Council President Herman Van Rompuy said in 2010:

What went wrong wasn't what happened this year. What went wrong was what happened in the first eleven years of the Euro's history ... It was like some kind of sleeping pill, some kind of drug. We weren't aware of the underlying problems.

(Barber 2010)[6]

This perspective generally has two main strands: (1) that core and periphery member states were too imbalanced when they adopted the euro and (2) that the structure of the monetary union had built-in design problems.

The *first* strand of this argument focuses on the structural imbalances between "core" member states – such as Germany Austria, the Netherlands, and Finland – and "periphery" member states – Greece, Ireland, Italy, Portugal, and Spain.[7] When member states agreed to eliminate nominal exchange rates and adopt the common currency, the most basic difference was in terms of current accounts – the difference between a country's exports and imports (Van Overtveldt 2011: 80–82). EU member states adopted the euro despite these differences because they expected that periphery countries would eventually converge with core countries in terms of prices and wages, which would enable the monetary union to maintain its stability (Bonatti and Fracasso 2013: 1023). However, at the time of the global financial crisis, such uniformity had not yet been fully achieved. The argument is that periphery member states had high external deficits alongside strong growth, while core member states – especially Germany – were busy tackling serious reforms to their social security structures with restrictive monetary policy, resulting in lower growth. Peripheral countries garnered significant capital inflows, both from international investors and from core EU member states, and this helped to finance housing and credit booms. Since these periphery countries had access to so much credit, they did not focus on domestic structural reforms

---

[6] Although this quote captures the perspective well, Van Rompuy went on to say that it was actually the very strength of the euro that caused leaders to ignore the signs of weaknesses. He criticized the "rumors and prejudices" circulating in the financial markets and compared markets to "packs of wolves," a reference to Sweden's finance minister Anders Borg's earlier statement that Anglo-Saxon financial markets amounted to a *rabid* "pack of wolves." He argued that investors benefited from the creation of the euro, and then sought to benefit from its downfall. For him, the solution was stronger regulation, especially targeting rating agencies and derivatives markets.

[7] For an extensive account of these imbalances, see Marsh (2012).

that would lead to rapid convergence with the core. The result was that wages and prices increased quickly, domestic demand grew, and economies like Spain and Ireland boomed.

Meanwhile, core member states gained large external surpluses – they were exporting much more than they were importing – as they sold their goods and services to the periphery. In particular, since the mid-1990s, Germany had restructured industrial relations, and in the 2000s reformed its labor markets and social security system, in order to enable a smooth reunification with East Germany and to ensure that over the long term it could continue to be a major exporter and support its aging population (Bonatti and Fracasso 2013: 1027). In light of this restructuring, its growth was relatively low and wages relatively flat in the years leading up to the Eurozone crisis. Indeed, this low growth stood in such contrast to the rest of the European Union that Germany was often referred to as "the sick man of Europe" (Mayer 2012: 81).

According to this perspective, when the global financial crisis reached Europe, core countries and other international investors suddenly pulled out of periphery countries, undermining the favorable growth the latter had been experiencing. This quickly exposed the trade deficits, housing bubbles, private debt, and highly leveraged banks that constituted the vulnerabilities within this block of peripheral countries (Bonatti and Fracasso 2013: 1024). Thus, the argument is that core-periphery imbalances meant that the Eurozone was doomed to experience a severe crisis – if not total dissolution – from the start. It was only a matter of when.

The *second* major strand of this perspective focuses more on institutional design flaws in the initial setup of the monetary union. As with the previous strand, proponents of this view argue that a serious crisis of the euro currency was inevitable (Van Overtveldt 2011: 83; Ash 2012: 2). Frequently mentioned problems with the design of the monetary union include: (1) there was no common responsibility for public debt, (2) banking systems remained national while the monetary union was supranational, (3) there was seemingly no lender of last resort, and (4) there were only weak mechanisms for enforcing fiscal discipline.

With regard to the lack of common responsibility for public debt (Pisani-Ferry 2012: 4–5), Barry Eichengreen explains:

Opponents of monetary union founded their arguments on asymmetric shocks. They argued that adverse shocks affecting some members but not others were so prevalent that locking them into a single monetary policy was reckless. If those asymmetric shocks hit heavily-indebted countries, then the latter would also have no capacity to deploy fiscal policy in stabilising ways. Absent coping mechanisms like a system of inter-state transfers, the only option would be a grinding deflation and years of double-digit unemployment. (Eichengreen 2009)

Thus, the argument is that public debt was in the hands of the member states, with no way of preventing massive destabilization in the event of a financial crisis. Some have suggested that the EU budget should have been bigger, closer to 5 percent rather than 1 percent of combined GDP, to give the EU some leeway for dealing with such imbalances.

This argument is closely related to a second oft-mentioned design flaw in the monetary union: banking systems were kept national while the monetary union was supranational. This meant that national governments were still responsible for the cost of banking crises and rescues. And, at the same time, banks were vulnerable to large government debt holdings (Pisani-Ferry 2012: 6). This particular aspect made the EU distinctive because in other federations – such as the United States – banks do not hold huge amounts of government debt, and even so, there is little vulnerability because the Federal Reserve can intervene and is not responsible for state debt. The federal government in the United States can only rescue *banks*, not states (Pisani-Ferry 2012: 8). Thus, the design of the European monetary union meant that banks and governments were mutually intertwined and could take on significant amounts of public debt without an overarching body to make difficult decisions, such as intervening or allowing banks to fail. As an aside, the launch of the euro actually served to alleviate some of this risk because portfolios became more diversified with increasing cross-border investments.

A third argument with respect to institutional design flaws is that the monetary union lacked a lender of last resort. As a result, when the global financial crisis spread to Europe, markets overreacted to the growth of Eurozone debt. When the European Central Bank (ECB) was created as part of the monetary union, it was given a near monopoly on decision-making power to keep inflation at around 2 percent. But since there have long been standard economic principles and well-known rules on how to do this, there was no need for the ECB to actually make discretionary decisions. Member states simply delegated the limited power of controlling inflation to the ECB, and little else. Of course, as I will return to later in the chapter, this quickly changed during the course of the crisis as the ECB eventually took on huge discretionary choices. But according to this perspective here, it was the lack of a formal lender of last resort at the outset of the crisis that constituted a major weakness in the design of the monetary union.[8]

A fourth argument about the flaws in the monetary union is that the Stability and Growth Pact had no teeth, and thus during the first ten years of the monetary union, when the economy was strong, euro member states lacked fiscal discipline (Pisani-Ferry 2012: 3). The adoption of the euro meant that member states did not face external constraint in terms of their current accounts because they did not have to worry about keeping the value of their national currencies within a certain exchange rate. Thus, they were only disciplined from *within* the EU (Alphandéry 2012: 5). However, from 1999 to 2008, half of the original twelve euro countries exceeded EU deficit rules, including France and Germany, but were not sanctioned. Moreover, the Stability and Growth Pact does not apply to private sector debt. The argument is that once the EU decided to adopt a lax approach to maintaining fiscal discipline, the euro was potentially in trouble. This kind of reasoning led to an immediate policy of austerity in reaction to the Eurozone crisis. As Jean Pisani-Ferry summarizes, "The euro area in its first ten years suffered from a lack of fiscal discipline, while from the standpoint of sustainability of public finances good times were wasted, and the credibility of fiscal rules was compromised" (Pisani-Ferry 2012).

While the perspective that the setup of the euro was fundamentally flawed from the start is compelling in many ways, it nonetheless suffers from some weaknesses in terms of explaining the origins of the Eurozone crisis. For example, it does not address the timing of the crisis. It is no coincidence that these apparent core-periphery imbalances became a problem precisely when the effects of the collapse of Wall Street served as an exogenous shock to the European market. Thus, a counterfactual should be considered. Would the Eurozone crisis have happened in the absence of the US subprime mortgage crisis? Indeed, would it have happened *at all*, given that Eurozone leaders were well aware of the need to achieve further convergence and were gradually achieving it?

Arguably, no. It was not necessarily true that prices and wages had to converge across Eurozone member states to create a stable monetary union. Such an achievement might be ideal, but it has not been accomplished at all in another monetary union: the United States. Prices and wages differ vastly

---

[8] It should be noted that even though the United States had a lender of last resort – the Fed – this was not enough to prevent the Great Depression. Thus, too much weight should not be placed on the existence of a lender of last resort (Stiglitz 2003: 128–129).

across the United States, and yet it is a very stable monetary union. If the global financial crisis had *not* occurred, one would expect peripheral EU countries to continue developing and growing, pursuing external finance at the favorable rates they were already enjoying. Eventually, convergence might have been achieved without a crisis. But even in the absence of pressure from Brussels, member states might have still chosen to structure their economies differently (versus Germany's conservative socioeconomic model), and this would have not necessarily resulted in severe crisis.

When it comes to fiscal discipline, the US case actually looks worse in some ways. Before the crisis, many Americans rushed to buy houses they could not afford, thanks in large part to predatory lending practices by financial institutions that knew they could not afford them. Meanwhile, many Europeans were saving their income. Indeed, according to the OECD, household savings in the Eurozone amounted to 16 percent of available income, while in the United States, this same figure was less than 4 percent. As US deregulation flooded the global market with cheap consumer credit, only a few member states – mainly Portugal and Spain – took advantage of this, and even in these cases this was a far more recent development than had been the case across the Atlantic (Sales 2011: 2). Thus, the piling on of cheap credit was nowhere near as entrenched of a problem in Europe as it was in the United States.

With respect to core-periphery imbalances, although initially the Eurozone crisis seemed asymmetric in its impact, it soon became symmetric. The external economic shock meant that *all* European countries suffered from low growth. Thus, the argument that built-in asymmetries within the Eurozone caused the crisis falls short. As Jean Pisani-Ferry (2012) points out, the susceptibility of a member state breaking common deficit rules during these years has *absolutely no relationship* to its degree of suffering during the crisis. Similarly, Paul de Grauwe and Yuemei Ji find that the surge in spreads for the peripheral member states was in no way connected to the increases in debt-to-GDP ratios (from government bailouts of domestic banking systems) (de Grauwe and Ji 2013: 15–36). As evidence of this, Spain and Ireland never exceeded deficit targets before the crisis. In fact, their debt levels as a percentage of GDP even *declined* in the lead-up to the crisis (OECD 2015). And yet, they suffered some of the most difficult hardships during the Eurozone crisis. Both Greece and Italy had high levels of public debt pre-crisis, but while Greece spiraled into a nosedive, Italy fared relatively well, all things considered. Moreover, the United States, with its current account deficit of over $730 billion in 2007 (which has long been the highest in the world) (Central Intelligence Agency 2015), did not face declining

TABLE 5.1 *EU Member State Average
Annual Growth, 1999–2007 (Eurostat)*

	Growth of GDP
Austria	2.6%
Belgium	2.3%
Finland	3.6%
France	2.2%
Germany	1.7%
Greece	4.2%
Ireland	6.1%
Italy	1.5%
Netherlands	2.5%
Portugal	1.8%
Spain	3.7%

global confidence in its currency or significantly increased borrowing costs during the global crisis. Thus, there is little correlation between pre-crisis debt or deficit levels and the impact of the crisis on each country.

In particular, it is important to recognize that the differences between "core" and "periphery" member states were actually not so clear-cut. In the late 1990s, one could easily clump Germany and Italy together on the one hand, and the rest of the EMU countries on the other. As Thomas Mayer notes with respect to this period, "With the notable exceptions of Germany and Italy, growth in most countries of the Eurozone was buoyant and inflation extremely well behaved" (Mayer 2012: 81).[9] With the introduction of the euro, Germany's economic growth was only a little better than Italy's and actually worse than Portugal's. As shown in Table 5.1, Eurozone countries experienced levels of growth from 1999 to 2007 with no clear dividing line between the so-called core and periphery.

In sum, the various arguments about fundamental flaws in the setup of the monetary union are convincing insofar as they describe the limitations the EU had in trying to deal with the crisis once it had already come about. At the time, European leaders needed crisis management tools that were more centralized. But it is difficult to say that institutional design problems constituted the root cause of the crisis without understanding the strong impact of the crisis of *confidence* – widespread negative

[9] This conclusion is based on data from Eurostat, ECB, Haver Analytics, and Deutsche Bank Research.

perceptions, lack of understanding, and market overreactions – that plagued Europe from the start, as I will return to in the next section of the chapter.

Third Perspective: Greece as the Real Problem

A third prominent perspective that tries to explain the causes of the Eurozone crisis underlines the fact that each country that succumbed to the euro's crisis of confidence did so for different reasons. Thus, it was not as clear-cut as core versus periphery. This perspective recognizes Greece's economy as the main problem (Manolopoulos 2011) and argues that the issues that undermined the other countries' economies were distinctive in each case. Greece was affected more severely than other Eurozone countries because the country had a high budget deficit of 14 percent and public debt of 115 percent of GDP in 2009 (Eurostat). Moreover, it had managed to hide this growing debt problem from the European Commission during the preceding years, thanks in large part to help from some of the very people on Wall Street who had played a key role in bringing about the global financial crisis in the first place (Paulo 2011: 17).

Greece had enjoyed strong growth through the early 2000s, but its economy was vulnerable in that it was based largely on tourism, shipping, and agriculture. Tourism greatly increased during this period, and the demand for Greeks to ship raw goods to China generated significant amounts of new jobs and services. Also, with low euro interest rates, housing prices more than doubled from 2000 to 2008, leading to a real estate boom (Manolopoulos 2011: 16). But the Greek state failed to encourage investment of this growth back into new technologies or other sectors of the economy, leaving the country's economy undiversified and relatively low-tech.

Meanwhile, consumer spending spiked as Greek citizens bought new homes and cars, businesses imported many more goods to satiate demand, and with the help of significant EU funding, new government spending went toward upgrading transportation and communications infrastructure. Eventually, public and private debt built up. By 2009, Greece's public debt had well exceeded the stipulations of the Stability and Growth Pact. Several experts have suggested that if the Greek government had only collected its taxes – in 2005, more than half of the population avoided paying taxes – the solvency problem could have been avoided (Inman 2012). Regardless, rather than finding a way to reduce public debt, the Greek government hid it from the EU with the help of Goldman Sachs' underhanded accounting (Bazli 2010; Scheer 2010). Thus, according to this perspective, the main problem was poor governance in Greece. When the sheer scale of its debt was finally discovered, Greece was downgraded by the rating agency Fitch, dropping to below "A" in 2009 and then downgraded further by other rating agencies in 2010, even after it received a substantial €110 billion rescue package from the Eurogroup (the organization made up of the finance ministers of the Eurozone countries). Looking beyond all of the complexities of how the Greek economy unraveled, it must be noted that Greece was still the *only* Eurozone country that had budgetary problems that did *not* stem entirely from the broader, global financial crisis.

This perspective clearly departs from the argument that core–periphery imbalances or problems with the monetary union as a bloc caused the crisis. It corrects a widespread misconception that all Western European countries had supposedly acquired high levels of public debt because of bloated welfare states *before* the crisis struck. As mentioned, Italy did have high public debt in the lead-up to the crisis, built up over the years, but unlike Greece, it fared pretty well through the crisis. Besides Greece and Italy, other EU countries had relatively *low* public debt, but still succumbed to the global crisis for different reasons. For example, Irish public debt was only 25 percent of GDP in the lead-up to the crisis. But when the global financial crisis hit Europe, Ireland was the first to go into recession. When the country's housing bubble collapsed, the Anglo-Irish bank was in trouble, prompting the government to bail it out, thus absorbing this private debt into public debt. This quickly increased public debt as a percentage of GDP. Therefore, the core problem in Ireland was that the financial sector was governed poorly, and this was not exposed until the US financial crisis mushroomed beyond Wall Street.

Spain also had its public debt under control and, like Ireland, had experienced a property bubble. When the global crisis hit, public debt quickly went up. Both Spain and Ireland are strong export countries, and thus both suffered when the global contraction decreased demand for imports. Portugal too suffered as a result of the global financial crisis. The country had very low growth in the decade before the crisis as its industrial sector was not competitive enough, and the global recession aggravated this. Before the crisis, the governments of Spain and Portugal had adopted policies that deregulated access to credit and enabled accumulation of private debt, creating some vulnerability. Within the Eurozone the crisis then began to spread. In 2012, Cyprus became another victim for a variety of reasons, including exposure to Greek debt. In 2010, 2011, and 2012 respectively, Belgium, France, and Slovenia were also subject to high borrowing costs as the contagion effect took hold (Davies and Sage 2011).

Thus, this third perspective emphasizes that other countries besides Greece went into crisis for different reasons, and all as a *result* of the wider global financial crisis. Indeed, as Pradumna Rana argues, public-sector overspending in Ireland, Greece, and other southern member states, as well as banking-sector problems in Ireland and other countries that came from financing a property bubble that the public sector guaranteed, were all *symptoms* of the crisis, and not causes of it (Rana 2012). The real problem from the start, however, was Greece, which was headed toward a serious liquidity crisis no matter what happened on the global stage.

While this perspective accurately describes the state of affairs in the lead-up to the crisis, and rightly points out that we cannot conceive of the Eurozone as a coherent bloc of "problem-economies," another step is still necessary to explain why a Greek solvency problem became an existential crisis for the whole EU. Even in the case of Greece, it is important to recognize that these problems became apparent only after everything went downhill in the United States, and then spread from Wall Street to the entire global financial system. Yes, the timing may have been a coincidence, and Greece clearly was headed toward a crisis anyway. However, it was not a foregone conclusion that this small economy would seemingly have the capacity to bring the entire Eurozone down with it.

What's Missing?

These three perspectives reveal various important structural aspects of the crisis, but all three fall short of telling the full story. It is clear that the global financial system and the rampant deregulation that had occurred since the Reagan–Thatcher era provide the context for the Eurozone crisis, but they cannot account for its timing. It is also true that Greece had real solvency problems that had reached a head because the country's leaders had hidden its mounting debt for so long, but this cannot account for the crisis' severity, impacting the entire Eurozone. Moving beyond the more structural explanations, the Eurozone crisis was fundamentally a crisis of confidence, and it is therefore necessary to come to an understanding of why confidence in Europe's economic, financial, and monetary viability precipitously declined.

Indeed, there was nothing inherently worse or more damaging about the monetary union as compared to other non-European, sovereign economies. Structurally, there was nothing to indicate that what happened in the Eurozone should necessarily have been worse than what happened in the United States, the UK, or Japan (de Grauwe and Ji 2013). As Pisani-Ferry notes, many Eurozone countries experienced increased government borrowing costs even though their economies were more sound than those of the United States, the UK, or Japan (Pisani-Ferry 2012: 3). The IMF's own calculations in 2011 showed that the United States was in a similar situation to Portugal, and Japan was similar to Ireland (IMF Fiscal Monitor). Spain and the UK faced similar fiscal situations, according to Paul de Grauwe, and non–euro area countries faced similar adjustments to euro area countries more generally (de Grauwe 2011). Since 2007, debt-to-GDP ratios had been increasing significantly faster in the United States and the UK than in the Eurozone. But in November 2011, the rate on a Spanish ten-year bond was 6.5 percent, while it was only 2.3 percent for the UK.[10] By this point, the United States had surpassed the Eurozone in terms of debt to GDP, and the UK was on the verge of doing so; they were fiscally worse off, but those two countries experienced none of the major spread increases that many countries in the Eurozone did, and therefore faced no sovereign debt crisis.

Surprisingly rapidly, the euro went from universal recognition as the second-most important currency in the world (Marsh 2012: 213) to teetering on the brink of collapse under a widespread metanarrative that it was doomed to fail. All European countries suffered from rising public debt. The global recession, credit crunch, and growth contraction meant that Eurozone governments were struggling to pay their bills. However, when they looked for refinancing in international markets, they were subject to significantly higher interest rates as a result of the lack of confidence. Peripheral countries were punished most severely, especially Greece and Ireland. In December 2010, Greece had to pay interest rates four times higher than Germany, and Ireland three times higher (Paulo 2011: 17). Even as the crisis intensified, the three countries that had the most strain in terms of public debt were Greece, Ireland, and Portugal, but taken together they only accounted for 6 percent of the Eurozone economy (Rogoff 2011). Nonetheless, the perception was that this was a Eurozone-wide crisis. Speculators bet against the viability of the euro,

---

[10] Similarly, in June 2011, the British budget deficit was at around the same level as Greece's – 10 percent of GDP – yet markets treated British bonds as a safe haven at the time. See Thomas (June 16, 2011b).

and rating agencies played a big role in building a contagion effect. And so the question becomes: why did this happen, and why then were Eurozone countries so vulnerable to this crisis of confidence?

I argue that to more fully understand the nature of this crisis, we must investigate its socially constructed dynamic. It is important to note that at no point did any member state contemplate leaving the euro, but there was nonetheless a perception that Europeans were not committed to the existence of the common currency. The widespread external belief that a member state might actually leave the euro was a serious miscalculation on the part of the international financial community. As German Finance Minister Wolfgang Schäuble put it in 2010, markets "do not understand the euro" (Atkins and Peel 2010). In effect, markets behaved irrationally in response to the impending crisis in 2009 because they neglected to take into account the political importance of the euro to Europeans.[11] German Chancellor Angela Merkel captured the political dimension well when she repeatedly said, "The currency union is our common destiny. It is a question, no more or less, of the preservation of the European idea. That is our historical task: for if the Euro fails, then Europe fails" (Hall and Peel 2010).

Going further, Emmanuel Sales argues that the euro has also had a moral dimension, writing that "[g]auging the euro zone against purely accounting and financial criteria is one sided in that it omits vital elements of history" (Sales 2011). His argument is that we must remember what Europe was like before the euro:

The corruption of the currencies after the Great War was the key factor in the social and political collapse of European society. From 1914 until the introduction of the euro in 1999, the value of the French franc was divided by twenty; the mark collapsed twice, the lira and the peseta became practically worthless. On every occasion the monetary policies that followed a return to peace led to deficit, national withdrawal, a reduction in demand and the impoverishment of the majority.   (Sales 2011: 2)

Thus, the moral roots of the euro stem from a desire to move past a history of arbitrary inequality during which there was a lack of common rules and individual rights. Perhaps markets would not have overreacted as they did if they had somehow internalized the meaning of the euro to Europeans beyond mere ostensible national self-interest.[12] In particular, as the

---

[11] For more on the political importance of the euro, see Marsh (2012); Mayer (2012: chapter 3); Mourlon-Druol (2012).

[12] For a historical view on the meaning of the euro to European policy makers and citizens, see McNamara (1998); Risse et al. (1999: 147–187); Risse (2003: 487–503).

systemic argument about global deregulation indicates, speculators and rating agencies were simply searching for short-term profits, and understanding this drive is of paramount importance in coming to understand the social origins of this crisis of confidence.

CONSTRUCTING THE CRISIS

As outlined in the first two chapters, there is a clear pattern that can be seen in the trajectory across the three crisis cases examined in this book. First, in each case, there is an event of some kind that is interpreted as a trigger for crisis based on societal perceptions and reactions. Second, these crises build in severity, with clear signs of integrational panic – including overreaction to events and amplification of preexisting tensions – until the crisis reaches its height in the third phase, with open talk of the "end of Europe," which can in turn lead to a self-fulfilling prophecy dynamic. In other words, as each crisis builds and reaches its height, there emerge tangible manifestations of existential crisis – such as social breakdown, economic turmoil, or political gridlock – because of the integrational panic that preceded. This section of the chapter examines the social dynamics behind the construction of the Eurozone crisis. Integrational panic is evident in instances of clear social overreaction to a perceived problem with EU integration, and I argue that this was the case when the euro was perceived to be under threat.

As in the Iraq case, the crisis trigger for this third case was external in origin. The subprime mortgage crisis that brought down Wall Street in 2008 served as a kind of pre-crisis trigger, but it did not yet signify the beginning of Europe's third existential crisis of the twenty-first century. As described earlier in this chapter, prior to the impact of the Wall Street crash, the Eurozone was doing well, having maintained a steady growth rate since the introduction of the euro. Indeed, it took about two years for the events that resulted from the Wall Street crash to begin to affect Europe in a way that began to be perceived as an existential crisis for the EU and its currency. Eurozone growth overall was negative in 2009, as the entire global economy contracted, but talk of the possible breakup or end of the Eurozone did not really reach a serious level until 2011. As already mentioned, many economists and public commentators have argued that the Eurozone was headed for crisis no matter what, but it actually took a massive destabilization of the global economy for the weaknesses in the structure of the Eurozone that they emphasize to rise to the surface.

Thus, when discussing triggers, a more immediate event needs to be found. An important moment was the realization of the sheer scale of Greece's debt, which finally came to light when Greece's newly elected prime minister, George Papandreou, announced in October 2009 that Greece's budget deficit would be much larger than the previous government had forecasted. The European Commission then confirmed on January 8, 2010, that there were indeed severe irregularities in the Greek Excessive Deficit Procedure. Nevertheless, from October 2009 to May 2011, the crisis remained one confined to Greece. But in May 2011, the perception grew that the Greek debt problem could potentially threaten the whole Eurozone. Indeed, it became apparent that Portugal required a bailout and that Greece would need a second bailout to avoid default. It was these two revelations that served as the crisis trigger for Europe. And yet, even at this point, these two countries only represented 3 to 4 percent of the entire Eurozone economy (Greece alone represented around 2 percent and Portugal an even smaller portion). So why then did the Greek debt crisis turn into a full-blown EU crisis in 2011, complete with "end-of-Europe" rhetoric?

The Role of the Media in Crisis Buildup

As in the 2003 European crisis over Iraq (Chapter 3) and the 2005 constitutional crisis (Chapter 4), the media played a significant role in interpreting events and advancing certain understandings (and not others) about this crisis. Specifically, it interpreted the Greek debt crisis as a wider European existential crisis, contributing to a growing sense of integrational panic among elites and the public. While the structure of the Eurozone did have some elements of weakness – and as I have argued, all economies do – a shift in perception underlined and repeatedly amplified by the media not only constructed a feeling of Europe-wide crisis, but caused international markets to react sharply against the future of the Eurozone.

A media frenzy signaled the buildup of the crisis from May to November 2011.[13] Figure 5.1 is based on reading *all* news stories across the four publications that mention the keyword "Eurozone," resulting in a total number of 2,069 articles. National newspapers in Europe and the United States published more articles on Greece in 2010–11 than they had in the five-year period from 2005 to 2009 (Tzogopoulos 2013: 64–67).

---

[13] See Chapter 2 for methodology.

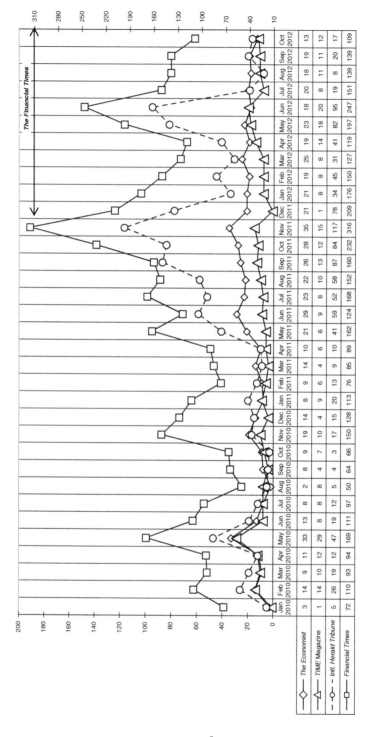

	Jan 2010	Feb 2010	Mar 2010	Apr 2010	May 2010	Jun 2010	Jul 2010	Aug 2010	Sep 2010	Oct 2010	Nov 2010	Dec 2010	Jan 2011	Feb 2011	Mar 2011	Apr 2011	May 2011	Jun 2011	Jul 2011	Aug 2011	Sep 2011	Oct 2011	Nov 2011	Dec 2011	Jan 2012	Feb 2012	Mar 2012	Apr 2012	May 2012	Jun 2012	Jul 2012	Aug 2012	Sep 2012	Oct 2012
The Economist	3	14	9	11	33	13	8	2	8	9	19	14	8	9	14	10	21	29	23	22	26	28	35	21	21	19	25	19	23	18	20	18	19	13
TIME Magazine	1	14	10	12	29	8	8	8	4	7	10	4	9	6	4	6	6	9	8	10	13	12	15	1	8	8	8	14	18	20	8	11	11	12
Intl. Herald Tribune	5	26	19	12	47	19	12	5	4	3	17	15	20	13	9	10	41	59	52	58	87	84	117	78	34	45	31	41	82	95	19	8	20	17
Financial Times	72	110	93	94	169	111	97	50	64	66	150	128	113	76	85	89	162	124	168	152	160	232	316	209	176	150	127	119	197	247	151	139	139	109

FIGURE 5.1 Eurozone crisis, volume of media coverage, January 1, 2010–October 31, 2012*

* In this figure, the right side Y-axis pertains to the *Financial Times*, while the left side Y-axis pertains to the other three media outlets. The *FT* publishes more stories in general as well as those related to the European region.

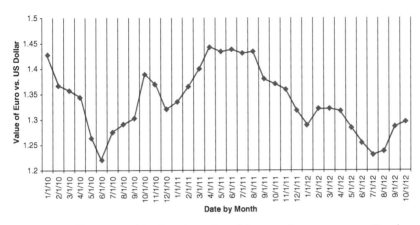

FIGURE 5.2 Eurozone crisis, changing value of the euro, January 1, 2010–October 31, 2012

And news coverage shifted from debate over what to do to help Greece to fears that the European project itself was in jeopardy. This negative media coverage even prompted Greek Prime Minister Papandreou to criticize journalists openly for their often inaccurate reporting and their repeated speculation that Greece was either on the verge of collapse or would have to exit the Eurozone (Tzogopoulos 2013: 6). This media frenzy reached its peak in November 2011 when Prime Minister Papandreou announced that he would put austerity to a popular referendum.

Moreover, the media's intense attention to the crisis had an influence on perceptions of Europe's economy worldwide. In comparing the volume of media coverage to the fluctuating value of the euro during the same period of crisis buildup (Figure 5.2), it is clear that shortly after each spike in media coverage about the crisis, the value of the euro declined. For example, the May 2010 increase in volume of coverage was followed by a June 2010 low for the value of the euro. The same is true following the frenzy in media coverage in November 2010, November 2011, and June 2012. In each case, the corresponding value of the euro reached a relative low point the very next month. A study by Mark Mink and Jakob de Haan also shows that 2010 news coverage about the Greek bailout significantly impacted bank stock prices throughout the Eurozone, even those that were not exposed to Greek (or other indebted member states') debt (Mink and de Haan 2012). Similarly, Roel Beetsma et al. find that there was a strong correlation between more news about a particular country – Greece, Ireland, Italy, Portugal, or Spain – and an increase in interest rate spread for that country, especially during the 2011 period of crisis buildup I have identified (Beetsma, Giuliodori, de Jong, and Widijanto 2013: 83–101). Moreover, they find a pattern of spillover from one of these countries to the others (even to northern member states, except Germany) whenever news coverage mentioned bankers' negative financial claims about that country. In multiple dimensions, this pattern suggests that the media was not merely reporting on the story, but to some significant extent actually driving it.

The socially constructed dynamic of crises is especially hard felt in the case of an economic or financial crisis because markets are fundamentally shaped and affected by perceptions, which can shift dramatically from day to day, as well as over the longer term.[14] As one investment banker put it: "This is classic 'buy the rumor, sell the news.' The equity market was up in anticipation. We priced it in ahead of time" (Benhold 2011). The media was instrumental in reporting what European leaders decided or did not decide to do, almost always with a negative spin (Figure 5.3). For example, in May 2011 when the ECB chief denied the need to restructure Greek debt, bond rates soared in reaction. This, of course, made it more difficult for Greece to recover, making the need to restructure the country's debt even more acute. Repeatedly, in the buildup of the crisis, markets reacted to negative perceptions.

There was even a fictional series published in *Le Monde* entitled "End of the Line for the Euro" (*Terminus pour L'Euro*), which was a twelve-part economic thriller about the demise of the euro, intended to entertain French readers over the weekends. The story takes place in 2012 and describes the downfall of various European banks for which the author uses the real names of leaders and big banks, such as Crédit Agricole and UniCredit. When a passage that was eerily similar to this fiction was published in the *Mail*, a British tabloid, the stocks of several French banks plummeted. Société Générale's stocks, for example, went down 15 percent in response to this (Kenney 2011). The French government promptly criticized the *Mail* for mistakenly interpreting *Le Monde*'s fictional series as real news, and the British tabloid retracted the story. But the damage was already done as speculators acted on the rumors as if they were real. As the editor-in-chief of *Le Monde*, Erik Izraelewicz, wrote in the Sunday–Monday edition:

---

[14] It has been well established in the literature that news coverage has an impact on financial markets. For example, see Andersen, Bollerslev, and Vega (2003); Albuquerque and Vega (2008); Aizenman, Joshua, Jinjarak, Lee, and Park (2012).

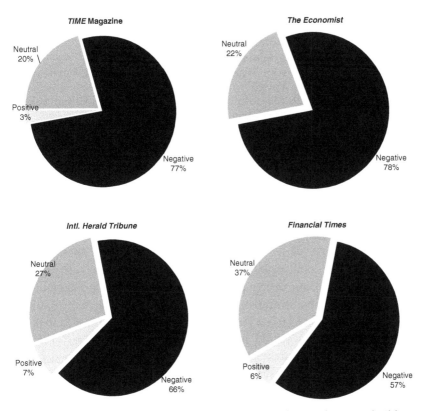

FIGURE 5.3 Eurozone crisis, neutrality of coverage during the crisis buildup, May 1, 2011–November 30, 2011

The reality is that our fiction had nothing to do with this crazy rumor. The paradox is that this case has come to illustrate something that our series denounced: the unacceptable role played by rumors in determining the fate of nations and businesses. (Pfanner 2011)

In addition to this rather dramatic tale of blatant crisis construction based on thin air, journalists played a significant role in casting the very real debt crisis in Greece as a crisis for all of Europe through their regular framing and spin. Typical of the tone at this point were statements such as "A Greek default will unleash a dynamic process that will threaten the Eurozone's financial stability, even its very survival" (Münchau 2011a). The covers of the *Economist* were particularly striking:

May 1, 2010	"Acropolis Now: Europe's Debt Crisis Spins Out of Control"
January 15, 2011	"The Euro Crisis: Time for Plan B"
July 16, 2011	"On the Edge: Why the Euro Crisis Has Just Got a Lot Worse"
November 26, 2011	"Is This Really the End?" (with an image of a euro coin going down in flames)

Many media reports and op-eds argued early on that either Greece would have to leave the EU or it would bring the rest of Europe down with it. News stories such as "It's Time to Admit the Euro Has Failed" (Sivy 2011) and "10 Reasons the Euro Was a Dumb Idea" (Gersemann 2011) became commonplace. Others predicted that the only way Greece could repair its own economy and save itself was to leave the EU.

Crucially, at no point in this period did the European Commission or any EU head of state suggest that Greece (or any other country) might have to give up EU membership or exit the euro. But this did not stop the media narratives. For example, a *Financial Times* op-ed stated, "A severe debt write-off by Greece and Portugal is a foregone conclusion; and in my view both countries would be better off without the euro" (Brittan 2011b). Other such statements were numerous, and they defined this as a serious crisis for Europe before other EU countries had even been drawn in to the mess. Two representative examples include:

Political turmoil is sweeping through Europe, toppling governments and threatening to undermine efforts to rescue the financial system and, ultimately, the euro zone itself.   (Donadio 2011)

The Greek financial crisis is neither Greek nor financial any more. It is a political crisis of the whole of Europe. Its solution is no longer financial, but political. It is no longer a matter just for Athens, but for Brussels. Indeed, it is now a Franco-German problem above all since their banks are most exposed ... Greece will never repay its debts. The numerous aid plans, even if they have so far succeeded in avoiding default, failed to clear the long-term liabilities. One must face the facts, which have been known for a long time: No common currency area can last without a dominant country or without some form of federalism (as in the United States). (Attali 2011)

As with the 2003 Iraq crisis and 2005 constitutional crisis, the media again took specific, confined problems and portrayed them as deep, Europewide turmoil before there was any basis for this. And as we shall see, this would again play a significant role in *making* it so.

From the early stages of the crisis, Eurozone leaders scrambled to craft both short-term and long-term solutions. Short-term solutions involved bailout packages, whereas long-term solutions looked toward creating the crisis-management tools that would enable the EU to respond more decisively and effectively in the future. After the initial summit to put together a Greek bailout package, Eurozone leaders held a special, emergency summit on July 21, 2011, during which they agreed on several far-ranging crisis resolution steps, including the creation of a €440 billion European Financial Stability Facility, more commonly known as the Eurozone rescue fund. But even as European leaders agreed on actions to take to alleviate the crisis, the negative media spin intensified, anticipating that these measures would fail before they had even been launched. In turn, investors started betting against other countries in the Eurozone, creating a contagion effect that began to take hold during the summer of 2011. Some representative examples of this negative framing include:

The measures agreed at last week's emergency summit brought the bloc back from the brink. But they also mark the first steps in a hazardous direction for the Eurozone – towards greater fiscal union .... But the nature of the sovereign debt crisis is such that without more integration, the euro will fall apart; its internal contradictions are so glaring.   (*Financial Times*, "The Euro," 2011)

The odds of a disorderly outcome to the eurozone crisis are also rising. So it is understandable that the risks on the horizon can seem overwhelming.

(Authers 2011b)

The latest Eurozone rescue package was too far from a solution to calm spirits for more than a matter of days … Spanish politicians are unlikely to agree on an austerity plan tough enough to calm markets before the November election. Silvio Berlusconi, Italy's prime minister, might fall and leave a political vacuum (although an anti-deficit technocratic government is more likely). And the worries about France, like those about the US, are easy to justify: it has been slow to cut a chronic deficit.   (*Financial Times*, "Cruel Summer," 2011)

Thus, a common theme in international news coverage was to criticize European leaders for not governing or communicating well in seeking a solution to the crisis. And yet, during the second half of 2011, Eurozone leaders were constantly in meetings with each other to work on solutions as the crisis grew beyond expectations. It was clear that leaders had their eyes on the long term and were not simply looking for a short-term fix. Naturally, agreements that require more integration and restructuring of EU financial mechanisms take time. Nonetheless, the media repeatedly described this process of dialogue and deliberation as a leadership and governance failure. For example:

As efforts to rescue Greece for a second time come to a frenetic climax, Europe's politicians and its financial markets seem to be stuck – still – in a dialogue of the deaf. Accountable to domestic voters, and accustomed to negotiations that start with opening positions from which they later compromise, European ministers have generated a political cacophony, failing to cohere around quick and clear messages to markets. (Castle 2011)

You can always gauge the temperature of the eurozone crisis by the blame game . . . This is as much a crisis of policy coordination as it is a debt crisis.
(Münchau 2011a)

European leaders have been drawn into one of the most agonised debates seen since the eurozone debt crisis erupted nearly two years ago. (Spiegel 2011a)

The eurozone's overall strategy, then, is marred by confusing and inconsistent tactics. Before long, this may lead to another string of cliffhanger meetings as policy is again outrun by events.
(*Financial Times*, "Second Thoughts on the Euro Rescue . . .," 2011).

It would be easy to chalk up the confusion to yet another example of the European Union's inability to communicate to financial markets. Except that days after the deal was struck, confusion still reigns. (Spiegel 2011c)

But there are strong reasons to doubt that a eurozone armed to the teeth with balanced budget amendments would be any better equipped to overcome its sovereign debt and banking sector crises than a eurozone without such rules . . . Such examples illustrate how eurozone politicians are artfully exploiting the issue for national or party political ends. Sustainable public finances are a good thing. But European policymakers are expending an awful lot of political effort in largely symbolic gestures. (*Financial Times*, "Artful Promises . . .," 2011)

In criticizing EU leaders as they strove to craft workable agreements, media coverage of their efforts contributed to a self-fulfilling prophecy dynamic. For example, Italian and Spanish government bonds were subject to increased pressure as early as July 2011, even though neither country had a solvency problem, nor did they need external help. And despite the growing sense of political failure portrayed in the media, many agreements among EU leaders were made on major issues relatively quickly. This timeline included, among other things:

May 2, 2010	Greece gets $146 billion in loans from the EU and IMF
May 9, 2010	European officials announce an agreement to provide nearly $1 trillion to support member states under duress.
November 21, 2010	Ireland gets $100 billion in financial support.
December 16, 2010	The EU establishes an emergency fund

July 2, 2011	Eurozone finance ministers agree to speed payment of funds that are part of the bailout package previously approved.
July 21, 2011	European leaders agree on a new $157 billion rescue plan for Greece that may include a selective default.
October 26, 2011	European leaders obtain an agreement from banks to take a 50 percent loss on the face value of their Greek debt.

Indeed, there were around twenty different EU summits from the beginning of the crisis until mid-2012, all dealing with discussing ways to move forward with economic integration (Vilpisauskas 2013). European Council President Herman Van Rompuy made clear in May 2011 that all EU member states were prepared to stand by the euro and not let it fail. But despite this, their progress was continually undermined by negative media predictions:

Even if it can be achieved legally and politically, it is far from clear that the half-hearted mix between eurobonds and national bonds that currently is being discussed will actually end the crisis. Such an arrangement would discourage fiscal discipline while possibly even increasing overall borrowing costs for indebted economies, as the national share of the bonds would face alarmingly high rates if eurobonds were implemented on existing debt.   (Parsson 2011)

At every stage of this process, from the first signs of trouble in Greece, to the spread of problems to Portugal and Ireland, to the recognition of Greece's inability to pay its debts in full, to the rise of debt spreads in Spain and Italy, the authorities have played out the stalemate machine. They have done just enough beyond euro-orthodoxy to avoid an imminent collapse, but never enough to establish a sound foundation for a resumption of confidence. Perhaps inevitably, the gaps between emergency summits grow shorter and shorter.   (Summers 2011)

Even when in October 2011 European leaders agreed to a far-ranging package, they were hammered with criticism (see Figures 5.1 and 5.3).

At the end of the summer of 2011, the media and the markets turned their attention fully to Italy, adding to the contagion effect, despite Berlusconi's protests. The Italian prime minister said in August 2011 that Italy was "economically and financially solid" (*Financial Times*, "UniCredit Advances Despite Volatility," 2011) and that speculators were to blame for sudden, skyrocketing borrowing costs. Indeed, he expressed his annoyance that markets seemed incapable of correctly evaluating the strength of Italy's fundamental economic indicators (Dinmore and Sanderson 2011). And yet, the spin continued, as the *Financial Times* reported it:

In less than three months, Italy has changed from a country whose fiscal and economic ailments are difficult but not impossible to cure into a country whose atrophied and self-serving political system threatens to destroy the Eurozone.   (*Financial Times*, "Fiddling in Rome ...," 2011)

At the height of the crisis in November 2011, Berlusconi refused an IMF loan, saying, "Italy does not feel the crisis. The restaurants are full, the planes are fully booked and the hotel resorts are fully booked as well." He described the bond sell-off as a "passing fashion" (Spiegel and Dinmore 2011).

The cycle of exaggerated and negative media coverage alongside market reactions was quickly transforming the Greek debt problem into a European-wide crisis. The widespread perception that the crisis would not be confined to Greece led to a contagion effect that became self-fulfilling,[15] with serious financial woes spreading from Greece to Portugal, and then on to Spain, Italy, France, Cyprus, and others. Whenever EU leaders agreed to a new program to end the crisis, they only gained a small window of breathing room before traders resumed their attacks, drawing more EU countries into their range. This was immediately reflected in the elevated cost of borrowing, which only served to worsen conditions. Then when EU leaders implemented austerity measures, it backfired, adding fuel to the self-fulfilling prophecy and negative media coverage. From the crisis trigger in May 2011 to the buildup of crisis during the subsequent few months, the EU had entered a downward spiral, with the media playing a central role in feeding these fears and making it so.

The Role of Elites in Crisis Buildup

Very few public figures recognized this largely disproportional ratcheting-up of crisis rhetoric. There were some exceptions, coming from former political leaders who must have felt more freedom to point out the obvious, such as former British Foreign Secretary David Miliband, who wrote in an op-ed, "I don't know whether to weep or laugh. Eurozone leaders have turned a €50 billion Greek solvency problem into a €1,000bn existential crisis for the European Union" (Miliband 2011). Similarly, former French President Valéry Giscard d'Estaing said in a speech:

---

[15] For more on the technical aspects of contagion, see De Santis (2012); Mink and de Haan (2012).

Greece is a great culture but a small country in our financial sphere and there is no basis for it rocking the euro at this point, had it not been constantly prodded by speculators and by banks from outside the euro area.

(as quoted in Rettmen 2011)

And former German Chancellor Helmut Schmidt added to this, stating, "This talk of a crisis of the euro is merely hot air emanated by journalists and politicians" (as quoted in Rettmen 2011). He described the atmosphere of the time as psychopathic and emphasized that it was really the Anglo-Saxon media that was to blame.

On occasion, when a member state was specifically under attack in the media, a leader would be prompted to respond, as Greek Prime Minister George Papandreou did in May 2011 when the German magazine *Der Spiegel* reported that Greece was using a threat to leave the Eurozone as leverage for easier terms on paying back debt (Erlanger 2011b). Papandreou attacked this reporting, stating unequivocally that this was evidence of widespread "rumor mongering." In fact, EU finance ministers had never discussed or even considered this possibility when they met in Luxembourg that month. Other EU leaders also denounced this suggestion, stating that the idea of any member state leaving the EU was akin to an "apocalyptic situation" (Ewing 2011). Even though the whole event was fabricated in the media, markets punished the euro in response, and the currency dropped to its lowest level since December 2008.

Seemingly in vain, EU leaders continuously attempted to calm markets and reassure investors that member states were committed to solving the crisis no matter what. For example, in June 2011, after a two-day summit in Brussels, Merkel said, "We have agreed that there will be a new program for Greece. This is an important decision that says once again we will do everything to stabilize the euro over all" (Castle 2011a).

The problem at the elite level was that these strong statements were the exception rather than the rule. A few former leaders spoke out, and some other current ones were prompted to do so in response to blatant fabrication. But in general, European leaders – both at the member-state and EU levels – were often weak in countering the negative crisis rhetoric. And in their inaction, they contributed to crisis buildup, letting the media and outsiders have the upper hand. They were warned about the lack of strong communication. For example, European Commission President José Manuel Barroso said that EU politicians should be faulted for "undisciplined communication" in the wake of the July 21 summit. But he also believed that the agreement did not go far enough. He wrote, "Markets remain to be convinced that we are taking the appropriate steps to resolve the crisis. Whatever the factors behind the lack of success, it is clear that we are no longer managing a crisis just in the euro area periphery" (Saltmarsh 2011).

Similarly, in August 2011, former French Finance Minister Christine Lagarde insisted strongly that Eurozone leaders needed to improve on their communication. She said, "Putting on my European hat for a microsecond ... we did not communicate it in a harmonised fashion, nor did we particularly speak with one voice ... The euro countries have been on the verge of the cliff and have actually understood that they have to come together" (Beattie 2011c). She urged them to "stick to the script" from now on. Unlike Barroso, Lagarde argued that Greece's first rescue package was not flawed, but rather it was the fact that Greece was suffering from "reform fatigue" (Beattie 2011a). There was an awareness of a climate of integrational panic among the leadership. It was not that European leaders were making the crisis worse, but that the messages they did put forward about the steps they were taking to resolve the crisis were not strong enough to inspire confidence and overcome the dominant crisis narrative. To add to this, if any leader's statement could possibly be construed as negative, this spin was certain to be amplified in the media.

Beyond government leaders, the wider community of experts and advisors contributed to a sense of crisis at the elite level, as well. Charles Grant, director of the Center for European Reform, said:

European leaders are divided over what policies you need. The euro is on the sick bed and the doctors cannot agree on the nature of the illness or the medicine they need to provide ... The track record shows that whenever they have been sailing into the abyss, the European body politic has summoned the political will and demonstrated its ability to rescue the Eurozone. Nevertheless, the process is tortuous, fraught, and open to all sorts of political risks.　　　(Castle 2011b)

Paul de Grauwe, economist and advisor to Barroso, said, "It looks like a real unraveling – everyone is taking their own position and as a result cooperation has become an impossibility" (Thomas 2011a). Simon Tilford, chief economist at the Centre for European Reform think tank said, "Short of the eurozone agreeing [to] a fully-fledged transfer union, it is hard to see how Greece can remain in the eurozone" (Chaffin 2011). In addition, an academic book entitled *The End of the Euro* was published in 2011 and promptly endorsed by the *Financial Times* as a convincing perspective, even though the author had had trouble finding a publisher in 2009 because the main argument "was considered so heretical" (Brittan 2011a).

As in the case of the Iraq crisis, some tone-setting statements also came from outsiders and then became widespread in the international media. Various actors from the IMF to the US government to rating agencies contributed to a sense of building crisis, all amplified in the media. For example:

> Writing for today's Financial Times, Professor Martin Feldstein of Harvard argues that "a default by Greece is inevitable" – this view is increasingly shared. But how might this occur and what are the likely consequences? None of the possible scenarios makes comfortable reading: Disorderly default; Orderly default; Staggering on; Leaving the euro. (Giles 2011)

> International Monetary Fund staff have provoked a fierce dispute with eurozone authorities, by circulating estimates that show serious damage to European banks' balance sheets from their holdings of troubled eurozone sovereign debt …. The analysis, which was discussed by the IMF's executive board on Wednesday, has been strongly rebutted by the European Central Bank and eurozone governments, who say that it is partial and misleading. (Beattie 2011b)

> The competition between the big two names in the ratings business is a hot debate in the markets. Some accuse them of engaging in a form of "competitive downgrading." (Milne 2011)

From further afield, Chinese Premier Wen Jiabao in October 2011 began to publicly chastise the Europeans for not stabilizing the euro successfully or restoring confidence in the market. This set the tone for an even more widespread sense of European failure: an outside leader from a rising power that itself was not even a democracy now felt justified in telling the EU what to do (Spiegel 2011b). And this was picked up in the media, with front pages of newspapers amplifying the statements, along with large photos depicting the Chinese coming to save the day. The idea that China might "rescue" Europe was embarrassing and could not help to restore any remaining confidence in the euro. Hans-Peter Keitel, president of Germany's BDI industry association, said in response, "Asking a non-eurozone nation to help the euro would give the other nation the power to decide the fate of the single currency. All help from them would come at some political cost" (Shirky 2011). Ultimately, China did not get involved, but the combination of media frenzy and a weak response from EU leadership led to the belief that a Greek default was virtually inevitable, and that this would mean the "death of the euro."

The Public

It might be easy to jump to the conclusion that EU citizens also played a strong role in creating and building up the crisis. Indeed, widespread protests – especially in Spain, Portugal, and Greece – were a common feature of the Eurozone crisis as it gained momentum. European publics became more skeptical of EU integration as the crisis grew, and elections showed increased numbers voting in favor of populist or extremist parties. Opinion polls at the time indicated that voters did not want to offer more aid to Greece because they thought that the country would not be able to pay back the loans.

It is important to note, however, that these protests were a *reaction* to the policy measures taken by elites to try to resolve the crisis, especially the drive toward austerity. The European public actually played only a small role in starting the Eurozone crisis, or ratcheting up the speculation of euro collapse. Instead, they were part of the general atmosphere of integrational panic. And as will be discussed fully in the next section, the public did play a substantial role in bringing underlying North–South tensions to the surface, forcing government leaders to take their concerns into account. Given the international nature of financial crises, the perceptions of non-Europeans arguably had a stronger impact on the social construction of crisis, but this would not manifest itself except in the financial sector, where speculators and investors make important choices about how they view various currencies.

In sum, to fully understand the causes and buildup of the Eurozone crisis, we must look beyond structural accounts to consider the socially constructed dynamic of the crisis. In particular, the media's coverage effectively channeled certain meanings or interpretations of events in a direction that emphasized threats to the EU's continued viability. It portrayed a Greek debt crisis that represented only 2 percent of the Eurozone economy as a threat to the very survival of the entire euro, and possibly even the EU itself. Thus, as in the other two cases, there was a clear point at which the media closed the gap between reality and worst-case scenario thinking through its volume of coverage and negative spin, and played a pro-active role in building up perceptions of crisis. Elites were also part of the crisis buildup. European policy makers were too weak in their communication efforts to counteract the contagion effect, and to stop the growing crisis in confidence internationally, while other elites made pessimistic statements, which then contributed to the negative media dynamic.

INTEGRATIONAL PANIC AND CATHARSIS

As with the 2003 Iraq crisis and 2005 constitutional crisis, once the Eurozone crisis took on a life of its own, Europeans eventually managed to turn it into an opportunity. The second half of this chapter traces the process by which the buildup of this crisis enabled a degree of catharsis to take place, subsequently leading to dramatic steps forward in economic integration. Full economic recovery is, of course, an ongoing process, especially in Greece and Spain, but the perception of existential threat to the existence of the EU was mainly settled in 2012. As with the other cases, the development of this crisis ensured that the strongest sources of pre-existing tensions – North–South differences – were openly aired. And Eurobarometer polls show that after the crisis, there was convergence in terms of North–South attitudes toward the role of the EU, indicating that a kind of societal catharsis took place.

I begin this section by outlining preexisting tensions and discussing how they were expressed openly as the dominant crisis narrative. I show that divisions between northern and southern Europe did not necessarily have to be the dominant narrative, considering the circumstances surrounding the crisis. But these divisions rose to the surface because they had already been a growing source of tension before the crisis had even begun. I then describe how leaders resolved the crisis with major advancements in integration, and why this was connected to the catharsis that occurred with the release of North–South tensions. Ultimately, this case shows once again how an event that might have been overlooked as relatively routine – dealing with debt in a small member state – was built up into a seemingly existential challenge through a period of integrational panic, but then turned into an opportunity to advance integration goals.

Preexisting Tensions

Liesbet Hooghe and Gary Marks synthesize the numerous studies that explain why specific kinds of tensions among member states have stood as stumbling blocks to the completion of the single market at various stages in the process. These include individual and national economic interests, communal identities, national institutions, elite attitudes toward the EU, political ideology, effect of integration on welfare provisions, and the nature of the debate among political parties about EU issues (Hooghe and Marks 2005: 436–437). At a basic level, these obstacles boil down to whether citizens favor more or less integration, and whether they are more supportive or skeptical of the EU. This body of research clearly points to the existence of North–South tensions stemming from differences in economic cultures.

In the lead-up to the Eurozone crisis, however, these North–South differences had emerged as an increasing source of concern. These tensions had been present arguably since the early years of economic integration, but they clearly intensified in 2008. There were several reasons for this. First, the global economic crisis put the entire European economy on shakier ground. Second, there was increasing evidence that the South was not being as fiscally conservative as the North. Along with this, new member states, such as Poland, made it their explicit aim to emulate the member states of the North rather than those of the South. Third, there was a growing sense of divide between those EU countries that had adopted the euro and those that had not. British Prime Minister David Cameron emphasized this aspect with his rhetoric about preventing the Eurozone from controlling the destiny of the EU (Miliband 2011). Fourth, the rise of German economic power alongside growing German economic leadership raised concerns and insecurity in other member states. Finally, with the tightening of domestic budgets and enlargement of EU membership, the division between net contributors and net detractors to the EU budget became more contentious. Before the onset of the Eurozone crisis, I argue that these tensions stood as obstacles to major innovations in the economic and financial spheres.

The origins of the Eurozone crisis were, however, not a consequence of these underlying tensions stemming from differences in economic culture. The tensions did not *cause* the crisis. Jörg König and Renate Ohr (2013) demonstrate through a composite index that ten years into the use of the euro, significant heterogeneity across Eurozone member states existed in various dimensions of economic integration, such as trade, labor markets, monetary union, capital markets, and institutional convergence. Some member states had more of a supply-driven strategy (export emphasis), while others had more of a demand-driven strategy (import emphasis, such as the United States) (Alphandéry 2012: 5). Nonetheless, none of these differences posed a serious problem because the European economy was generally healthy until the worldwide economic contraction in 2009 (Eurostat). Indeed, many of these differences are similar to what occurs within any federal-style system. But it is clear that the preexisting societal tensions between northern and southern member states nevertheless emerged as the dominant narrative once the crisis got going.

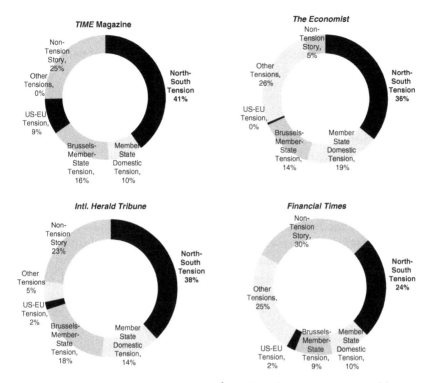

FIGURE 5.4 Eurozone crisis, nature of tensions in news coverage, May 1, 2011–November 30, 2011

The Crisis Narrative

As with all crises, there are multiple tensions that rise to the surface, but the one that stood out in the crisis narrative of 2011 was the hostility between northern and southern member states (e.g., see Figure 5.4).[16] In effect, the crisis became an excuse to discuss these specific preexisting tensions much more openly, especially as there had long been a language of stereotypes surrounding North–South differences. Northern Europeans were assumed to be "hard-working, law-abiding people who live within their means," while Southern Europeans were "work-shy, rule-bending, and profligate" (Mahony 2012).

On October 15, 2011, there were widespread protests in Europe, especially in the southern region as part of the greater Occupy

---

[16] See Chapter 2 for methodology.

movement, which originated in the United States as Occupy Wall Street. However, this was largely a non-European movement, and it did not target EU issues. It was entirely concerned with the global financial crisis and its ramifications, such as inequality, capitalist greed, and government corruption. Thus, this round of protests should be viewed separately from the protests that specifically had to do with the Eurozone crisis and EU policies. EU-oriented protests were most intense in Greece, Spain, Portugal, and Cyprus. The main purpose in these was to campaign against austerity, but the specific message was to speak out against EU decision makers (van Gent, Mamadouh, and van der Wusten 2012). For example, in Greece in February 2011, there were protests specifically targeted at Merkel to express opposition to austerity measures as a condition for bailouts. These protests escalated just a day after the EU and IMF agreed to write down the country's debt, leading to the cancellation of a long-planned military parade. The same thing happened the following year when Merkel visited Greece, and also in Portugal during her stop there on November 12, 2012. In a much more orderly atmosphere, protests broke out in Germany where 100 tents were set up opposite the headquarters of the ECB to demonstrate dissatisfaction with its purchases of Eurozone bonds and its refinancing of banks. In Spain, half a million demonstrators marched to a main square in Madrid, while nearly as many also gathered in Barcelona. And Italians had the worst social unrest in thirty years. Thus, popular protests continued well past the height of the crisis, which is to be expected considering that these protests were a reaction to the launch of new crisis-driven austerity policies.

The media once again played a major role, this time in spreading and sharpening the stereotypes of North–South differences as ostensibly underlying causes for the growing problems in the Eurozone:

Taxpayers of northern Europe do not want to bail out what they perceive to be profligate and lazy southern Europeans. Yet their elected politicians cannot contemplate the alternative of sovereign default because that would put the whole European banking system at risk.   (Plender 2011)

Some events that garnered media attention bordered on the absurd:

European Union policymakers were bickering about the latest unhelpful proposal for tackling the crisis: flying the flags of states with high budget deficits at half-mast. The origins of this bizarre idea lie in the northern European, Protestant notion that debts are sinful and demand public humiliation. Treating economics as a morality play is one reason the European crisis is not over.

(*Financial Times*, "Democracy's Slow Cure for the Euro ...," 2011)

Of course, playing up the tensions between Greece and Germany was at the heart of this:

> Greece, they say, should leave the eurozone for its own good, as well as the Continent's. Some German economists argue that others in the 17-nation currency union, like Portugal or even Italy, might need to leave as well ... Meanwhile, Germany's attitudes draw plenty of publicity in Greece and other stricken euro countries, where they feed stereotypes of arrogant, domineering Germans and stoke the resentments that are already deeply straining European unity .... "We don't care about staying in the euro," said one protester, who gave his name only as Dimitris. "It would be costly, but at least with the drachma we would be able to control our own currency and our own future." ... "People believe Greeks don't pay our taxes and we don't want to work," said Christos Manolas, a Greek businessman. "That's a myth perpetuated by the Germans." ... Mr. Manolas cited a study published in June by the French bank Natixis, which found that Greeks and other south Europeans worked more hours than Germans, though the German economy was more productive. (Ewing and Alderman 2011)

And some coverage emphasized North–South tensions, while also reporting on the need to overcome them:

> The German analysis, shared by the Dutch and others in prosperous northern Europe, like the Finns, sees as the main problem the indiscipline and profligacy of others, especially in the south, like Greece, Portugal, Italy and Spain, which have run up high debts or fiscal deficits .... Mr. Papandreou, acutely aware of this strain of thought and the threat it poses to Greece, sought on Tuesday to calm passions. "We must stop blaming each other for our different weaknesses and unite together with our different strengths," he said in a speech to a business group in Berlin. "Even Germany depends on Europe, its biggest trading partner, for growth and jobs." ... "If there is austerity everywhere, where is the engine for growth?"
> (Erlanger 2011a)

Of course, at the outset, there was a variety of ways in which Europeans could have talked about the Greek debt crisis, and this narrative did not necessarily have to center on North–South tensions. Other tensions about the crisis that arguably would have made much more sense in this context were blame for US neglect in upholding financial regulation, criticism of Wall Street, criticism of the global banking sector for greed and corruption, questioning of capitalism in general, and complaining of growing inequality between the rich and the poor. However, these were either far less prominent or entirely nonexistent in the media coverage, again demonstrating the socially constructed nature of the crisis during its buildup phase. For example, from May 1 to November 30, 2011, the *Financial Times* and the *International Herald Tribune (IHT)* focused on US–EU tensions only 2 percent of the time in their coverage of the

Eurozone crisis (Figure 5.4), even though this was the main cause of global economic crisis and of the subsequent contagion effect within Europe. Even tensions between Brussels and the member states or tensions within member states appeared far less frequently in coverage compared to North–South tensions.

As the crisis gained momentum, France and Germany took the lead in trying to find a solution. This was a natural development given that they have the biggest economies in the Eurozone and have been traditional leaders throughout the evolution of the EU. In reaction to their leadership during the Eurozone crisis, however, many Southern Europeans were highly critical, especially when it came to German Chancellor Angela Merkel's role. As media rhetoric and societal narratives within Europe became increasingly intertwined, southern member states' reactions added fuel to the fire of the media's coverage. Indeed, the backlash from some southern member states became so severe that for the first time since the founding of the ECSC there was open talk of "the German problem" again, and various other forms of highly controversial German bashing. Thus, Europeans were talking about these preexisting tensions in far more blunt and exaggerated terms than they had been before the crisis. For example, op-ed columnist Gideon Rachman wrote,

> Any taboos about references to the Nazi occupation of Greece have been dropped long ago. Across southern Europe, the 'ugly German' is back – accused of driving other nations into penury, deposing governments and generally barking orders at all and sundry.
>   (Rachman 2012)

Many older Greeks could remember the Nazi occupation of Greece and felt that they were legally entitled to reparations. And Germany's attitude toward Greece throughout the crisis brought these feelings out into the open. For example, in a speech in Germany in May 2011, at the beginning of the crisis, Merkel uncharacteristically castigated Southern Europeans for being lazy and not working hard enough. She said, "It's not just about getting further into debt in countries such as Greece, Spain and Portugal. People should not be allowed to receive a pension before their German peers" (Dempsey 2011).

Breaking down the North–South narrative further, media content analysis of the international coverage of the crisis indicates that there were four main aspects to it: (1) criticism of the South for being fiscally irresponsible, (2) criticism of Germany for being too iron-fisted, (3) tension between net detractors and net contributors to the EU budget, and (4) tension between euro and non-euro EU member states

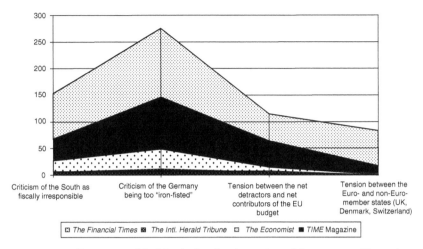

FIGURE 5.5 Eurozone crisis, North–South sub-tensions, May 1, 2011–November 30, 2011

(Figure 5.5). But when the crisis reached its height in November 2011, the dominant narrative expressed in the media was the problem with Germany's behavior. Forty-five percent of the coverage in *Time* magazine, 54 percent in the *Economist*, 48 percent in the *IHT*, and 39 percent in the *Financial Times* focused on this. There was a shift from blaming the South for being fiscally irresponsible to blaming the North for not offering its support, and in particular, blaming Germany for being too iron-fisted.

The openly expressed backlash to Merkel's leadership was at times severe. Daniel Brössler wrote in the newspaper *Süddeutsche Zeitung*, "Merkel is failing to secure German demands in Europe, and she has not succeeded in winning Germans over to the rescue of the euro" (Cowell 2011). Kevin Featherstone, an EU expert at the London School of Economics, said, "It reinforces a shift that we have seen in recent years for Germany to become rather more focused on its own national interests rather than sacrificing for some defined European interest. Germany is not giving up on Europe, but it is certainly frustrated" (Ewing and Dempsey 2011). As the *Financial Times* reported it:

So far, Germany and its fiscally hawkish allies – Finland, the Netherlands and others – are putting their feet down and saying no …. Germany and other countries with a record of strict fiscal prudence oppose e-bonds, describing them as a form of "sweet poison" or fatal temptation. According to politicians [in] the Christian Democratic party, the senior partner in Germany's ruling coalition, e-bonds would enable less disciplined nations to piggyback on the strong German credit rating and would impose higher interest rates on the country's debt.

(Barber 2011)

Former British Prime Minister Gordon Brown struck a similar tone in an op-ed in the *IHT*, writing, "Germany's recent failure to act from a position of strength endangers not only the country itself, but the entire euro project that Germany has spent decades developing" (Brown 2011). Other stories in the *IHT* echoed this sentiment, placing blame squarely on Merkel:

Each day Europe inches closer to a full economic meltdown, but Chancellor Angela Merkel of Germany is still blocking what is needed: a real bailout of Europe's weakest economies by their richer neighbors or the European Central Bank ... But German officials are still insisting that their profligate neighbors need to pay for their sinful ways – and that Germany's virtuous taxpayers will not be made to foot the bill. Until recently, European leaders argued that they could quell the crisis with an underfinanced rescue fund and stiff austerity policies imposed on borrowers to re-establish their creditworthiness. Investors are unpersuaded, and the crisis keeps spreading ... What makes this even more absurd is that Europe has the resources – if Germany would drop its objections.

(*International Herald Tribune* 2011)

The reality was that the German chancellor was willing to embrace Eurobonds, but only alongside greater fiscal integration. Thus, she saw it as a longer-term goal. Indeed, her finance minister, Wolfgang Schäuble, made clear that he saw this crisis as an opportunity that would not only enable southern European countries to increase competitiveness, but that would enable all member states in the Eurozone to take big steps toward fiscal union. The French leader agreed as well.

This emphasis on Germany as the main problem may be somewhat surprising, given that the German economy itself was not suffering directly in light of the Eurozone crisis, nor were Germans destabilizing the euro directly. But Germany – as the "pack leader" of the northern member states – was criticized for its unwillingness to act quickly enough, for the austerity measures it required of the Greeks, and for the control from Brussels that was a condition for any bailout. This points to the socially constructed nature of crises and the sorts of difficulties that arise once integrational panic sets in: the story had become that the real source of the crisis was not so much the financial hardships experienced by countries in the South, but Germany's stubbornness. The implication was that no country should obstruct the ability of Europe to move forward and save itself from the crisis. No one should begrudge the sacrifice required to support the common good of European solidarity and recovery, especially Germany. This narrative was a far cry from the actual roots of the crisis: the confluence of the Wall Street subprime crash and revelations about Greek debt.

Crisis Height

The crisis reached its height in November 2011 as Greece's prime minister unexpectedly announced that he would hold a referendum on the terms of the second EU bailout package, which raised alarm across Europe because the assumption had been that the Greek leader was determined to accept the terms that came with it. Many recognized that Papandreou was taking a democratic approach in light of months of public protests, but at the same time, EU leaders were distressed because such a move would take time and in the meantime would put everything at risk. Papandreou was well aware of the greater ramifications of the referendum. He said, "This is not a question of only a program. This is a question of whether we want to remain in the eurozone" (as quoted in Voigt 2011). The reaction in the markets was immediate as shares in European banks nosedived and equity markets registered massive losses. The EU was truly at the brink, and for the first and only time during this crisis, EU leaders violated a long-standing taboo, openly stating that there was the possibility that a member state could leave the euro. Of course, the media went even further, with dramatic claims such as: "Unless something very drastic happens, the eurozone could break up very soon" (Münchau 2011b).

Shortly after his announcement, Papandreou backed down from the idea of a referendum, replacing it with a confidence vote on his leadership. This created confusion in the markets: at least seventeen times in a twenty-four-hour period, the value of the euro to the dollar vacillated up and down. At this high point in the crisis, markets also started attacking Italy and pinned reactions to whether or not Berlusconi would step down. Despite the frenzy surrounding Italy, many understood that this was more about politics than actual economic concerns:

If Mario Monti, the former European commissioner, becomes Italy's next prime minister, he can take some comfort from the fact that although his government is deep in the red, his country overall is still one of the richest in the world ... The irony, therefore, is not only that the eurozone easily has the funds to save Italy, but so does Italy itself. The trick becomes one of reallocation.

(*Financial Times*, "Remember the Assets" 2011)

At this point, a dose of reality crept in: "What's the point of being an active investor when attitudes towards entire asset classes are ruled by fears that the eurozone is doomed rather than the merits and valuations of individual companies?" (Guthrie 2011) and "Currency traders are complaining that they are 'bored' with the euro crisis and turning to increasingly esoteric areas in an attempt to make money as they continue to be baffled by the single currency's strong performance" (Ross 2011).

Thus, November 2011 was a time of mixed feelings and chaotic reactions. France came unjustifiably under attack again when the S&P index mistakenly implied an impending downgrade of the country's triple-A status. Bond yields for France rose sharply despite having no economic basis for concern. Investors started asking whether France was headed in the direction of Italy, and then started acting on these hunches. Money was flowing to the UK, even though it was on the verge of recession, because markets saw it as a haven of some kind from ostensible instability on the continent. Meanwhile, nearly 80 percent of Germans believed that the euro would survive and 56 percent approved of Merkel's leadership, which was an increase of more than 10 percent since the previous month (Peel 2011).

In hindsight, the about-face on the Greek referendum combined with the start of Mario Draghi's presidency of the ECB – which began with an immediate cut to the interest rate and the creation of a three-year, long-term refinancing program to give liquidity to the European banking system – signaled a change in the direction of the Eurozone crisis. The day after the Greek referendum idea was abandoned, Poland's central bank governor declared, "Nobody should think that the euro will collapse, will disappear. No matter how long the way, I think that the bet against the Euro is gone" (Cienski 2011).

From Crisis to Opportunity

Because recovery from this crisis, more than the other two cases analyzed in this book, was to a great extent at the whim of volatile external markets, international speculators, and the pain of austerity (a policy that had clearly backfired), the crisis had a resurgence in mid-2012 before the existential threat was finally put to rest. Throughout the crisis, EU leaders were constantly and strongly criticized for their inaction, inability to speak with one voice, national selfishness, and so on. Issues such as disagreements on how to recapitalize banks were described as deep rifts among EU member states, especially France and Germany. But the main question – whether to support the euro no matter what – met with wide agreement among EU leaders. A major step in scaling down the crisis came when the new ECB head, Mario Draghi, started to buy EU member states' government bonds in November 2011. In addition, that same month Berlusconi resigned, and the Italians appointed Mario Monti to run a technocratic government. Greeks also appointed Lucas Papademos to replace George Papandreou in leading a new Greek unity government. As an economist and former vice president of the ECB, there was much more confidence in his ability to steer Greece in a good direction. But it was not until Draghi said in London in mid-2012 to an audience of business leaders that he would "do whatever it takes to preserve the euro" and added, "believe me, it will be enough," that markets finally calmed down (McHugh 2012).

As the crisis began to weaken, there was growing talk of the greater importance of Europe for preserving peace, and enabling all European countries to prosper. The overarching narrative featured less talk of the North–South divide and started showing more signs of solidarity. This resolution narrative began to creep in as early as November 2011, at the height of the crisis:

> Take away the south and the "new euro" would skyrocket, sinking the north's economies in the process. The German and Dutch economies are on steroids thanks to a cheap exchange rate .... Should Greece be forced from the euro, Germany and Holland are going to wind up like Switzerland before it decided to intervene in the currency markets. The northerners need the Greeks and Italians as much as the southerners need them. (Henkel 2011)

> From an economic point of view, the eurozone has what it takes to solve its debt crisis without any external help. It must do so. The 20th century started with a small Balkan state blowing up the world. History must not be allowed to repeat itself in the 21st. There is something deeply wrong with the global economy if a small country like Greece can become such a big threat.
> (*Financial Times*, "The World Needs a Cannes-do Summit ...," 2011)

But the sense that the Eurozone had finally stepped away from the brink took a few more months to fully develop. Leaders made explicit ties between the survival of the euro and the survival of Europe, among other things. As indicative of this turn toward recovery, on March 3, 2012, French President Sarkozy said, "It is the first summit since August 2011 which has not been a crisis summit ... It is a huge relief to see European summits dedicated to subjects other than the financial crisis, and a huge relief to see the financial crisis no longer dominating the headlines day after day" (as quoted in Peel 2012). As the concept of integrational panic anticipates, the "end of Europe" rhetoric had quickly disappeared, and the focus returned to the real core of the problem, which was Greek sovereign debt, and now, the aftermath of detrimental austerity strategies in other peripheral states.

It is important to recognize that resolving the existential phase of this crisis by achieving more integration was not necessarily a foregone conclusion. Many economists assumed that the only way out was to give up on the common currency, and they had produced models showing all of the ramifications of this action and how it would play out (Chicago Society Conference 2012). Others were also pushing in this direction. London's Mayor, Boris Johnson, argued that it was "remorseless logic" to stick by the monetary union by tightening fiscal integration. He said, "I think it would be absolutely crazy to decide the solution to the eurozone crisis is to intensify fiscal union and try to create an economic government of Europe. I really can't see for the life of me how that is going to work in the long term" (Parker 2011).

Nevertheless, with the end of Europe's crisis of confidence came a number of big steps forward in terms of fiscal integration, including a European fiscal compact to maintain balanced budgets,[17] transparency rules that allow Brussels to monitor national budgets, a permanent European Stability Mechanism,[18] the eventual creation of a fiscal union, and increased powers to the European Central Bank. Some even more far-reaching initiatives that would have never been discussed seriously before the crisis were also put on the table, such as a financial transaction tax, a European finance minister, Eurobonds, a mechanism to temporarily ban speculative trading, a ban on rating agencies addressing sovereign debt, a European monetary fund, and an EU rating agency. In sum, European leaders used the crisis as an opportunity to push forward with renewed consensus and integration. As Germany's finance minister, Wolfgang Schäuble, put it:

In addition to the harmonized monetary policy we have at the European level with the European Central Bank, [we need] stronger institutions to oversee the implementation of a commonly agreed finance policy. That is what I call fiscal union. We need to take big steps to get that done. The crisis shows that we

---

[17] The Commission has the authority to require spending cuts of member states, or impose large fines if they are found to be in violation of the rules.
[18] To replace the European Financial Stabilization Facility and European Financial Stabilization Mechanism in July 2012. This €500 billion rescue fund can be spent without the approval of national parliaments.

need it – now in particular. That is why crises are also opportunities. We can get things done that we could not do without the crisis.

(as quoted in Peel and Wiesmann 2011)

For some time, the ECB had begun a program of buying bonds on the open market. Under Mario Draghi's leadership it had effectively become a lender of last resort for Europe. Even though some of these ideas will take some time to fully implement, it is significant that such a far-ranging level of fiscal integration is even being discussed. Before the crisis, talking about these various provisions, such as Eurobonds or a European finance minister, would have been impossible, in large part because of underlying tensions. Even uttering the words "fiscal union" would have caused deep alarm. After the crisis, this had now changed completely.

The new EU monetary union has vastly increased powers, and it is now much more difficult for member states to change the rules in place.[19] If governments break the Stability and Growth Pact rules, they can now be automatically fined unless a qualified majority of 65 percent of the population and 55 percent of the member states agree to allow it. The banking union means that the EU can close down particular banks that are not performing well. The fiscal compact requires Eurozone countries to run a small budget surplus. Member states can still make decisions on economic governance, but if any government gets closer to breaking the rules on borrowing, it will gradually lose this discretion to the EU. There is also now much more collectivization of risk (at the level of around €2 trillion) through bailout funds and new EU powers to handle systemic risk.[20] EU agencies have more influence in this respect than before the crisis, and the ECB is now far more powerful. It can engage in long-term refinancing of banks (at the level of €1 trillion), lend to member states on a short-term basis, make discretionary and political decisions, and generally "do whatever it takes to save the Euro," as Draghi put it during the crisis.

Catharsis

The puzzle is, why did EU integration move forward so dramatically in the wake of such a severe crisis? As with the previous cases studied in this

---

[19] Christopher Lord calls these innovations the "four Cs" – coerce, constitutionalized, conditional, and collectivization of risk.

[20] By contrast, in the United States, the federal government is not responsible for state-level debt, allowing states within the union to go bankrupt as happened with California in 2010. For comparison of EMU with the United States, see Van Overtveldt (2011: 62–63).

book, is catharsis part of the explanation? In this crisis, I argue that the public was an important dimension that served as a prerequisite for elite-level agreement on major reforms. As Jacques Delors said in a speech at *Notre Europe:*

> [A] return to grass-roots opinion is a necessity ... within the Eurozone, there is a rift between the north and the south and we must not underestimate its impact on grass-roots opinion.   (Delors 2012)

One important indicator of whether North–South tensions declined as a result of the crisis is to examine citizens' "desired scope of European policy-making" (Vössing 2005). Shortly after the peak of the crisis in early November 2011, there was acknowledgment of the need to have public support to move forward with more integration:

> As Europe edges toward fiscal union, decision-makers need to know that they can rely on popular support. For this to happen, the onus must be placed on the very forces which have failed so far. Political parties must do what they were created for, which is to mediate among society's conflicting interests. Technocrats are giving them some breathing space. They cannot waste it.
> (*Financial Times,* "In Defense of Democratic Politics ...," 2011)

The Autumn 2008 Eurobarometer survey found that 45 percent of EU citizens thought that their own national government alone should make decisions about the economy, and 51 percent thought that these decisions should be made jointly with the EU (Standard Eurobarometer 70.3: 11). Table 5.2 breaks this down in terms of northern versus southern member states and shows that before the crisis, southern member states were generally *more* in favor of EU economic integration than northern member states. Thus, there was a clear difference in northern and southern views on this issue.

Did this change after the crisis? The Eurobarometer survey stopped asking exactly the same question, but still posed comparable questions in Autumn 2014, and with a more fine-tuned breakdown on the role of the EU. It is clear from the data that after the crisis, northern and southern member states have converged in their views on the question of the EU's role in dealing with the economy. Rather than having a spread of around 15 percent difference in the North versus the South, in 2014, support for the EU's role in tackling the crisis in terms of regulating financial institutions, approving member states' budgets, and governing through a banking union had well less than a 10 percent difference across core northern versus southern member states. It is also noteworthy that

TABLE 5.2 *Desired Scope of European Economic Policy Making, 2008 (Standard Eurobarometer 69) vs. 2014 (Eurobarometer 82 Annex)*

	2008		2014		
	Economic decisions should be made at the national level	Economic decisions should be made jointly with the EU	EU should have a more important role in regulating financial institutions	EU should approve member states' budgets in advance	EU should have a banking union
Core southern member states					
Cyprus	32%	65%	66%	54%	69%
Greece	54%	46%	61%	54%	58%
Italy	40%	53%	64%	56%	60%
Portugal	45%	50%	79%	70%	77%
Spain	44%	49%	73%	59%	75%
Average South	43%	52.6%	68.6%	58.6%	67.8%
Core northern member states					
Austria	49%	47%	67%	54%	69%
Finland	76%	23%	59%	49%	67%
Germany	68%	29%	68%	48%	75%
Netherlands	44%	55%	69%	60%	85%
Average North	59.25%	38.5%	65.8%	52.8%	74%

attitudes toward the EU's influence in general increased dramatically across the board.

Another important indicator of the effect of the crisis on North–South tensions is citizens' "desired content or direction of policies on the European level" (Vössing 2005). Here, the data from the 2013 survey is even more revealing. Table 5.3 shows strong evidence for the emergence of newfound common views on the content and direction of EU economic and financial integration.

In terms of the desired content or direction of EU policies, the high percentage of agreement in response to the questions of whether member states should work or will have to work together more closely in the area of finance and the economy is striking. In 2008, 52.6 percent of citizens in southern member states thought that economic decisions should be made jointly between the member states and the EU, and 38.5 percent of

TABLE 5.3 *Desired Content or Direction of Policies, Autumn 2013: Percent Agreement (Standard Eurobarometer 80 Annex: 112–118)*

As a consequence of the crisis …	member states *should* work together more	member states *will* *have to* work more closely together	the EU will be stronger over the longer term
Core southern member states			
Cyprus	98%	97%	45%
Greece	92%	88%	42%
Italy	82%	74%	50%
Portugal	91%	78%	50%
Spain	93%	88%	61%
Average South	91.2%	85%	49.6%
Core northern member states			
Austria	78%	74%	46%
Finland	92%	90%	62%
Germany	93%	90%	57%
Netherlands	89%	86%	58%
Average North	88%	85%	55.75%

citizens in northern member states also took this position. In 2013, a similar question resulted in an average of 91.2 percent from southern member states and 88 percent from northern member states believing that EU member states should work more closely together. Beyond this extremely high level of support for working together more closely, these responses also indicate convergence in northern versus southern attitudes.

The question of whether the EU will be stronger over the longer term as a result of the crisis garnered a somewhat optimistic response across both northern (55.75 percent) and southern member states (49.6 percent). Given the uncertainty of the period immediately following the crisis, the answers to this question elicited a high number of "don't know," but it is still significant that the number of citizens in agreement is relatively similar across core northern and southern member states, despite the very different experiences of the two regions during the crisis. By contrast, before the crisis in spring 2008, the average percentage of agreement to the statement that "things are going in the right direction" in the European Union was 41.6 percent among citizens in southern member states and 37.75 percent for citizens in northern member states (Standard

Eurobarometer 69).[21] Thus, this was not a source of North–South tension even before the crisis, but the increased level of optimism about the longer-term prospects for the EU, combined with very high levels of support for member states working together, does suggest that there was a sense of post-crisis catharsis. Since 2013, optimism in the future of the EU, support for the common currency among euro countries, feelings of being an EU citizen, and trust in EU institutions have all noticeably risen (Standard Eurobarometer 83 2015).

Overall, comparison of opinion polls before and after the crisis supports the idea that the crisis served as an opportunity to release tensions related to North–South differences in economic cultures. While these tensions did not cause the crisis, they had been intensifying beforehand, they were openly expressed during the crisis, and they were weakened post-crisis. Member state leaders were then able to move forward with new levels of economic integration that will likely increase the future legitimacy of the EU as an economic power in world politics. Indeed, more than half of Europeans believe this to be true, and systematic studies show that more financial integration will lead to more development and growth for the EU economy (Guiso, Jappelli, Padula, and Pagano 2004). With the convergence of popular opinion, political leaders, experts (and epistemic communities), and EU institutions were able to move Europe much closer to fiscal union.

CONCLUSION

With regard to outcomes, this chapter makes the case that a significant factor in enabling leaders to push forward with integration after the Eurozone crisis was the broad-level catharsis that took place across northern and southern Eurozone countries. With this crisis, compared to the others, the recovery period will likely be longer because the austerity measures that policy makers chose for dealing with the crisis ended up exacerbating the impact of the crisis in many member states. There are tangible structural problems to overcome, and this will take some time. At least in the short to medium term, there may be greater differences between those that suffered in the crisis and those that weathered the storm. Moreover, implementing new agreements on the functioning of the

---

[21] The breakdown was Greece 46 percent, Portugal 41 percent, Cyprus 47 percent, Spain 48 percent, Italy 26 percent, Germany 37 percent, the Netherlands 46 percent, Austria 27 percent, and Finland 41 percent.

monetary union will take time. What matters, however, is that significant breakthroughs have been made in terms of agreement on new policy areas that will substantially affect the future of the monetary union.

This particular crisis has spurred more analysis about its consequences than the other two. Indeed, numerous studies advance different perspectives on how the crisis has impacted EU integration. Many scholars contend that there has actually been an *intensification* of the North–South divide in the wake of the crisis (Torreblanca and Leonard 2013: 1–6). They typically cite the southern region's plummeting trust in national governments and political parties, while northern citizens' trust in national institutions remains about the same as before the crisis (Eurobarometer as cited in Alonso 2013). Or they argue that the creditor countries in the north do not want to bear the debt burden of those in the south, while those in the south feel as though the EU has placed them in an economic "straight-jacket" (Torreblanca and Leonard 2013). Much of the media and public commentary focuses on the dire circumstances associated with growing Euroskepticism, citing declining trust overall in the EU (Rohac 2013). There is also the assumption that if these two trends are at work – and yet, European leaders continue with significant steps toward more integration – there must then also be a growing democratic deficit.

I would suggest that the premises of these two views on the effects of the Eurozone crisis are actually somewhat flawed. First, in terms of the claim that the North–South divide has grown even stronger, in this chapter I have cited a significant amount of evidence to the contrary: after the crisis, northern and southern views have converged in support of prioritizing the EU as the level that should decide economic policy, and the overwhelming majority believes that EU member states should and must work more closely together. In addition, if northern and southern member states have different levels of trust in their *national*-level institutions, this says nothing about tensions *between* these two regions. Moreover, it is important to recognize when that public trust declined, it did so *further* for national-level institutions than it did for EU-level institutions (Standard Eurobarometer 80: 5). Thus, studies that only consider trust in the EU fail to realize that decline in trust was present for *all* democratic institutions, and there is consistently *more* trust overall for EU institutions as compared to national institutions.

Second, while opinion polls indicate that Europeans were less trusting in democratic institutions *in general* immediately after the crisis, this does not in itself answer the question of whether or not citizens supported further integration. As Serricchio et al. write there is "a distinction between mass attitudes towards the current workings of the EU and mass attitudes towards the project of European integration" (Serricchio, Tsakatika, and Quaglia 2013: 52). In other words, critics of the EU and its policies were not *necessarily* skeptical of the EU overall. For example, Greek citizens had declining trust in the EU, but they still overwhelmingly wanted to stay in the EU and keep the euro after the crisis (Nanou and Vernet 2013). More generally, opinion polls indicate that European citizens maintained their confidence in financial institutions between the pre-crisis era and 2012 (Manchin 2012b). Gallup polls also indicate that Europeans still held the belief that if they worked hard, they could get ahead. For the most part, they maintained their faith in meritocracy of the European employment sector (Manchin 2012a). The November 2013 Eurobarometer survey shows that more than half of Europeans were optimistic about the future of the EU. In spring 2015, this increased to 58 percent. At the same time, pessimism about the future of the EU steadily declined from 46 percent in spring 2013 to 36 percent in spring 2015 (Standard Eurobarometer 83 2015: 12). The same is true for support of the single market and common currency among Eurozone countries, which rose to nearly match the pre-crisis high of 70 percent in spring 2015 (Standard Eurobarometer 83 2015: 25). Thus, an overemphasis on trust – either toward national or supranational institutions – can be misleading.

If there is a growing democratic deficit as a result of the Eurozone crisis, it likely stems more from participatory practices and negative media discourses than from individual preferences or attitudes (de Wilde and Trenz 2012). It is concerning that trust in both national and European-level institutions is lower than during the early 2000s. Democratic representatives must work hard to repair this. However, the EU continues to enjoy greater trust than national governments for the most part. And as the crisis resolution literature indicates, during times of crisis, leaders gain more decision-making power than during non-crisis times. Thus, as Europe continues to recover from the crisis, taking advantage of the stronger levels of integration it has agreed to post-crisis, it is important for leaders to restore power and influence to its citizens.

References

Aizenman, Joshua, Yothin Jinjarak, Minsoo Lee, and Donghyun Park. 2012. "Developing Countries' Financial Vulnerability to the Euro Crisis: An Event Study of Equity and Bond Markets." NBER Working Paper Series, 18028.

Albuquerque, Rui and Claria Vega. 2008. "Economic News and International Stock Market Co-movement," *Review of Finance* 13: 401–465.

Alonso, Sonia. 2013. "A Perfect Storm: Europe's Growing North-South Divide." *Policy Network*, September 12.

Alphandéry, Edmond. 2012. "The Euro Crisis," *Foundation Robert Schuman*, Policy Paper 240: 1–13.

Andersen, Torben G., Tim Bollerslev, Francis X. Diebold, and Claria Vega. 2003. "Micro Effects of Macro Announcements: Real-Time Price Discovery in Foreign Exchange," *American Economic Review* 93(1): 38–62.

Atkins, Ralph and Quentin Peel. 2010. "Financial Markets 'Do Not Understand the Euro.'" *Financial Times*, December 5.

Attali, Jacques. 2011. "The Crisis Is in Brussels, Not Athens." *International Herald Tribune*, June 19.

Ash, Timothy Garton. 2012. "The Crisis of Europe: How the Union Came Together and Why IT's Falling Apart," *Foreign Affairs* 91(5): 2.

Authers, John. 2011a. "Leadership Required to Stave Off Fresh Meltdown." *Financial Times*, London, August 6.

Authers, John. 2011b. "Toxic Mix Puts Profits and Stocks into Limbo." *Financial Times*, London, July 30.

Balzli, Beat. 2010. "How Goldman Sachs Helped Greece to Mask Its True Debt." Der Spiegel, February 28.

Barber, Tony. 2011. "Four Steps to Fiscal Union." *Financial Times*, London, August 12.

Barber, Tony. 2010. "Strong Euro Hid Crisis, Says EU Chief." *Financial Times*, London, June 4.

Beattie, Alan. 2011a. "Europe to Deliver at the End of the Day." *Financial Times*, London, August 1.

Beattie, Alan. 2011b. "IMF Clash with Eurozone Authorities." *Financial Times*, London, September 1.

Beattie, Alan. 2011c. "Lagarde Pleads for European Unity over Greek Rescue Plan." *Financial Times*, London, August 1.

Beetsma, Roel, Massimo Giuliodori, Frank de Jong, and Daniel Widijanto. 2013. "Spread the News: The Impact of News on the European Sovereign Bond Markets during the Crisis," *Journal of International Money and Finance* 34: 83–101.

Benhold, Katrin. 2011. "US and European Markets Rise on Optimism Over Greek Vote." *International Herald Tribune*, June 29.

Bergsten, Fred C. 2012. "Congressional Testimony: The Outlook for the Euro Crisis and Implications for the United States." *Peterson Institute of International Economics*, February 1.

Bonatti, Luigi and Andrea Fracasso. 2013. "The German Model and the European Crisis," *Journal of Common Market Studies* 51(6): 1023–1039.

Brittan, Samuel. 2011a. "The Euro Is Still Far from Out of Danger." *Financial Times*, London, July 29.

Brittan, Samuel. 2011b. "Who Is Winning in the Race for Recovery." *Financial Times*, London, May 13.

Brown, Gordon. 2011. "The Euro Zone's Cure Starts with Germany." *International Herald Tribune*, August 21.

Buti, Marco, Servaas Deroose, Vitor Gaspar, and João Nogueira Martins. 2010. *The Euro: The First Decade.* Cambridge: Cambridge University Press.

Castle, Stephen. 2011a. "Europeans Agree to a New Bailout for Greece with Conditions." *International Herald Tribune,* June 24.

Castle, Stephen. 2011b. "In Debt Crisis, EU and Markets Stuck in a Dialogue of the Deaf." *International Herald Tribune,* June 11.

Central Intelligence Agency. 2015. *The World Factbook.* Washington, DC: Central Intelligence Agency. Continually updated; available at www.cia.gov/library/publications/the-world-factbook.

Chaffin, Joshua. 2011. "Athens Faces Turmoil If It Decides to Abandon the Euro." *Financial Times,* London, July 18.

Chicago Society Conference. 2012. "Post-crisis: Perspectives on the Sovereign Debt Question." International House at the University of Chicago, May 12.

Cienski, Jan. 2011. "Poland Pledges Commitment to Euro." *Financial Times,* London, November 5.

Cowell, Alan. 2011. "Scrutiny of German Leader Builds as Debt Crisis Rattles Europe." *International Herald Tribune,* June 19.

Davies, Nigel and Alexander Sage. 2011. "Spain, France Borrowing Costs Raise Contagion Alarm." *France 24,* November 17.

De Grauwe, Paul. 2011. "Managing a Fragile Eurozone," *CESifo Forum* 12(2): 40–45.

De Grauwe, Paul and Yuemei Ji. 2013. "Self-Fulfilling Crises in the Eurozone: An Empirical Test," *Journal of International Money and Finance* 34: 15–36.

De Santis, Roberto A. 2012. "The Euro Area Sovereign Debt Crisis: Safe Haven, Credit Rating Agencies and the Spread of the Fever from Greece, Ireland and Portugal." Working Paper 1419, European Central Bank, Frankfurt, Germany.

De Wilde, Pieter and Hans-Jörg Trenz. 2012. "Denouncing European Integration: Euroscepticism as Political Contestation," *European Journal of Social Theory* 15(4): 537–554.

Delors, Jacques. 2012. "Consolidating the EMU, A Vital Task." Speech, Jacques Delors Institute, Paris, December 7.

Dempsey, Judy. 2011. "Merkel's Blunt Talk Offends Debtor Nations." *International Herald Tribune,* September 6.

Dinan, Desmond. 2013. *Ever Closer Union: An Introduction to European Integration.* Boulder, CO: Lynne Rienner Publishers.

Dinmore, Guy and Rachel Sanderson. 2011. "Berlusconi Insists Italy Will Survive." *Financial Times,* London, August 4.

Donadio, Rachel. 2011. "Greek Turmoil Raises Fears of Instability around Europe." *International Herald Tribune,* June 16.

Eichengreen, Barry. 2009. "Was the Euro a Mistake?" *VoxEU,* January 20.

Erlanger, Steven. 2011a. "Europe Nears Agreement on Bailout Fund That May Be Inadequate." *International Herald Tribune,* September 27.

Erlanger, Steven. 2011b. "Greek Leader Irked by Speculation on Debt." *International Herald Tribune,* May 7.

Ewing, Jack. 2011. "S.&P. Cuts Rating on Greek Debt, Shaking Confidence." *International Herald Tribune,* May 9.

Ewing, Jack, and Judy Dempsey. 2011. "Europe's Economic Powerhouse Drift East." *International Herald Tribune*, July 18.

Ewing, Jack and Liz Alderman. 2011. "Some in Germany Want Greece to Temporarily Exit the Euro Zone." *International Herald Tribune*, August 10.

Financial Times. 2011. "Artful Promises: Constitutional Amendments Will Not Save the Eurozone," London. August 25.

Financial Times. 2011. "Cruel Summer." August 4.

Financial Times. 2011. "Democracy's Slow Cure for the Euro: Northern Europeans Treat Economics as a Morality Play." Editorial, London, September 17.

Financial Times. 2011. "Fiddling in Rome: Italy Needs Economic Reform but Berlusconi Cannot Deliver," London. September 22.

Financial Times. 2011. "In Defense of Democratic Politics: New Political Class Must Arise from Technocratic Interlude," London. November 26.

Financial Times. 2011. "Remember the Assets." November 11.

Financial Times. 2011. "Saving the Euro, Saving Europe: A Comprehensive Plan Is Needed to End the Debt Emergency," London. July 19.

Financial Times. 2011. "Second Thoughts on the Euro Rescue: Eurozone's Latest Strategy Fails to Dispel Market Doubts," London. July 29.

Financial Times. 2011. "The Euro." July 25.

Financial Times. 2011. "The World Needs a Cannes-do Summit: The Global Economy Is in Peril," London. November 3.

Financial Times. 2011. "UniCredit Advances Despite Volatility," London. August 4.

Fossum, John E. 2014. "Democracy and Differentiation in Europe." Workshop at 5th International Conference on Democracy as Idea and Practice, Oslo, January 8.

Gersemann, Olaf. 2011. "10 Reasons the Euro Was a Dumb Idea." *Time*, November 25.

Giles, Chis. 2011. "Alternative Scenarios All Point to World of Political Uncertainty." *Financial Times*, London, June 23.

Guiso, Luigi, Tullio Jappelli, Mario Padula, and Marco Pagano. 2004. "Financial Market Integration and Economic Growth in the EU," *Economic Policy* 19(40): 523–577.

Guthrie, Joanathan. 2011. "The Death of Skill." *Financial Times*, London, November 11.

Hall, Ben and Quentin Peel. 2010. "Europe: Adrift Amid the Rift." *Financial Times*, London, June 23.

Henkel, Hans-Olaf. 2011. "The Euro-Zone North Needs the South." *International Herald Tribune*, November 11.

Hooghe, Liesbet and Gary Marks. 2005. "Calculation, Community and Cues: Public Opinion on European Integration," *European Union Politics* 6(4): 419–443.

Inman, Phillip. 2012. "Primary Greek Tax Evaders Are the Professional Classes." *The Guardian*, September 9.

International Herald Tribune. 2011. "Germany's Denial, Europe's Disaster." Editorial, November 29.

International Monetary Fund, Fiscal Monitor, September 2011.

James, Harold. 2012. *Making the European Monetary Union*. Cambridge, MA: Harvard University Press.

Kenney, Caitlin. 2011. "The End of the Line for the Euro." *wbur*, August 12.

Kirkegaard, Jacob F. 2011. "Congressional Testimony: The Euro Crisis: Origins, Current Status, and European and US Responses." *Peterson Institute of International Economics*, October 27.

König, Jörg and Renate Ohr. 2013. "Different Efforts in European Economic Integration: Implications of the EU Index," *Journal of Common Market Studies* 51(6): 1074–1090.

Kouvelakis, Stathis. 2012. "Introduction: The End of Europeanism." In *Crisis in the Eurozone*, edited by Costas Lapavitsas, et al. London and New York: Verso.

Krugman, Paul. 1998. "The Confidence Game: How Washington Worsened Asia's Crash." *New Republic Online*, October 5.

Lapavitsas, Costas, et al. 2012. *Crisis in the Eurozone*. London and New York: Verso.

Mahony, Honor. 2012. "National Stereotyping – The Eurozone's Other Story." *EUobserver*, February 22.

Manchin, Anna. 2012a. "Many Europeans Believe They Can Get Ahead with Hard Work." *Gallup*, March 14.

Manchin, Anna. 2012b. "Opinion Briefing: Confidence Deficit in the EU." *US Foreign Policy Opinion Briefings*, February 2.

Manolopoulos, Jason. 2011. *Greece's "Odious" Debt*. New York and London: Anthem Press.

Marsh, David. 2012. *The Euro: The Battle for the New Global Currency*. New Haven, CT: Yale University Press.

Mayer, Thomas. 2012. *Europe's Unfinished Currency the Political Economics of the Euro*. New York: Anthem Press.

McHugh, David. 2012. "Draghi: ECB to Do 'Whatever It Takes' to Save Euro." *Bloomberg Business*, July 26.

McNamara, Kathleen R. 1998. *The Currency of Ideas: Monetary Politics in the European Union*. Ithaca, NY: Cornell University Press.

Miliband, David. 2011. "Don't Leave Europe to the Skeptics and Federalists." *Financial Times*, London, November 15.

Milne, Richard. 2011. "Big Two Vie to Spot Risks: Agency Rivalry." *Financial Times*, London, September 21.

Mink, Mark, and Jakob de Haan. 2012. "Contagion during the Greek Sovereign Debt Crisis." DNB Working Paper 335.

Mourlon-Druol, Emmanuel. 2012. *A Europe Made of Money: The Emergence of the European Monetary System*. Ithaca, NY: Cornell University Press.

Münchau, Wolfgang. 2011a. "Don't Blame Moody's for a Messy Euro Crisis." *Financial Times*, London, July 10.

Münchau, Wolfgang. 2011b. "The Eurozone Really Has Only Days to Avoid Collapse." *Financial Times*, London, November 28.

Nanou, Kyriaki and Susannah Vernet. 2013. "The Eurozone Crisis Has Increased Soft Euroscepticism in Greece, Where Greeks Wish to Remain in the Euro, but No Longer Trust the EU." *LSE European Politics and Policy (EUROPP)*, Blog, available at http://blogs.lse.ac.uk/europpblog/2013/03/02/greece-euroscepticism.

OECD. 2015. "Ireland" and "Spain" data. Available at www.oecd.org.

Parker, George. 2011. "Johnson Attacks Osborne on Crisis." *Financial Times*, London, October 19.

Parsson, Mats. 2011. "UK Would Need Larger Share of Eurobond Issuance." *Financial Times*, London, August 29.

Paulo, Sebastian. "Europe and the Global Financial Crisis: Taking Stock of the EU's Policy Response." *Foundation Robert Schuman*, April 2011: 17.

Peel, Quentin. 2011. "Germans Confident of Euro's Survival." *Financial Times*, London, November 12.

Peel, Quentin. 2012. "Merkel Injects Note of Caution to Collective Sigh of Relief." *Financial Times*, London, March 4.

Peel, Quentin and Gerrit Wiesmann. 2011 "Crisis Provides Opportunity for 'Fiscal Union.'" *Financial Times*, London, October 30.

Pfanner, Eric. 2011. "Source Sought for False Story on French Bank." *International Herald Tribune*, August 14.

Pisani-Ferry, Jean. 2012. "The Euro Crisis and the New Impossible Trinity," *Bruegel Policy Contribution* 1: 4–5.

Plender, John. 2011. "Time for Eurozone Policymakers to Grasp the Nettle." *Financial Times*, London, July 13.

Rachman, Gideon. 2012. "Germany Faces a Machine from Hell." *Financial Times*, London, February 13.

Rana, Pradumna B. 2012. "Misdiagnosing the Eurozone Crisis: Perspectives from Asia." *VoxEU*, September 22.

Rettman, Andrew. 2011. "EU Institutions Hit Back at Markets, Rating Agencies." *EUobserver*, October 20.

Risse, Thomas, Daniela Engelmann-Martin, Hans-Joachim Knope, and Klaus Roscher. 1999. "To Euro or Not to Euro? The EMU and Identity Politics in the European Union," *European Journal of International Relations* 5(2): 147–187.

Risse, Thomas. 2003. "The Euro between National and European Identity," *Journal of European Public Policy* 10(4): 487–503.

Risse, Thomas, Daniela Engelmann-Martin, Hans-Joachim Knope, and Klaus Roscher. 2008. "To Euro or Not to Euro? The EMU and Identity Politics in the European Union," *European Journal of International Relations* 5(2): 147–187.

Rogoff, Kenneth. 2011. "The Euro's PIG-Headed Masters." *Economics Business & Finance World Affairs*, June 3.

Rohac, Dalibor. 2013. "Fewer Europeans Trust the EU." *Washington Times*, November 26.

Ross, Alice. 2011. "Forex Traders Look beyond the Euro." *Financial Times*, London, November 21.

Sachs, Jeffery. 1997. "The Wrong Medicine for Asia." *New York Times*, November 3.

Sales, Emmanuel. 2011. "The Euro's Stability: The Need for True Reform of Financial Activities." *Foundation Robert Schuman*, July 2011.

Saltmarsh, Matthew. 2011. "European Stocks Skid Amid Lack of Action." *International Herald Tribune*, August 4.

Scheer Robert. 2010. "It's Greek to Goldman Sachs." *The Nation*, March 1.

Serricchio, Fabio, Myrto Tsakatika, and Lucia Quaglia. 2013. "Euroscepticism and the Global Financial Crisis," *Journal of Common Market Studies* 51(1): 51–64.

Shirky, Clay. 2011. "Business Wary of Foreign Help: Political Cost." *Financial Times*, London, October 28.

Silver, Nate. 2012. *The Signal and the Noise: The Art and Science of Prediction*. London: Penguin.

Sivy, Michael. 2011. "It's Time to Admit the Euro Has Failed." *Time*, September 12.

Soros, George. 2012. *Financial Turmoil in Europe and the United States*. New York: Public Affairs.

Spiegel, Peter. 2011a. "An Elusive Debt Resolution." *Financial Times*, London, July 20.

Spiegel, Peter. 2011b. "China Presses Eurozone Leaders." *Financial Times*, London, October 22.

Spiegel, Peter. 2011c. "The Shaky Basis of the Greek Rescue." *Financial Times*, London, July 27.

Spiegel, Peter and Guy Dinmore. 2011a. "Berlusconi Brushes Off Debt Crisis." *Financial Times*, London, November 5.

Spiegel, Peter and Guy Dinmore. 2011b. "Merkel Warned on Bail-Out Impasse." *Financial Times*, London, July 15.

Standard Eurobarometer 69. 2008. "Public Opinion in the European Union – Annexes." Fieldwork March–April 2008. Published December 2008.

Standard Eurobarometer 70. 2010. "Public Opinion in the European Union." Fieldwork October–November 2008. Published June 2010.

Standard Eurobarometer 70.3. 2010. "The European Union Today and Tomorrow." Fieldwork October–November 2008. Published June 2010.

Standard Eurobarometer 80. 2013. "Public Opinion in the European Union – Annexes." Fieldwork November 2013.

Standard Eurobarometer 83. 2005. "Public Opinion in the European Union – First Results." Fieldwork May 2005. Published July 2015.

Stiglitz, Joseph. 2003. "Democratizing the International Monetary Fund and the World Bank: Governance and Accountability," *Governance* 16(1): 111–139.

Summers, Lawernce. 2011. "The World Must Demand that Europe Act to Rescue Its Currency." *Financial Times*, London, September 19.

Thomas, Landon Jr. 2011a. "In Europe, Rifts Widen Over Greece." *International Herald Tribune*, May 23.

Thomas, Landon Jr. 2011b. "Weak Economic Data Belies British Optimism." *International Herald Tribune*, June 16.

Torreblanca, Jose I. and Mark Leonard. 2013. "The Continent-wide Rise of Euroskepticism," *European Council on Foreign Relations* 79: 1–6.

Tzogopoulos, George. 2013. *The Greek Crisis in the Media: Stereotyping in the International Press*. Burlington, VT: Ashgate.

Van Gent, Wouter P.C., Virginie D. Mamadouh, and Herman H. van der Wusten. 2012. "Political Reactions to the Euro Crisis: Cross-national Variations and

Rescaling Issues in Elections and Popular Protests," *Eurasian Geography and Economics* 54(2): 135–161.

Van Overtveldt, Johan. 2011. *The End of the Euro: The Uneasy Future of the European Union*. Chicago: Agate Publishing.

Vilpisauskas, Ramunas. 2013. "Eurozone Crisis and European Integration: Functional Spillover, Political Spillback," *Journal of European Integration* 35 (3): 361–373.

Voigt, Jenna. 2011. "Europe Suspends Greek Aid." *Financial Times*, London, November 3.

Vössing, Konstantin. 2005. "Nationality and the Preferences of the European Public toward EU Policy-Making." *European Union Politics* 6(4): 445–467.

6

Conclusion

The evolving European order, which centers on the process of European Union (EU) integration, is characterized by both incremental change and critical junctures of crisis. This book has grappled with the latter. Even a casual look at the history of the EU since its inception in 1957 shows that at numerous junctures through its development, the EU (or EEC/EC) has been depicted as being in severe crisis, even on the verge of dissolution. Not only does the EU continually survive the repeated occurrence of existential crises, it ultimately seems to thrive on it. Many of the EU's most serious crises have served as catalysts, rather than genuine setbacks, for European consensus and integration. The overarching explanation for this phenomenon is key. Why do European crises continually defy popular and media-driven expectations? Why do they instead end up further restoring, and even often legitimizing, European order? What enables a strengthening of political will and resolve to find new areas of consensus among European decision makers?

In this book, I have endeavored to explain both the puzzle of the repeated occurrence of EU existential crises, as well as of renewed post-crisis consensus. With regard to the first, while most explanations of crisis focus on systemic or structural flaws in the European institutional structure, this book argues that we cannot fully understand the nature and severity of these crises without recognizing the role of societal reaction to events and the nature of social narratives about crisis, especially those advanced by the media. In other words, although many political, economic, and social developments can prove to be challenging problems for Europe, certain events more than others become construed as crises when people *perceive* them to be, and when they define them as such. Thus, the EU is plagued by episodes of integrational panic – periods of overblown, existential crisis in which social narratives about events build up the perception that the end of Europe is at hand.

Second, I have argued that even though social reaction to events plays an important role in constructing crises, these narratives about crises in turn provide the means to openly air underlying societal tensions that would otherwise remain below the surface and impede further integration. The concept of catharsis captures this process. At the societal level, these tensions often have to do with differences in identity, political culture, and attitudes toward the EU. At the elite, political level, they often have to do with national interest, geopolitics, and attitudes toward other countries, especially the United States. Crises, as opportunities to find solutions to real obstacles, also give Europeans at both the popular and elite levels an occasion to use language that would otherwise be considered confrontational. The three main case studies of this book show how this process develops and evolves. Preexisting tensions tend to shape the terms of each crisis' dominant narrative, turning these episodes into opportunities to speak frankly. In each case, post-crisis catharsis repeatedly creates a window of opportunity for more consensus among EU leaders, and for the emergence or strengthening of the European public sphere. Thus, what might at first appear to be episodes of failure to agree or work together can also be viewed as triggers for future success.

A central conclusion of this book is that the EU ultimately has staying power. It is not only resilient in the face of these crises, it eventually finds strength from them. This is all the more crucial to recognize in the face of widespread misperceptions that the EU is continually on the verge of falling apart. Indeed, a closer examination of the Iraq, constitutional, and Eurozone crises for the EU demonstrate that misperceptions actually play a significant role in building these crises through exaggerated media reports in the first place.

In this concluding chapter, I begin by summarizing the main findings of the book. Then, to illustrate the importance of integrational panic in creating a self-fulfilling prophecy dynamic, I consider non-cases of crisis, or the "dogs that didn't bark." These are instances in which societal actors, for a variety of reasons, do not pick up on potential crisis triggers, and as a result, a crisis narrative anticipating Europe's demise does *not* emerge. Finally, I end with some of the main implications for the phenomenon of integration by crisis.

SUMMARY OF FINDINGS

The book examines three major crisis case studies of particular notoriety: the 2003 Iraq crisis, the 2005 constitutional crisis, and the 2010–12 Eurozone crisis. Table 6.1 summarizes the properties of the three cases. As discussed in Chapter 3, scholars have advanced various explanations for the origins of the 2003 Iraq crisis for Europe: (1) diverging views on member states' relationships to the United States, (2) the inability for EU leaders to agree on foreign policy, and (3) deep divisions between eastern and western member states' strategic culture. Although these arguments give us the context for the crisis, they do not go far enough in explaining how the crisis reached such existential proportions. The Common Foreign and Security Policy (CFSP), and especially the European Security and Defence Policy (ESDP), were still new, and member states had a history of not seeing eye-to-eye when it came to unprecedented, high-stakes foreign policy challenges. However, in this particular case, the media and elites quickly defined Iraq as a major crisis for Europe, and integrational panic at the elite level built up early on. In December 2002, a media frenzy fed the growth of a strong crisis narrative, equating the question of whether or not to join the United States in invading Iraq as a question about the legitimacy of EU integration. This might have played out as simply a case of diverging preferences over foreign policy, but the media portrayed European debates over Iraq as having larger, longer-term, and more serious implications for

TABLE 6.1 *Case Studies Summary*

	Crisis Trigger	Main Actors Constructing Crisis Narrative	Perceived Stakes	Crisis Narrative-Tensions	Level of Catharsis
Iraq (2003)	Should the EU support the US in invading Iraq?	Media, elites	Enlargement, CFSP	Big Three, East–West	Elites
Constitution (2005)	Will member states be able to pass the Constitutional Treaty?	Media, elites, public	Integration	Public–elite	Public and elites
Eurozone (2010–12)	Greek debt; will the EU stand by the euro?	Media, elites, public	The euro, the EU	North–South	Public and elites

EU policy, amplifying certain tone-setting statements that leaders articulated in frustration. The socially constructed nature of this crisis is all the more apparent considering that European publics were largely homogeneous in their opposition to the war. After the crisis reached its height, it nonetheless became an opportunity for integration. Pre-crisis tensions among elites, especially among the Big Three and within eastern versus western European countries, formed the backbone of the crisis narrative, and the open expression of these tensions ultimately resulted in a sense of catharsis. This crisis ended with new levels of integration in the area of security and foreign policy, and in particular, the 2003 European Security Strategy.

In the case of the 2005 constitutional crisis (Chapter 4), there are also many explanations for how this grew into an existential crisis that brought Europe to the brink: (1) the treaty represented too much integration for Europeans, (2) the public was actually indifferent to the treaty and voted based on other issues unrelated to it, and (3) the public was manipulated by the "no" campaigners as often happens during unreliable referenda processes, and used the referendum as an excuse for a protest vote. Not all dimensions of these arguments are supported in the empirical record surrounding this case. Moreover, these arguments do not explain why the ratification process threatened the existence of the EU, while previous initially negative referenda votes on EU treaties did not. My analysis of media coverage and public reaction at the time shows that the crisis was fully under way well *before* the French and Dutch people voted "no" on the treaty. So, given that the Constitutional Treaty introduced relatively modest changes, especially in terms of its impact on regular European citizens, why did even the possibility of a negative outcome become defined as an existential crisis for Europe? An initially failed ratification process would represent a setback for Europe's leaders, but a plan had long been in place on how to proceed in this eventuality. In other words, it was not totally unexpected. Moreover, the mere chance that ratification would be stalled did not necessarily mean the "end of Europe." A closer look at the narratives surrounding this crisis shows how integrational panic grew, and demonstrates the socially constructed nature of it. The media certainly contributed to a sense of impending crisis with its amplification of conflict among elites, predictions of referenda failure, and exaggerated claims about the consequences of a negative vote. The crisis narrative brought preexisting public–elite tensions of various sorts into the open, and eventually led to a kind of societal catharsis. This crisis ended with newfound consensus – ratification of the Lisbon Treaty –

and more importantly, it led to significantly increased societal integration and public engagement with the EU.

Finally, why did the 2008 global financial crisis, originating on Wall Street with the sub-prime mortgage crisis, eventually impact the EU as an existential crisis (Chapter 5)? In the case of the 2010–12 Eurozone crisis, the various common explanations in the literature for the events leading to this crisis also have strengths and limitations. Some argue that (1) the cause originated from the structure of the global financial system, with high levels of deregulation over the decades; others emphasize (2) the flaws in the design of the euro itself; and still others (3) focus the blame on out-of-control Greek debt. It is evident that each of these explanations helps to explain the general crisis of confidence that emerged in the European economy. However, as with the other crises, I contend that any explanation of the Eurozone crisis must also grapple with the socially constructed nature of it, especially in terms of how the media amplified a crisis narrative of North–South divisions, and was a driving force behind integrational panic. The self-fulfilling prophecy aspect of crises is most tangible in this case. In 2008, the only Eurozone country with a major solvency problem was Greece, and its entire economy only amounted to 2 percent of the Eurozone total. There was no immediate reason for why such a small-scale liquidity crisis would eventually manifest as a full-blown crisis for Europe. The monetary union had its share of structural weaknesses – all economies do – and these became exposed as the Greek crisis grew. I demonstrate how the Eurozone was no worse than other economies in terms of these vulnerabilities, yet the euro suffered disproportionately in international markets. Eventually, with this crisis too, Europeans emerged with the opportunity and political will to move forward with integration and the better functioning of the common market. The dominant crisis narrative from 2010 to 2012 openly voiced preexisting North–South tensions in European society. These tensions, related to differences in economic cultures, had been present for decades, but they did not *cause* the crisis. The tensions did, however, intensify in the lead-up to the crisis and were strongly aired during the height of it. Far-reaching agreements in economic integration, particularly the creation of a banking union, came with the catharsis that followed, and this was coupled with a demonstrated convergence in North–South attitudes toward Europe.

In some respects, contagion effects drove all three of the crises for the EU. The case of the Eurozone crisis is obvious, but contagion also occurred in the other crises. The constitutional crisis was really about

France and the Netherlands, and possibly the UK as well. However, it truly became a *European* crisis as the narrative about the potential for a failed referendum in one of the member states spread, and the reaction to the actual "no" votes in France and the Netherlands reverberated throughout Europe. A main reason for this was that the media and elites had equated any negative outcome with the failure of Europe as a whole. The same is true for the Iraq crisis, in which a debate that was mainly focused on how the Big Three (i.e., France and Germany versus the UK) would respond to President Bush's call to invade Iraq, quickly metastasized into a crisis for all of Europe, with a particular emphasis on which side the Central and Eastern European states would support and what this meant for the future of the Union. In all of these crises, as they reached their height, there was a strong sense that the EU could not continue to exist in the way that it did. And yet, after each crisis, the easing of tensions brought a return to reason and normalcy, and the true nature of the EU integration project was reasserted.

It is worth noting that consistently over time, majorities of Europeans continue to *want* the European project to work. They trust Brussels institutions more than their national governments. They identify increasingly not just with their own nations, but with Europe as well. They especially support a stronger and more effective Common Foreign and Security Policy, and they do not want to give up on the euro. There is an underlying belief everywhere in Europe that EU integration is a good thing, and that it is the right thing to pursue. These attitudes are evermore present each time Europeans come face-to-face with the potential of the EU's demise. More generally, we can recognize catharsis when there are new insights, reevaluation of past problems, and solutions for overcoming them.

At the same time, the concept of integrational panic may face the criticism that by looking through this lens, almost everything appears to be socially constructed to the point that reality – that is, real-world circumstances – drops away. For example, while one scholar may look at an episode of societal panic and determine that it was an exaggeration, another may look at the same event and find that society's reaction made perfect sense. There is risk in judging behavior as well as in challenging the nature and degree of reactions from the media, European leaders, and society more generally. Indeed, the biggest challenge in examining the socially constructed nature of crises is to recognize the extent to which societal reactions are normal and rational, and the extent to which they are disproportionate and overblown. As David Garland writes, "We need, however, to be careful here lest we attribute too much efficacy to 'panics' and too little to rational reactions to underlying problems – although it is often empirically difficult to disentangle the two" (Garland 2008: 16). Of course, the only way to respond to this risk is to engage in careful empirical research, to trace crisis narratives (particularly the *timing* of their escalation), and to consider whether the crisis really had to play out in the way that it did. In this respect, a brief reflection on counterfactuals is valuable.

THE DOGS THAT DIDN'T BARK

The EU's crises over the Iraq war, the Constitutional Treaty, and the Eurozone show a broad-level pattern in the way that Europeans respond to and deal with crises and their triggers. Each case demonstrates the importance of media and societal narratives about events, and how this ultimately feeds into their resolution. But what happens if a crisis narrative does not build? Richard Ned Lebow writes extensively about the importance of contingency in explaining events in international relations, and the value of considering counterfactuals to demonstrate this (Lebow 2010). While I will not try to construct a story of what might have been, this section highlights a few examples of potential crisis cases that failed to materialize in the same way as the crises in Chapters 3, 4, and 5. These examples show how potential crisis triggers may not grow into anything more in the absence of integrational panic.

Although this analysis is simply a brief, illustrative overview compared to this book's three main case studies, the factors to look for are the same. Is there a crisis trigger of some kind that prompts division among EU actors? Does the narrative about events take on a quality that is out of proportion with the particular events and that reflects other underlying societal tensions? If integrational panic builds, is there a self-fulfilling prophecy dynamic that picks up momentum? Or, instead of these qualities, does the EU react to crisis triggers with a measured response, and tackle these challenges as fairly routine?

As mentioned previously, the French and Dutch "no" votes in the 2005 constitutional crisis were actually far from unprecedented, as a number of previous treaty agreements also resulted in initially negative referenda. In particular, the 1992 Maastricht Treaty that created the European Union itself underwent both a difficult negotiation process and an initially failed ratification process. The Maastricht Treaty had two parts: the first was the Economic and Monetary Union and the second was the Political Union.

The latter, especially its Common Foreign and Security Policy (CFSP), created the greatest controversy. At first, it was difficult to reach consensus between the British and Danish representatives who opposed CFSP, and the German and French representatives who supported it. Spain and Greece also threatened to block compromise on political union for their own reasons, and representatives of the Commission and the Parliament demanded increased powers. The main controversy over CFSP in 1991 was that the governments of several member states were concerned that it would supersede the authority of NATO, thereby alienating the United States from European affairs. The three main CFSP points up for consideration were the so-called Asolo list of areas that would come under joint action, the procedure for implementing joint action, and whether the issue of defense would be portrayed in the treaty as federal or intergovernmental.

Eventually, with EU ambassadors playing a strong role, the terms of the treaty were agreed to at the level of statesmen, but ratification then took an additional two years to complete (Cross 2007: chapter 6). This included a protracted, eighteen-month political struggle in the British parliament, where Tory Euroskeptics did not want to approve the Maastricht Treaty at all. For them, the treaty's strong moves toward increased supranationalism – particularly in regard to majority voting on issues that would impact British politics – represented the "end of the road" for their cause. Indeed, the Maastricht Treaty was described as an "immensely damaging episode for the Conservative party" itself (Rice and Owen 1993: 6. Things were no better in Denmark, where a referendum held on June 2, 1992, rejected the new treaty, albeit by a slim margin. This meant a reopening of negotiations and resulted in the introduction of some new measures to satisfy the Danes. Almost a year after the first, negative referendum, the Danish people finally voted to approve the treaty. Ratification difficulties were even present in the very heart of Europe, where there was real concern that the French referendum might fail, and in the end it only passed by a narrow margin.

Despite this rocky process of agreement, the Maastricht Treaty eventually went forward, and there was no sense of existential crisis threatening Europe during this period. This is particularly significant in comparison with the Constitutional Treaty, as Maastricht made far greater strides in furthering the integration process, and yet there was no talk whatsoever of the end of Europe, the possible departure of member states, or the death of EU integration when the ratification process stalled. There was no media frenzy or sharp elite-level response. Reactions were measured and discussions reflected the nature of the issues at stake. In sum, integrational panic did not take hold.

The EU has also faced numerous foreign policy challenges since the launch of CFSP that might have developed into full-blown crises in the same way that the Iraq crisis played out. In particular, Kosovo's bid for independence, Russia's incursion into Georgia, and the effort to deal with instability and violence in Libya stand out as issues that significantly divided member states, yet none of these led to major existential crises for the EU. A closer look at each of these challenges is instructive.

After years of conflict, on February 17, 2008, Kosovo declared independence from Serbia. The reaction on the part of various EU member states brought about immediate division. EU foreign ministers tried at first to arrive at a common stance, but then determined that each member state should take its own position. Cyprus, Greece, Romania, Slovakia, and Spain refused to recognize Kosovo, while the other twenty-two member states did (see Caspersen 2008; Davidson 2011). In December 2009, Spain, Romania, and Cyprus went so far as to give depositions against Kosovo's independence at the International Court of Justice, the UN's highest legal body, while Germany, France, the UK, and the Netherlands spoke in opposition to this view at the same hearing (Rettman and Krasniqi 2009). It would be easy to think that if divergence over the Iraq invasion in 2003 could lead to the buildup of crisis, then so could an issue as central to European foreign policy as the Balkans region. After all, the inability of the EU to act independently during the 1998–9 Kosovo War was what triggered the idea for the European Security and Defense Policy in the first place. But now, merely ten years later, not only did division over Kosovar independence fail to trigger a crisis for Europe, member states were still unanimously able to agree to launch a rule of law mission (EULEX) in Kosovo to help train police and justice officials in maintaining order and stability.

Why did this event play out without crisis? First, the media narrative was more concerned with the situation in Kosovo rather than the EU's reaction to it. Second, policy elites actively sought ways to get around the disagreement through the clever use of language and timing. Third, the general public did not become highly engaged with the issue. Another dimension to consider is that in the lead-up to the events in Kosovo, there were no overwhelming tensions brewing under the surface among EU member states. It was a period of relative calm and quiet.

Also in 2008, the Russia–Georgia War divided member states on foreign policy. Some sided with the Georgian government, going so far as to provide them with nonmilitary aid and publicly condemning the actions of the Russian government. Others did the opposite, accusing the Georgian government of provoking the conflict with Russia in the first place. In late August 2008, member states gathered for a crisis summit to discuss the war, and the divide became even more apparent. Britain, Poland, and three Baltic states called for harsh sanctions on Russia while France, Germany, and Italy, each heavily reliant on Russian energy, opposed such sanctions. This level of fragmentation was not unlike the breakdown in agreement over whether to join the United States in invading Iraq in 2003, except this time the stakes were arguably much higher given that the Russia–Georgia War was much more in the EU's backyard. Moreover, with the benefit of five more years of working with CFSP, one might expect that such disagreement among member states would have appeared even more controversial, and would have triggered an even more significant crisis reaction. However, an existential crisis narrative was virtually absent from coverage of these events, and thus, internal disagreement was not perceived to be strong enough to prevent the EU from acting alongside the UN and OSCE to broker negotiations between Russia and Georgia. Eventually, in October 2010, this "troika" of organizations helped push Russia to remove its troops from the disputed village of Perevi. Although the EU was able to participate in the negotiation process, it did not quite take the lead because the UN and OSCE remained a big part of the picture. Furthermore, as a result of their reliance on Russian oil, certain member states prioritized national preferences over acting multilaterally through the EU. Nonetheless, this significant crisis trigger still did not result in integrational panic. As with Kosovo's bid for independence, the media and elites did not define the Russia–Georgia War as threatening the existence of the EU. Preexisting tensions did not rise to the surface, and the European public did not rally around the issue. Once again, with no integrational panic, there was no existential crisis.

In the case of the 2011 Libyan war, there was again division in Europe over how to approach a thorny issue of foreign policy, and this led to an initially fragmented response (IISS Strategic Comments 2011). This seemingly distant conflict became significant to the EU because US President Barack Obama called for Europe to take the lead, seeking to emphasize a post–Bush-Doctrine world. At first, EU member states were in a state of disarray. On February 17, 2011, they called for an "immediate end to violence" but could not initially agree on sanctions against the family of Libya's leader Muammar Gaddafi (Italy, Malta, and Cyprus were opposed, while France, Germany, and the Netherlands were for it).

The member states also could not reach agreement on a no-fly zone, and the new EU High Representative, Catherine Ashton, did not appear to be able to lead them to a stronger common stance on this issue. Italian Prime Minister Silvio Berlusconi had just signed new investment deals with Libya, and did not want to risk throwing those into question. British Prime Minister David Cameron was the first to call for a no-fly zone, while French President Nicolas Sarkozy unilaterally announced military action against Gaddafi's forces. Given the various separate actions and announcements across Europe with respect to the Libyan uprising, the possibility of a common EU military operation was quickly taken off the table, and certain European member states proceeded under the umbrella of NATO.

The Libyan war might have served as a crisis trigger given that the 2009 Lisbon Treaty had recently been implemented, and its primary aim was to ensure a stronger foreign policy for Europe. While some have bemoaned the EU's slow and sloppy response to Libya, it is nonetheless clear that this crisis trigger did not lead to a full-blown existential crisis for Europe. And it is worth noting that the United States itself was internally divided on how to respond and had yet to develop its own position (Szabo 2011). Nevertheless, this conflict did demonstrate that the EU still had some work to do in order to fulfill the promise of CFSP, and it is clear that when the EU faces unprecedented foreign policy questions in which the use of force is on the table, agreement on a common approach is not always straightforward. However, in this case the social reaction to the Libyan war was more or less in proportion to the circumstances. Despite the fact that Europeans had to resort to using NATO – a failing that some describe as a crisis for the viability of the Lisbon Treaty – and the fact that the EU showed that it still needed to rely on US military resources, there was yet again no buildup of integrational panic. Indeed, to the contrary, as EU leaders grappled further with their different viewpoints, by late February 2011 they were able to launch an official embargo on equipment that Libyan authorities could wield for internal oppression, bring sanctions against Gaddafi and his supporters, and enforce travel bans and asset freezes. In early March of that year, the Commission proposed the Partnership for Democracy and Shared Prosperity with the Southern Mediterranean, an incentive-based approach, which aimed to bring four billion euros of aid to the region in 2011–13, contingent on progress in judicial reform, corruption, and human rights. And by April 12, 2011, the EU also agreed to extend its sanctions to Libya's energy companies to force Gaddafi from power. Shortly after this, the EU deployed its own mission, EUFOR in Libya, to help move around aid supplies and refugees in support of the UN. Thus, this foreign policy crisis not only shows the EU's ability to avoid integrational panic, but also its capacity to find areas of consensus upon which to hook a common approach, even in moments of apparently significant division.

Looking to the future, there are numerous possible crisis triggers that lie in wait during the second decade of the twenty-first century and beyond. It is impossible to predict exactly what new challenges Europe will face, but certain issues may be fertile ground for this even if they do not initially result in crises. Russian aggression under Putin's leadership is clearly a growing area of concern. The EU dealt with Russia's 2014 incursion into Ukraine without succumbing to internal crisis (see Cross and Karolewski 2017). Rather, the Russia–Ukraine conflict from 2013 to 2015 was primarily a crisis for Ukraine, not an existential threat to the EU. It was a crisis in which the EU was a key actor, and indeed, because the conflict began with Ukrainians taking to the streets in support of closer ties to the EU, Europeans felt obligated to be involved. But at the same time, the EU did quite well at responding coherently with a strong sanctions regime against Russia and with ongoing diplomatic actions. This may change if Putin's aggression escalates, particularly if he turns his attention to other Eastern European countries.

The 2016 British referendum to leave the EU – commonly known as Brexit – also has the potential to lead to crisis narratives about the future of the EU, possibly escalating to an existential level, and triggering other member states to hold membership referenda of their own. However, the main narrative in the wake of the British referendum was much more about the ramifications for the UK than about integrational panic for the EU. Indeed, considering the unanticipated outcome of the British vote, and significant potential this had to destabilize the EU, the Brexit referendum was clearly a case of the "dog that didn't bark." European leaders were firm from the beginning that Brexit is about the British, and that there was no reason for it to pose a serious threat to the integrity of the EU itself. Indeed, some member states had already reconciled themselves to the possibility of the British leaving the Union, and many were actually fed up with the UK for continually holding them back from further integration. In the immediate wake of the referendum, the EU quickly established a strong common stance, with the launch of the new Global Strategy and agreement on the creation of a true defense union, among other things. Nonetheless, as preparations for the UK's departure from the EU actually play out, the anticipation of how this will impact the EU and other

Euroskeptic member states could be enough to spark a self-fulfilling prophecy in the future.

Several other possible crises have already proven to fall in the category of "dogs that didn't bark," although that could still change. The Greek debt crisis during the summer of 2015 had the potential to serve as a serious crisis trigger for Europe, particularly considering that it followed on the heels of the 2010–12 Eurozone crisis and had a similar starting point. In some ways, the temptation for media and elites to get caught up in doomsday scenarios may have been even stronger given the unpredictable and daring maneuvers of Greek Prime Minister Alexis Tsipras. Yet, in 2015 the EU was also in a period of post-Eurozone crisis catharsis (see Chapter 5). European society had only recently stood at the apparent brink of economic collapse and had come through with even stronger resolve to repair the damage and move forward. If anything, the 2015 Greek debt crisis demonstrated that the EU could and would continue without Greece, if necessary, and it would not succumb to a downward spiral so soon after surviving the previous financial crisis. As a result, strong talk of Europe's demise was noticeably absent during the summer of 2015. Instead, the focus was specifically on Greece and what would happen to the country in the event that its leaders could not find a compromise with Europe and the IMF.

Just around the time that Greece found its way back onto more solid ground, the migration and refugee crisis presented a growing challenge for Europe as the unprecedented rise in the number of people making their way to Europe's borders from the Middle East picked up speed. Despite much talk of this as a crisis for Europe, it did not have the properties of an existential threat to EU integration up through the Autumn of 2015. European leaders largely shared the view that refugees seeking asylum should be allowed into Europe, and the sharp increase in refugee flows was mainly a logistical challenge to solve in terms of processing people and figuring out a way to distribute them across EU member states in a timely and fair manner. The crisis was serious, but it was largely so for the refugees themselves. In early 2016, this crisis took on some elements of existential threat to the EU's political order mainly stemming from increasingly vocal anti-immigrant rhetoric coming from far-right parties. Unprecedented situations such as the migration crisis do have the potential to lead to integrational panic if the EU takes too long to find a common approach and if media attention amplifies the problems leaders are trying to solve. A few tone-setting statements uttered in exasperation could add fuel to the fire, particularly if far-right parties are able to capitalize on this.

If refugees are connected to terrorist threats or attacks, such as those in Paris in November 2015, and this then triggers division among Europeans on how to respond, the possibility for the rise of integrational panic is there.

These "dogs that didn't bark" again show that the EU possesses a high level of resilience in the face of challenges and, indeed, is able to find ways to move forward when an event does *not* escalate into a full-blown existential crisis. Of course, in these cases of "dogs that didn't bark," we can observe that the EU does not typically choose solutions that are as fundamental and broad ranging as it does when existential crises create moments of opportunity, but it can still function in reaction to problems that spur division within. And yet, the goal of this book is to show a general pattern across the crises that *have* occurred. So a key question is: why do some events not develop into integrational panic? As we have seen, the EU has faced numerous divisive junctures related to major foreign policy challenges, and not all have resulted in integrational panic. Agreement has also broken down during multiple treaty ratification processes, and many have been met with a more or less business-as-usual response. A comparison between the 2010 and 2015 Greek debt crises is particularly instructive. Taken together, the examples discussed in this section illustrate that crisis triggers – oftentimes as significant as those leading to the Iraq, constitutional, and Eurozone crises – have come and gone without much fanfare. The cases described here thus clearly show that the nature of the crisis trigger does not provide an explanation in and of itself.

As I have demonstrated throughout, a key source of integrational panic is the nature of media coverage. One could speculate about why journalists choose to cover one story and not another, and why some stories precipitate a media frenzy while others do not. A lull in other newsworthy events in the world or a shift in popular interest could tip the scales in the direction of a closer focus on Europe, and to negative effect. Of course, events in Europe could very well warrant that type of attention, and typically this happens when there is "bad news" to sell. Of course, the media is not the only societal actor focusing public attention, but media coverage is often necessary to make people aware of significant events and to help frame the terms of public debates on issues. Interest groups may also need to be coherent and influential enough to define and frame crises. If leaders make certain tone-setting statements (such as "old Europe" versus "new Europe" in the case of the Iraq crisis) or if symbols of crisis emerge that can rouse popular concern (such as the image of a dead refugee child being pulled from the sea), there may be a mutually constitutive effect between various societal actors and the media. The evidence also strongly suggests that integrational panic is more likely when pre-crisis tensions are more palpable. Just as US elections can be a chance for American publics to blow off steam, EU crisis triggers may be tipping points for European publics to voice their growing concerns, whether they stem from East–West, North–South, public–elite, or other types of tension. As debates about preexisting tensions become intertwined with a growing sense of crisis, this dynamic may be enough to lead to questions about the very viability of the EU itself, thus creating momentum for integrational panic. Future research can further explore the underpinnings of this question, but it is likely that a variety of factors potentially feed into the development of such crisis narratives. This is a highly context-specific and contingent process, even while being part of an overarching crisis pattern. For the purposes of understanding the nature of EU integration and its trajectory, the far more important question is the impact of the existential crises that *do* occur.

INTEGRATION BY CRISIS

European integration has largely involved incremental processes and gradualism, but there is also a dynamic by which integration is achieved in spurts, usually following major crises. Are there longer-term consequences of integration by crisis for the greater trajectory of the EU? Altogether, the three cases of existential crisis examined in this book suggest that a European public sphere seems to be gaining strength over time, particularly with the resolution of each round of crisis. After the European crisis over Iraq, a visible public sphere emerged for the first time, and after the constitutional crisis it strengthened. Of the three, the Eurozone crisis has required the longest period of recovery, but just three years after the existential threat was resolved, identification with the EU among its citizenry had never been higher. Thus, the societal panic that characterizes existential crises in Europe often serves to awaken the citizenry and to galvanize them around issues of concern, even if it means that they end up being critical of certain aspects of EU integration in the process.

Despite the fact that crises can help to break down previously existing barriers to consensus and integration, I would still argue that a gradualist approach is preferable in terms of protecting the longevity of the European project. On the one hand, repeated EU resilience in the face of crises may finally teach the lesson that there is no reason to "panic": the EU has proven that it will survive. But on the other hand, repeated crises may wear down the fabric of European society and tarnish the image of Europe around the world. Crises provide a kind of integrational boost, but this is still a dangerous and undesirable path for Europe. These episodes of turmoil should not be sought out as a means of pushing through otherwise controversial policies. At some point, there is the distinct risk that a self-fulfilling prophecy dynamic will go unchecked, actually resulting in the permanent breakdown of European integration. And this would certainly represent a monumental setback in human efforts to find ways to cooperate and achieve peace in our world. Rather, incremental processes, which have always been at the core of advancing the European project, have met with much more success in terms of achieving long-term stability and augmenting Europe's image.

The problem with integration by crisis is that it feeds into a meta-narrative about Europe that is deeply flawed and detrimental to the common goals that Europeans share. This metanarrative informs even basic observations about the EU, especially when it is in the midst of a crisis. This metanarrative includes assumptions that (1) the EU is too difficult to understand because its institutions are too large and unwieldy; (2) the EU is generally dysfunctional and is only capable of dealing with largely "useless" details, such as regulations and the minutiae of bureaucracy; (3) the EU has no political, security, and ideational underpinnings, and member states are held together simply by the desire to trade with one another and benefit from economic profit; and (4) the EU almost never speaks with one voice externally because member states are far more interested in upholding national interest. Altogether, these misconceptions of what Europe means to its own people lend themselves easily to perceptions that the EU is weak and always vulnerable to policy challenges and external shocks. Ultimately, this metanarrative should be corrected in order to mini-mize the risk that the soft power of the European model – and what it represents for peace and cooperation – is irretrievably harmed. It is also arguably better for the sake of democracy to make key decisions about the future of Europe when not in the throes of crisis.

Yet, at the same time, the cumulative effect of integration by crisis to date provides much more reason to be optimistic about the future of Europe in world politics than one might assume without considering the underlying nature of these crises. Crises create opportunities for Europe, and this is far more important than the cliché implies. The cumulative effect of these crises has not been to slow down or to reverse the integration that has been achieved thus far. Indeed, what the crises over Iraq, the constitution, and the Eurozone have revealed is that even in the face of extreme adversity, and even when the easy route of freezing or rolling back integration is on the table before them, Europeans routinely choose more Europe, not less. They are not forced to do so. The EU would still function, as it has in the past, without a banking union or a new treaty, and with a weaker public sphere or a poorly defined foreign policy. But instead, time and again, Europeans resolve these crises with renewed political will to push the boundaries of existing integration into new areas. This unprecedented experiment with international cooperation and integration contains many lessons on how to overcome differences among states and across societies more generally. Recognizing and understanding the EU's successes in overcoming seemingly insurmountable obstacles show that Europe is actually built on a strong foundation in the twenty-first century. Moreover, the road ahead does not have to be one in which change requires crisis.

References

Caspersen, Nina. 2008. "From Kosovo to Karabakh: International Responses to De Facto States," *Südosteuropa* 56(1): 58–83.

Cross, Mai'a K. Davis. 2007. *The European Diplomatic Corps: Diplomats and International Cooperation from Westphalia to Maastricht.* Basingstoke: Palgrave.

Cross, Mai'a K., Davis Cross, and Ireneusz Pawel Karolewski (eds.). 2017. "Europe's Parallel Foreign Policy: The Ukraine-Russia Crisis," *Journal of Common Market Studies*, special issue, January.

Davidson, Jason W. 2011. *America's Allies and War: Kosovo, Afghanistan, and Iraq.* New York: Palgrave Macmillan.

Garland, David. 2008. "On the Concept of Moral Panic," *Crime Media Culture* 4(9): 16.

IISS Strategic Comments. 2011. "War in Libya: Europe's Confused Response," volume 17, comment 18, April.

Lebow, Richard Ned. 2010. *Forbidden Fruit: Counterfactuals and International Relations.* Princeton, NJ: Princeton University Press.

Rettman, Andrew and Ekrem Krasniqi. 2009. "EU Group of Three to Attack Kosovo Statehood at UN Court," *EUobserver*, October 16. Available at http://euobserver.com/9/28842.

Rice, Robert and David Owen. 1993. "Maastricht Ratified as Rees-Mogg Bows Out." *Financial Times*, August 3, p. 6.

Szabo, Stephen F. 2011. "Why Merkel Matters," German Marshall Fund Blog, June 6.

Index

CPSIA information can be obtained
at www.ICGtesting.com
Printed in the USA
LVHW01s1940250118
564002LV00015B/245/P